Seventy-Seven And Counting

Seventy-Seven And Counting

The Somewhat Gay Life of Brian

A Memoir

Seventy-Seven and Counting

Cover image: Kristaps Strazdins and Eva Strazdina

ISBN 978-1-7393239-3-6

This book is a work of non -fiction. I have done my best to recall events and people as accurately and as kindly as possible. Apologies for any lapses of memory.

British Library Cataloguing in Publication Data.
A catalogue record for this book is available from the British Library.

3 5 4 2 1

First Published in Great Britain
Hawkwood Books 2024
Blackpool Enterprise Centre FY4 1EW

Printed and bound in Great Britain by CPI Group (UK) Ltd.
Croydon CR0 4YY

PUBLISHER'S INTRODUCTION

I first met Brian in the early twenty-first century, and that is about as precise as I can be. He ran a guest house in Blackpool for a fascinatingly varied clientele. As I grew to know him better, I saw and appreciated his unique take on life. This assumed perspective was confirmed when, in the Autumn of 2020, he moved to Latvia, for no other reason than it offered him quiet independence and a whole new start at the age of 75. Since then, I have grown to know him more through Messenger and Facebook. This memoir was born from those many chats and entries.

I'm the first to admit that it is a haphazard enterprise, neither chronological nor plotted, but that is its charm, if you free yourself to enter Brian's psyche. As far as I can tell, he is not hidebound by dogma, prejudice or traditions. Possibly from surviving an often brutal upbringing with a violent father and even more violent brothers, he muddled through with his wits, humour and resourceful mind.

If you are fussy about grammar and syntax, accept my apologies but I wanted to keep Brian's authenticity and idiosyncratic voice, even at the expense of language purity. Nevertheless, it has still endured countless hours of editing.

The book, I hope, transcends the musings of one man's life to tell us all something about free thinking and the lives we choose to live. There are some disturbing episodes described, and though not always expressed in the King's English, in fact perhaps more so for that reason, are as sad as they are shocking, with insights into the consequences of abuse many of us face quietly, alone and forever. There's also something touching about a single human soul speaking so candidly and originally, not knowing whether there are any listeners out there at all.

Well, there was one, at least.

LOOKING AHEAD

Forty-eight hours until I start my journey, stepping through a curtain into a new life. At least, what should be a journey of forty-eight hours becomes one of days - a covid test in Manchester necessitating a three-night hotel stay, collecting the result shortly before departure. I loll about in my hotel room, watching the drunks and drug addicts wander past and the ladies of the night plying their trade. Manchester City Centre is somewhat seedy, definitely not a place to step out after dusk.

In my mind's eye, I wistfully conjure up the scene of arrival in Latvia, a land I have never visited. My country house awaits, the garden and lawns, as far as the eye can see, right up to the door of my residence. New friends, standing out in the flower beds greeting me on the other side of enormous bay windows. I imagine my first sortie out into the city and environs, evenings sitting out in the balmy stillness, under the palm trees, watching for passing flocks of flamingos and wildebeest herds quietly grazing...

I will need a lawyer to arrange all this, and I have one, waiting for me. He will guide me through the quagmire of administrative procedures, find me an estate as befits my new life, a house, huge gardens that I don't have to mow or dig. Plans are already afoot for the building of an attached summer house to host the odd garden party. Meeting new friends - I expect that soon I will be needing a social secretary to organise my diary of events. Dignitaries will want to meet me, anxious to be included in the next banquet. Perhaps I should speak to the local council about setting aside an area for coach parking and tourist buses.

I am realistic enough to know that things might be ever so slightly different, in which case I will be looking for the nearest camping shop in Riga to purchase a cheap tent to take into the local woods.

GREETINGS!

Hello again, my lovely friends!

I have been just so busy over the past few weeks. Skips, Zoom meetings, well the one, actually. I had been invited by my friend to join a writers' group or something like that. Great fun to talk with some articulate authors from around the world. I have been asked to produce something and in my rushed state and lack of imagination I have combined some of my posts on Facebook outlining my adventures in Latvia and elsewhere.

Thinking of all the things that have happened reminds me what a hectic, frustrating and fun time it has been, for the most part. I've even made a few friends on the way that are life to me. I make no apologies in not writing anything new or wondrous. Perhaps when brain and time come to a confluence I will try again.

IT'S ME AGAIN!

What have I been doing this week? Monday, it was my final trip to PMLP office to collect my new ID.

"Looks like you will all have me around for another five years at least."

The immigration department, and especially the lady I have been dealing with over several visits, has been so kind and helpful. Within a few minutes of arriving, I had my card and I remarked to her that it was a shame that we might not see each other again for five years. She laughed. I thanked her for her kindness and helpfulness and as a parting request asked her if she might look at a message I had on my mobile sent from the Post Office that was all in Latvian of course.

Atgadinam, ka no 11.01.2021 pasta nodala Riga-4 LV-1004 atrodas Jums adresets sutijums LD034614073BE (01131) ar summu apmaksai 0.00 EUR. Vairak neka 80 pasta nodalu izsniedz sutijumus ari sestdienas! Ieskaties.

She said that I had a parcel awaiting for me, I had nothing to pay and kindly input the address I had to go to into the Bolt app on my mobile phone so that I was able to call for a taxi to take me there. Minutes later, I am on my way, arriving happy and joyful, the first time alone in a local Post Office.

Great. Just a couple of customers in there, got my queuing ticket, wait two minutes and I'm at the counter, greeting the female assistant with a cheery, "Hello, good morning!" She stares back at me blankly, muttering, "No English," with a sour stare.

This place being a local post office, I was prepared that they might not speak English. I showed her the message on my mobile and passed the phone to her. She looked and said curtly, "Not here." She passes my mobile to her colleague who, glancing at it, repeats, "Not here."

She found an A4 sheet of paper and hastily scribbled an address, almost unreadable, thrust it and my mobile back to me and continued to stare. Thanking them, thinking the lovely lady at immigration must surely have got it wrong, I left, slightly disappointed but undaunted.

Now I am outside in the street, trying to decipher the handwriting to put into my Bolt App. Impossible. I cannot find the address. Luckily, a man is standing nearby, smoking. I saunter up to him and ask, "Do you speak English, please?" "A little", he replies. I show him the scribbled A4 sheet with the address and ask if he could input it into the App for me. He says, "The handwriting is bad," but looking at the choices says, "Yes, it is the main Post Office in Riga," and kindly inputs it. With great cheer, I thank him and within minutes I am yet again back in Riga, outside a large office on a corner with a big, blue band around it.

Happily, I breeze in, full of confidence, and take my queuing ticket, delighted that I have mastered this device, although I'm not sure why there are so many buttons on it. Pressing one brings my ticket out. Super, no waiting at all. Reaching the counter, I said,

"Do you speak English please?"

"A little," comes the response.

I explain to her that I am here to collect a parcel and at the same time show her the message on my mobile. She looks carefully at it and replies,

"You are at the wrong place. You have to go to the office shown on the message."

"Bloody buggeries!" I thought.

I went on to say that this was the place I had already been to and they insisted it was here not there. She plays with her computer, checking my parcel's location.

"No, it is not here, you have to go back. It is there."

She was kind and apologetic, sorry that I had been sent to the wrong place by the local post office. Never mind, gritting my teeth, mainly to stop them chattering standing on the street in minus 17 degrees, I once more order a Bolt taxi.

Soon, I am back again where I started and yes, I could see the same ladies through the window glaring back at me. No customers at all that I could see in there now as I nod and point at the queuing machine, as if to say, 'Do I need to take a ticket?' It seemed a bit pointless with no customers at any of the six windows, but no response, they just keep staring. I take a ticket. On the screen, I am next. What a surprise!

The same woman as before.

She stares back at me, not a word.

I ask if anyone there speaks English. She barks back, "No English!" with a scowl. Clearly my charm and good looks are having no effect at all. I get my mobile out and show her the message. Yet again, of course, the message was in Latvian, but again she barks, "No

English!" and doesn't look at it.

Although I am unaware of him, another customer is now waiting at a different counter. He comes over, a Latvian gentleman, and asks me if there is a problem.

"Yes, actually, there is," and I show him my mobile with the message.

"Yes," he says, "I was listening. Give me your mobile."

With that he holds it up to the screen and demands that the woman reads it, thrusting it into her hands over the screen. She glances at it and with a huff and sour look says nothing but proceeds through a door to the side, returning a couple of minutes later with my parcel, roughly shoves it at me and maintains her silence and black looks.

I cannot believe the pain to get something from the post office! I must make sure never to order anything ever again that might end up there.

Finally, one more taxi ride and this time back home. My landlady sees me coming back and enquires what I have been doing. I relate my story and show her the message on my mobile. She is horrified and says I should write and complain. I say to her, I will not do anything, life is too short. After all, I am the foreigner, and no one would place any credence on my moans anyway. The office was full of miserable women behind the counter. No apology for making me go around town in taxis or wasting my time, just glares for being a foreigner, or perhaps looking like a former husband that had abandoned her for a friendlier, better looking model. If it was the latter, I could quite understand; I would, too. It is a matter of checks and balances. I meet far more nice people here and only a few nasty ones. Part of being an adventurer and independent is the challenge of dealing with people.

My landlady called me last night to say that she was so incensed by my treatment that she had called the office by phone to complain, not just about me, but, as she says,

"This Post office is near here, on Satiksmes Street. So many people have problems with them! Someone has to do something about it because such people should not work in public service. It's not right. If they are not able to read the message on your phone and find your post, it's wrong. It's their job and they're getting money for it!"

She said that she had spoken to the manager who stated that indeed there was no one who spoke English on duty that day. It was pointed out to her that no conversation was needed, all the information was on the phone. However, an hour later the post office manageress telephoned my landlady and said that after checking, she could only sincerely apologise and promised to do something to improve customer service.

All hail my wonderful landlady who shadows my every move and tells me off for trying to be so independent. If I was normal and forty years younger, I would want to marry her.

Later that evening, I decided to tackle another ongoing issue which was cancelling my Virgin mobile phone SIM. I have been paying charges for it since September despite not using it, in fact destroying it on arrival in Latvia. I had tried to cancel it months ago but, as with all call centres, especially in the UK, you can wait an hour for anyone to answer and then it takes another thirty minutes to resolve, by which time I had to add money to my LMT mobile account to continue the call.

I did manage in the end. After two calls, going through security, listening to their music on a loop whilst being passed to someone trying to convince me to stay, keep the card on hold, bla bla bla.

Over the moon to get an email from Virgin minutes after ending the conversations with a whole team desperate not to lose my money, to say it was finally cancelled, except of course I would have to pay for January. A pleasure.

That is all I did Monday.

Tuesday it was a visit to my friends, not getting back until two on Wednesday morning, having been force fed, plied with wine and cigarettes and lots of laughter. Out early to get my shopping. I can't wait to spend all evening and most of the night watching the Inauguration of the new President of the USA and the demise of Trump.

NEW YEAR'S DAY 2021

I spent yesterday with friends, ostensibly for drinks to see in the new year, staying over in the guest room. From 3 p.m. until 3 a.m., a sumptuous roast turkey dinner, wine and champagne, talking for twelve hours solid. The hostess, who had tirelessly been working all day cooking and serving, retired to her bed just after midnight, whilst the host and I continued pontificating on the world, sharing stories, getting more ridiculous and outrageous after every refill of the wine glasses. I could not keep my eyes open a minute longer and had to retire myself, much to the chagrin of the host who clearly has much more staying power than me.

It felt odd sleeping in a strange location, but also luxurious with piping hot water on tap and heating in abundance. The guest room is a luxurious apartment with lounge, kitchen, bathroom and every conceivable amenity. I slept soundly until 7.30 this morning, waking to complete silence. Perhaps another few hours dozing? Best not to move around for fear of disturbing the hosts in another part of the building, themselves sleeping soundly, too.

10.30 a.m. I had to get up, let the cat out and spend an eternity primping and preening myself.

Midday. I telephoned the host to enquire if he was up and about. No chance! Sounding dead to the world, my hosts were clearly sleeping in a tad longer.

1.15 p.m. I could wait no longer. Not wanting to disturb them, I decided to slink away home and leave them in peace. Drat! My shoes were behind a locked door to the music room, so with just socks on my feet, I quietly left, hoping I would not be stopped by the local police thinking that I might have escaped from an institution. I arrived home with soaking, cold feet, the rooms now also freezing cold having had no heating for the past twenty-four hours. It nevertheless was a pleasure to be back into my minimalist familiar surroundings. Another hour, with the heaters on full blast, the log burner roaring away and coffee at hand plus the pot-noodle I had brought back with me for emergencies. Great to sit back and reflect on the previous festivities, a surprising turnaround from what I was originally going to do, which was precisely nothing.

I considered a few resolutions, habits I might change or new adventures for the new year. I decided that I would cease my ridiculous videos and give everyone a break from my nonsense. Only after the passage of time when your guard is down to perhaps come bursting back to annoy you all with my odd lifestyle and provocative views of life in Latvia. For now, I am going to concentrate on my own little fortress and see if pottering in the garden is what I am best suited for.

ANOTHER LONG EPITOME FROM BRIAN

(Ed. Yes, I know, 'epitome' is not the right word, but hey ho, Brian is a modern Mrs Malaprop, and it's his memoir, not mine)

This time on the difficulties of being insular, private and of strong moral values, but at the same time gregarious and loving meeting people. Now that I am in Latvia, in spite of the lockdown, meeting online and occasionally, when it is safe to do so, visiting friends who are totally unaware of my strange ways and beliefs. I now have new friends that live not far away, twenty minutes' walk along and under the elevated overpass and along the railway track. These shortcuts soon learnt, I have visited a few times and they often invite me to share dinner with them, to which I always decline but nevertheless end up doing so, reluctantly, I might add.

Why am I appearing to be such an ingrate?

My antecedents from childhood have woven those experiences into my life choices, actions and foibles. So much so that I might appear aloof, un-caring or anti-social. A great example is that of being uncomfortable eating with others, however close I might be as a friend or partner. I love being invited for an evening of bonhomie, drinks flowing, the chatter, the cosines of sharing the warmth surrounded by friends here in Latvia, enhanced by a log fire crackling away, flickering flames and low lighting as mirth and conversation wile away many hours without noticing the passing of time.

"So, what's the problem?" you might ask.

Two-fold. The first, is that I never accept anything without contributing something, be it gifts or a simple invitation. Except once, here in Latvia, when I received the best and only present this Christmas, an electric blanket, now one of my most treasured possessions. Normally, as I said, I refuse gifts of any kind, and make it known, for fear really of being caught in a cycle of how to return the favour. What do I do - buy them a bigger one, buy them something they don't want or need in return? Soon to be like so many homes, filled with trinkets and ornaments, pots and pans, garish pairs of socks and underwear that will spend the next decade or two cluttering up the house, moving home with crates of junk. Even worse than present-giving is the thought that you might just be a charity case and can have our cast-offs. Actually, I don't mind the latter so much, if it is something they were going to put into the trash. I have had some great things, but only when someone has said, 'We are throwing this or that out with the trash,' when I will ask if I might have it. That is great.

Back to being invited out for a soiree with friends. Bearing in mind the limitations to my budget, I have to take something to the party, be it a bottle of wine, flowers or food. Therein lies a problem. Mostly, I am invited by people way above my social standing, successful, articulate and intelligent, who fortunately appear to like my company. They, of course are generous hosts, kind and caring. It would be an insult to take advantage of their largess in entertaining me by arriving with nothing, much less than the cheapest bottle of plonk or some withered flowers from the graveyard passed earlier. So, I must restrict my attendances simply because I'm not able to contribute in a meaningful way. As much as I might yearn to go somewhere, I do have to balance this with my resources - fares, drinks and contributions to the food on offer. So, mostly, I respectfully make excuses, like duties that preclude my attendance.

That was the first problem. Now for problem number two.

Without expanding on the subject of my childhood, it will suffice to say that food or meals came many times from neighbours and free school dinners. School holidays was when I would try to earn money to buy cakes and sweets or sandwiches to supplement our lack of decent meals at home, when no one would be hanging out of a window in the street shouting, 'Brian, Brian, come up here and have dinner.' Fabulous at the time, although I hated being asked to have a wash first. Now, seventy years later, I fear, the embarrassment of sharing a meal with anyone. It is a trial that hopefully ends quickly. How much should I eat, to be polite? Dare I leave anything? What is this strange food, and will it be ghastly? I am used to only the simplest foods, bread, potatoes, vegetables cooked as they are, no enhancements, no sauces, garnishes or gravies. I hate the formality of buffets or bowls of food in the centre of the table for every diner to help themselves. Do I dare take two Brussel sprouts, two carrots, two slices of that beautiful roast beef? Best not, I think. Don't want anyone to know that actually I could eat the whole lot. So, my standard answer to, 'Would you like more?' or 'Do you want to try the cheeses?' is to decline and say that it was all wonderful, but I could not eat another thing. Some dinners can go on for an hour or longer as I keep up with the conversations, looking at the centre of the table, watching others dip in frequently to take more of everything but daring not to myself, laughing with everyone at the appropriate time, stifling a yawn whilst pushing around what I have on my plate to confirm to the hosts that I am indeed enjoying what I have.

There you have it. Just one of my quirks, I guess.

Mostly, I am considered, I think and hope, to be the perfect guest, polite, respectful and can talk on many subjects, having lived many lives in this one. Ask me about my views on the world, religion, quantum physics, politics or the theory of relativity and I will have a view. I know nothing about such things, and when the going gets tough and I am trying to stifle another yawn, disguising it as a cough, I say anything, completely off the subject. Or medical issues that old folk like to talk about, including the range of tablets they are on. They are walking encyclopaedias on every medication known to man. The only thing I have is arthritis in all my joints; thankfully I do not have the full ritus!

At that point, my ignorance is abundantly clear and creates mirth!

RESIDENCY

Brian's ever unfolding story retiring to Latvia.

Yesterday, another visit to immigration to collect my temporary residency card. It will be changed again in January, following Brexit.

O8.40. First in.

Sadly, first out.

They would not release it because I could not show I had private insurance for the first year. My S1 certificates and E11 card were not sufficient. I had hoped my insurance was organized. However, contacting my friend and legal advisor Rick, I was told to stay put and wait whilst he enquired online for an insurer. Yes, came the reply, for forty-five euros.

"Wow, buy, buy, buy now!" I shout.

Getting in touch with them, he is informed that actually, on seeing how old I was, it would be six hundred euros! He searches again. All the time I am waiting, freezing to death. Half an hour later, he calls me. Result, he has found a travel agency that could arrange it for me, three months at fifty-four euros. Great. However, not from today but tomorrow. The immigration office had insisted that it would have to be from today. Tomorrow was not acceptable to release my card.

Rick advised me to go back again and use my charm to see if they would accept my new, lovely policy. Immigration downloaded it from my phone and with some slight reluctance and a lot of charm from me, issued my card, reminding me that I would have to have another year's private insurance in January when collecting the new full-term card. The staff really are nice and super friendly, only the systems make it so difficult. Rules are rules, even if we don't understand them. Plus, I still needed to open a Latvian bank account as Revolut is not recognized in Latvia.

Still not heard from the Latvian National Health Service yet. I had dropped into their post box my S1 forms, passport copy and address. So, very happy. I have my card now, but still things to do.

A long walk to the station and cutting through the shopping mall, I pass a shop selling e-scooters. On a whim, I bought one. Now, I can travel and explore without walking for longer than thirty minutes with pain in my feet. Plus, it gives me another reason to continue my quest to live here, however difficult.

Forgot the gin and shopping. I had my shopping trolley filled with spare wheels and parts, plus a scooter under my arm. It was a taxi back home. For the moment, I think I will take a week off chasing my tail and waiting for the frost to dissipate.

SOME THOUGHTS ON LGBTQ+

Something quite different to the usual posts. Maybe you have a view, maybe not, but do feel free to comment. I won't be offended. I have posted to some relevant groups here in Latvia. It is a banner that I have carried for the past sixty years and still do so, as a retired Englishman in Riga. I am in my seventies now and have been gay for as long as I remember, even from six or seven years of age. I fought for gay rights over many decades, had a partner for twenty-six years and another for fifteen years. Now I am single again. I saw Latvia as a challenge to help promote understanding of LGBTQ+ through my own years of campaigning whilst being subjected to abuse, loss of employment, eviction from housing and police harassment when the UK was where Latvia is now, struggling to recognize everyone's right to peaceful co-existence and accepting that, although we are not all of the same orientation, we nevertheless contribute to society as a whole.

The challenge here appears to be making initial contacts. Obviously, the language is a major stumbling block, plus of course my age, although that should be a positive given my many life experiences. As in England fifty or sixty years ago, it is left to the brave souls who live mostly in peace to promote a fair and accepting society whilst many sit on the side-lines watching, or worse, denying who they are for the sake of self-preservation.

LGBTQ+ should not be about an insular group but be pushing the boundaries. It was never meant to be solely a place for random meetings and private parties, as fun as that may seem, but working together to show a united front.

MORE SHOPPING

Back to reality and shopping. So many shops, so cheap and such good quality, we went from one to the other, my bags getting heavier and heavier with all the clothes I'd bought. Arriving in Riga with only three shirts, three pairs of trousers, an overcoat and jacket, hat scarf and gloves, I was dramatically bereft of clothing. Twenty-five items of clothing later, plus a pair of Logitech speakers, that incidentally I had been admiring in the electronics store earlier in the day, too much to carry, we left them all in the last shop and went for something to eat. At last, a hot meal! Yummy. Then collect everything, a taxi back to Rick's where he gives me even more, plus a pair of patent leather shoes.

Absolutely shattered by now, a bucket of Turkish tea awash with tea leaves, more of a meal than a drink, it was time for me to call for another taxi to take me home, requesting and receiving assistance with all my bags.

So nice to get home. Nine-thirty. I had been trolling around all day and my feet were seriously giving me gip. Sorry slipped into the vernacular of London for a moment. I set up my weather-station while my speakers played flawlessly through the TV aerial, then I collapsed into bed.

Not a bad first day overall and certainly made up for being in isolation for ten days. I was able to see lots of people, talk to everyone and feel alive again.

Later today, my lawyer and his friend Denis have invited me to a concert, which means another trip by taxi into town, although now I have a selection of clothes to wear. All these taxi rides and snacks in restaurants and buying so many clothes in the charity shops is running down my limited amount of money. I had brought with me a sort of three months buffer zone of funds to ensure I could pay the rent and still buy some food, so must be careful.

SHOPPING

I have just returned from the first foray on my scooter. Brilliant, but cold. I will love it, I know, especially when we emerge from winter. However, I know that next week I shall once again be chasing the authorities on my various quests.

My first day out of isolation started with an exploratory walk to find the train station, for reference. Twenty-five minutes to walk to and only seven to come back. I blamed the sun on my phablet obscuring the screen!

Rather bleak station with no ticket office or machine plus no idea what side of the tracks to be on for the city. With travel quite difficult to organise and adjust to with apps and paying via a card, I am a bit reluctant to spend euros on individual journeys, such as taxis. If I use the card for my UK bank, it costs me twice as much with all the charges.

Not to be daunted, I did order a taxi via the Bolt App. Wow, so easy and efficient and cheap. Fortunately, I do live on a short road, so inputting the wrong house number was no problem for the driver as he could see some old crone waving at him down the road.

I'd guessed the destination point, the mega shopping centre, where my lawyer had taken me on the way from the airport ten days earlier and was able to recognise that it was on a confluence of major roads. Using the app, I took a chance and stabbed the screen with my finger, hoping that I would not be dropped off at some out-of-town car breaker in the middle of an obscure industrial zone.

Bingo! The exact place I wanted to be.

The first task was to look for a shop that sold shopping trolleys. No luck. All these shops cater for the young upwardly mobile wanting designer tat, but I did buy myself a man bag, or messenger bag, after going in and out of almost every shop on the first floor.

The real purpose of my trip was to buy food, of which by now I had just half a packet of biscuits left and some stale bread. Opposite the huge food outlet was an electronics store where I thought I might amble around. Stroking the microwaves, looking at all the lovely things I could purchase once I had a lease and was assured of staying, I continued to perambulate each aisle, making a mental note of everything. I eventually left the store having purchased a weather station, a printer lead, plus a Phillips superior digital antenna which did absolutely nothing when I set it up at home and which I donated to charity.

Onwards into the Mega Food Store, grabbed a trolley and proceeded with my plan to walk every aisle. After all, I had all day.

The first aisle was plants and garden stuff, admiringly thinking that I could get some on a later visit. To my left were all the deodorants. Picked up some, including aftershave, bits and bobs and a humungous pack of cheap metal clothes hangers to complement the two I already had.

My mobile alerts me to a message from my lawyer. Would I like to drop into his place for lunch and a jaunt to all the charity shops in Riga. I said yes, give me a minute to pay for what I had already in my basket, text me the address and I would get a taxi. Gleefully dashing to the checkout, I was soon on my way again. Oops, minus any food shopping!

Love the taxis. Dropped off on the street with time enough for a cigarette before my lawyer came out of the building opposite to meet me. A look around his beautiful apartment and then it was off to the charity shops.

SCOOTING

Having cleared an escape route path to the street today, this is what I was faced with. The elevated road runs along where I live. The first real test for my electric chair in the snow.

Failed miserably. Three times, members of the public helped push me through snow drifts to get onto the pavements. A long line of traffic behind me on the roads as the normal footpaths became impossible with the cambers allowing me to slide into the roads or get stuck where they had not been properly cleared. Nearly ran out of charge with all the power being used to extricate myself so often.

However, I did make a superb shopping trip with bags and boxes filled to the brim and the extra weight helping me to keep a grip on the roads. Absolute relief when getting back home and a parent from the school helped me up the pavement to my gate.

Looks like it will be a bus or taxi for any further trips.

Minus 12 degrees now, so pleased to be back in the warm.

Keep warm everyone and if anyone wants my help to get or do anything, just ask.

AN INVITATION

My first invitation to a social soiree this festive season.

Given the first journey out for nearly two weeks, last Monday, effectively trapped by the snow, I decided that for last night's event I would take the much safer option of not using my mobility scooter and having random strangers dragging, pushing and lifting me out of the snow at the sides of the road or having long lines of traffic behind me as I ambled along at top speed. To save costs of taxis, I decided to go by bus, only using a taxi for the return journey. A great plan. Taking my shopping trolley with me to get more supplies at a corner store to see me through the festive season.

A change in the weather today, only one degree and rain. At least I wouldn't be too cold on the journey. Actually, less than two kilometres away if I were to walk, take the shortcuts under the motorway overhead road and cut along the railway lines, but the snow was still too deep.

So, the plan was to take a bus from my road, almost into the city centre and then a tram from there to my ultimate destination. Timings worked out, suitably dressed, looking like a telly tubby, off I went to my bus stop. Ten minutes early, in spite of the rain. I was not risking being late and the bus zooming off without me. Standing in the darkness of my street in the rain, getting concerned that my bus did not arrive as expected whilst all the time getting wetter and wetter. I could have easily called a taxi, blow the expense, but as it happens, although I know where I am going on several different routes, I can never remember the address, so that was out.

Eventually, the bus appeared, much to my joy, just ten minutes late. Leaping aboard, an uneventful and short journey, the only slight problem is that it is pitch dark outside and misted windows inside. Looking at the onscreen display does give one an indication of progress. Un-pronounceable names that mean nothing to me but a voice announcement of the stops. Great, no problem. The bus eventually halts in the dark by the river and the voice says, bla, bla,

bla, National Bibliatic. Leaping up, I am off the bus, watching it squish away and realising that the, bla, bla, bla was actually announcing the next stop! What a bitch.

So now, crossing the road, sinking deep into the snow piled up and dashing across to the other side, taking an icy path. It was not a long walk, but a slippery and slushy one, my canvas shoes decidedly damp. I did not anticipate doing anything but a short walk before starting out this evening and had thought that I would not turn up at a fine dining experience in my boots.

Anyway, not too far. I skirted around the national library to shorten the route, missing what looked like in the distance a blaze of Christmas lights and music blaring out, but I did have a tram to get and only a couple of minutes to get it.

Obviously, I missed it.

Undaunted, I went to the bus/tram/trolleybus stops opposite the national library. Not a bad place to wait because there is some cover there, under the trees. Lots to watch as it is a major transit hub, so comings and goings of all types of transport.

The bus stop pole with all four sides lists every route except mine, of course. There were a few blank spaces so maybe mine had fallen off. Time for a cigarette and just see if the Number 10 tram might appear. No, it didn't , so I asked a nearby young man if he spoke English? Yes, no problem, how can I help with a great welcoming smile.

"Am I at the right place for my tram?" I had done this route earlier in the year and was sure I was standing in the correct place. Like me, he scanned every side of the bus stop routes to no avail. Another gentleman came along and asked the first man, if he could help.

"Where are you going?" he asked. I replied, "I don't know, but it is that direction," waving my arm. "It's the number 10 tram I need."

Problem solved, there are about four routes that do not stop here at the side of the road but in the middle of the road by the iron railings. Great. And at least my location from memory was only half a width of road out. Thanking the gentlemen profusely, I cross the middle of the road and with the glow from my mobile phone, I could see the timetable. Just eight minutes to wait, time to work out exactly where the doors open when the tram stops so I will not have to dash through the slush dragging my trolley, hoping to get aboard before the doors crank closed.

Along the tram comes. I'm on, much to my relief, and can see even less out of the windows on this as it goes into the dark roads. There is the electronic board inside, but again I recognise nothing. I do know where to get off, by keeping my eyes glued on the doors as they open and close at every stop until I recognise bits of buildings at my stop.

The woman driver beckons me in front of her tram to cross onto the other side of the road in front of her tram. It's still raining and now there are great puddles of rain and slush everywhere. A stop into a great local shop and I fill my shopping trolley to the brim. If there is going to be an earthquake or tsunami, I know I will survive.

Eventually, arrive at my host's home, let myself in and park my trolley near the door in the hall. Much too heavy to traipse upstairs with it, and wary of damaging the beautiful new tiles. Naturally, wearing so many clothes, long thermal underwear, thick but warm ripped trousers with jogging trousers over them so no-one would notice, a thick shirt, heavy zipped pullover many times too big so I have to roll back the ends of the sleeves to my elbows, bought in a charity shop for just a few euros, but super warm. My hat with lovely earmuffs that my hostess on an earlier occasion had sewn elastic on to stop it flying off in the wind when careering at full pelt on my scooter. Scarf, gloves, shoes, heavy double lined, fur collared coat, now profoundly wet.

I was not stripping naked in the hall, but even so, with so much clothing and organising myself to appear casual and well dressed, takes some time. As is my habit, I tend to talk to myself or the trolley whilst so doing.

The hostess knew I had arrived and assumed I was talking to someone in the hall. No, I told her, I was calling the cat.

Anyway, I had arrived and to a great gin and tonic. Wow, the gin was in a bottle with a picture of an orange on it but called itself apple something. It was actually Booths that had been decanted for travel into a plastic container. It tasted special all the same.

Watched the hostess as she prepared and laid out foods from around the world, mostly European, strange looking blobs of this and that with equally strange names. A selection of equally fine and expensive wines to accompany every well planned and orchestrated course of which there were many.

There were to be only two other guests, incredibly late, but at least the evening could start. Everyone appeared to love the fare and quaffed with delight.

Four women and myself, three smoked, and that included the hosts, and two did not, one of whom after a while said she was feeling sick with the cigarette smoke and pouted and glared. I did suggest that opening a window behind her would help, especially if she went outside and could easily talk to us through it. She was not amused.

It always amazes me that people knowingly step into someone's home where they know smoking is always taking place and then want to dictate and throw a tantrum. Anyway, no one took any notice and we all carried on. Windows were opened for her and a bucket offered to be sick in, should she so desire.

From there the evening took a downward spiral as I asked her friend whether she was single, married and what she worked at. Did she have children or a boyfriend? I must admit, I did forget her name so often that the guest who objected to the smoke so vociferously went into a rage, saying how disrespectful of me to keep deliberately forgetting her friend's name or where I lived, getting angrier all the time.

So, the evening came to a close, the two girls leaving, one of the hostesses then went into a deep sleep mid-sentence, the other clearing away the debris from the evenings fare.Then wrestling and cajoling hostess number one up-stairs to bed, left me to turn out the lights.

Calling a taxi on my mobile phone, at least my address is registered so the application asks if I want to go home. Yes, perfect! Four euros plus a three euro tip was well worth it that time of the night, plus my now heavy shopping trolley that the driver retrieved from the car boot and hiked it over the snow mountain outside my gate.

That was yesterday 11th of December 2021, and weeks yet of merriment, parties and non-stop fun ahead.

For myself, I have decided that I really should not be in anyone's company other than my own for at least another month. This could save many corrosive skirmishes or even an international incident. So, loads of fun and love to you all. I am considering going to St Tropez instead.

TIME FLIES

Where have I been for the past two months?

Living the life of a hermit!

Somehow, during last autumn, most of my friends being away on holiday, working abroad or living in the countryside, I got used to my own company and friends in the garden - the birds, the moles and other furry things scampering around. Hacking away at the trees, mowing designs in the lawns etc.

Then came the snow even more than last year. Having to dig a path through to my gate to go shopping, my electric chair being bogged down in the snow no less than three times on one shopping trip on December 16th. Three times, members of the public helped push me out of the snow drifts at the side of the road.

Fortunately, my planning for bad weather this year included having at least two months of food and necessities in stock, twice the volume of briquettes to keep me as warm as toast. Loving the idleness of winter, staying up late, sleeping in until the afternoon and a reluctance to tread outside as I had last year. Somehow, I must have got older or more susceptible to the cold, or perhaps it was that I had lost the laces to my boots or maybe just being lazy, which is probably the real reason.

For the first time in a month, and during a lull and slight thaw in the snow, I did manage last week to go by taxi shopping, my shopping trolley, a giant haversack and a large shopping bag, all filled to the brim with another month's supply. Amazing timing because the next day, the snow returned.

The beginning of this week, the snow melted. I charged my electric pram in the expectation of being able once more to drive around and maybe visit friends. But no, the snow has returned.

Most know that I am an avid reader of news around the world, watching news channels, following the politics with great interest and tutting to myself when things go bad.

Listening to what some of you have said about so much of my posts being deleted before you or any might have seen them. Actually, they were never deleted but put into the archives, thinking that after a day or two, they would be of no real interest to anyone else but me for memories. So, I have restored from my archive all that was there to my posts. It does make reading long and perhaps tedious, but then, if one is laying in hospital in an iron lung and can't afford to pay for the hospital television, it would keep one occupied. Should anyone delve deep enough through all my posts, they are now in no particular order and some are repeated, a bit like my brain.

This is, by the way, something of an apology for my lack of posts and visits. However, I can confirm that I am still well, vibrant and happy. My brain is hurting now, so I will stop, until the next time.

Happy weekend everyone in the snow!

NEW YEAR REFLECTIONS

A break in the weather today, Wednesday. Sunshine and a gentle breeze. A great chance to shop for the new required PP masks, announced to be law from two days ago. Fabric masks are not allowed in any circumstances, be it on transport or in shops and other public places.

Fortunately, I did have a rather old and grubby one, so at least I thought I would be able to emerge into the world of Latvia and purchase some new ones.

I was going to go by bus, leaving with a few minutes to spare. I trudged to the bus stop only to discover I had forgotten my mobile phone, an absolutely necessary piece of kit for ordering a taxi for the return with my shopping. Sadly, trudged back along the road to collect it and glanced at the bus zooming past. Never mind, I ordered a taxi instead.

Along it came, the driver putting his cloth mask on as I boarded. Soon at Riga Plaza, fifteen minutes prior to it opening. However, the doors swished open and in I walked, pleased to be wearing my now regulation mask and brandishing my Covid certificate for the security guard to scan. But wait! He was wearing a cloth mask, much to my surprise.

On into Maxima. Fewer customers than staff and absolutely everyone in a cloth mask. Asking if I could purchase a new regulation mask, the answer was a firm 'No', "but we do have a pack of five cloth masks." Perhaps, I thought, they might be trying to sell the old masks first. Crossing to the pharmacy opposite, they too only had cloth ones. Then to the Bank, the cigarette shop. Still no one wearing the new ones.

Does seem odd that the rules were absolute and mandatory and not a regulation mask to be had or seen anywhere. Great planning!

Russia and the Ukraine situation appears to be getting worse, my worry being, should it all kick off, there could easily be a glitch in banking and IT, so it seemed prudent to ensure enough cash withdrawn to survive any money market crashes and be able to honour one's own commitments. Similarly, the reason for another big shop was to secure enough essentials - food, cigarettes and libations - should the supply chains be disrupted. I would urge others to take similar precautions.

I do hope that Putin will resist his aims of taking back Ukraine and indeed Georgia and later Lithuania and Latvia too, although the last two have done the most to legitimise their governments and of course are in NATO. I worry firstly for Ukraine and then Georgia, not so sound and free from serious Russian influence with a great deal of reported corruption and avoidance of basic human rights.

Back home again, warm and cosy. Maybe next week I will be digging trenches and erecting Anderson shelters, if anyone knows now what they are. Fortunately, I know a former freedom fighter that was one of those Wood People fighting for Latvia's freedom and also a joyful and incredible woman of great age. I am sure she could teach me much in any skirmish.

Looking now for where to buy camouflage paint for my scooter, to be able to make forays out at night across front lines to carry out acts of disruption, should the worse come to the worse.

Stay safe everyone. There is nothing wrong with thinking about the worst that could happen and planning for it, although hopefully it would be a waste of time. Have a great weekend, snow or no snow? At least I have my shopping.

Post: **https://www.facebook.com/LatvianMFA/posts/307407571416142**

MY BRIEF PHILOSOPHY

Freedom of thought, spirit and communication leads to an inner peace and happiness, even though that may bring harshness and even poverty of friends and living, cannot surpass the freedom of true honesty of one-self. These alone bring inner self-respect. Moreover the realisation that others through their own hardships and personalities may not feel able to follow your ethos of life and for that you have to also respect their trials in life by being friends and still giving respect. My eyes see, my ears hear, I hope also my heart feels.

A LONGER THAN USUAL POST

Good day everyone!

Rather a long post and I do hope that you manage to read it all. A few paragraphs you would have read before in some of my history, however, do stay with it.

A couple of months ago, in addition to my normal news reading and video watching on Facebook, I came across a predator hunting group live video of them catching, surrounding, interrogating and handing the miscreant over to the police. Since then, I have watched so many, as there are up to a hundred of these groups throughout the UK and they all combine and share knowledge plus posting the stings daily that are happening.

On some of these groups, I have anonymously posted some of what is written below for awareness of what it is like from a child's perspective and give support to what are termed as survivors or grooming and rape in childhood. The effects being suicides, drug abuse, alcohol abuse, fractured relationships for life and abandonment from their own families. Even worse is the abuse that happens to many from their own family members and neighbours.

I share this with you so that you also understand my strange and distant manner, why I don't ever contact anyone first and never accept anything.

I would be happy if anyone shared my comments to all hunter groups, for them to be aware that all survivors, people like me, draw great comfort to watch the stings and to be aware that so many like me can bring some sort or closure to all the angst. Too late for me to be aware of the reasons now, I have always felt so different, maybe I could have done something to help, although I doubt it.

My closest friends in the past have questioned if I was really gay, mainly because of my unwillingness to engage in sex, even my partners, for whom I felt sorry for and happily paid for them to seek that part of a relationship elsewhere. However, I am gay and do have the same dreams as anyone else, a strong man, a loving man, someone to cuddle up to, warmth and hugs, but just forget the rest.

This is the most I have revealed as it doesn't matter too much now at the end of my life, there is so much more that even so, now I could not speak of.

So, carry on hunting teams. You are a real blessing to all of us survivors that few of our colleagues and friends would realise. Everyone knows that I am gay, but I am equally afraid of men too and trust no one. Single, widowed and isolated, with the exception of a few really good guardians and one especially in particular. For now, I am now happy with the entertainment value of all the hunter groups, in watching the people squirm and come up with excuses that have been caught grooming children via the medium of the internet.

Amazingly, I have suffered from reverse grooming in the recent past, flattering but frightening at the same time. The same grooming scenario but for money or an easy life. Being a gay widower now brings them out like flies to manure in the hope of an easy life, an inheritance. Who in their right mind would even contemplate a wrinkled old geriatric unless they really were of a strong disposition.

Times have changed so much. In my childhood, being saved from some man bundling me into a van at the age of four, from being ravaged at 5, raped at 7, a neighbour taking me to a park and the toilets and forcing me to sit on his lap, tied up and fondled from 11 until 15 regularly every week until I left school and did not want to do it anymore because I earnt a wage and did no longer need his money. Plus, he had found another lad to tie up in the cellar. I point out that from 11 years old I was expected to work to feed and clothe myself. Nothing too sinister. All he would do is strip me, ask me to relieve him after untying me, and I would get ten shillings, a lot of money to me then. I hated it, but apart from fondling for a couple of hours, in between serving customers in the shop, he never attempted anything else. To be fair, he did each year remember my birthday which no one else did, even in my family, and gave me another ten bob. He would ask to see my school reports and reward me similarly. There were others equally kind and caring in their own way, which made me think that they were so, because interspersed with those were the real, evil monsters.

In later years, I would give advice to groups of teenagers coming out into the gay world and their parents about staying safe, never going home to someone else's house without telling a friend, staying always near an open door or window, not accepting more than one drink and most importantly being able to run fast. All else failing, I gave a few self-defence moves, some not so pleasant but effective. Even now at my age, I feel competent in defending myself.

Going to a cinema then to watch a film, or worse, the cartoon cinemas on Waterloo and Victoria railway stations was a real danger with some pervert coming and sitting next to you and soon a hand on your leg, frozen as it moved slowly up, pushing it aside and changing seats to be in the same situation yet again, some offering money to go to the toilets with them. Twice I remember being saved by others, adults sitting nearby realising what was happening.

I blamed myself and still do, because I did not run fast enough, or even enjoyed the attention and sometimes gifts from someone just for being cuddled and fondled, to be loved. I regularly seemed to be friends with all sorts of people. Perhaps it was my cheerful and trusting disposition. I thought that that was what love was. Only if they guided my hand to touch them was something that I hated, but actually some did not and I was happy to just sit on their laps, enjoying the caresses. Home was violent, extreme, knives, guns, police, all part of the mix. So, love elsewhere was so comforting, if a little uncomfortable at times.

Amongst all those were genuine caring people that loved me to keep them company, listening to their stories, sharing laughter. I remember the old man sitting late at night in his roadside tent, guarding the materials for digging the road works in St Johns Wood, London. A green tent, the red lamps and the hot brazier with the kettle always hot on top.

I stopped to warm my hands, he offered me tea and an up-turned bucket to sit on and we talked for an hour or two before I began my walk back home in the early hours of the morning.

Yet another really caring person was when I was a teenager, after finishing work at an off licence at 10.30 at night, I would go to an almost derelict shop in a back street where the tenant, a Canadian ex-soldier who had stayed after the end of World War Two, lived in absolute squalor. The shop window was just stacked high with old televisions and other rubbish, obscuring any view in or out, excluding any daylight too. He had no carpets or furniture, save for his ancient rocking chair. Helping him for a couple of years, he always wore exactly the same clothes, never changing and never washing. He did not have a bath or any facilities other than an old sink and cold tap. Not even a kitchen. He had no official papers and subsisted by purchasing 200 old TV sets at a time from Radio Rentals and DER, ex rentals that could not be repaired any more. I would then help him until 2 am, breaking them down, salvaging every part, the screws, valves, aluminium chassis, which he would then sell for scrap along with the valves at street markets, finally burning the cases in an open fire in the back room, half in and half out of the fireplace, kicking the cabinets piece by piece into the fire as they burnt. The smoke in the room was horrendous, with that and the gloom from a 25-watt bulb and amongst it all he had a coffee pot, battered, completely black from being put in the fire, always loaded with coffee and salt. Yuk. It was vile. I never got paid but I would accompany him to the scrap yards to sell his scrap and a treat for a fry-up in a café. His van was equally ancient, not an undamaged panel, several paint jobs over the years, bald tyres and the engine always needed coaxing and a lot of bad language before it would start. No road tax or insurance of course. Sometimes I would come across TVs and radios that I could get going again and take them home. Loving playing with electricity, I had them in the bedroom that I shared with my father. He would not sleep with my mother because he had emphysema, occasionally unable to breath. I had a cylinder vacuum cleaner tied to the top of an open window, the hose reversed to force air into my father's mouth when he shouted he was dying and then packed up breathing. It was successful. I had installed a fuse box, extension leads, breakers and always had at least four televisions and a couple of radios that I would be working on and would give them away to anyone that did not have one.

Whilst I was breaking them down in the Canadian's back room, he would be rocking away in his rocking chair, singing old cowboy songs. He was an ex-rodeo rider from Calgary in Canada, his legs horrendously scarred from that occupation. Before he was called up to the army, he worked building the Canadian roads into the wilderness, not tarmac, just high roads of dirt. His language was the coarsest I have ever heard. His toilet was down the drain in the backyard, his bed in a room above, no lights, curtains and an old iron bedstead covered in old clothes and blankets. No wardrobe or drawers, just a pile of rags, his clothes, in the corner. He never washed them ever. Eventually he had to leave to avoid the inland revenue tax officials, lack of rent etc. He had told me where he was going and it was around 35 miles. He wanted me to visit him and I could stay the night in a caravan if I wanted. The last time I saw him was when I cycled, an old bone shaker, but with class because I had tied on the handlebars a Dansette portable radio with a huge battery in it, from Brixton to Guildford. It seemed to take forever but at least I had the radio at full blast all the way.

He was living in half of a caravan that had been in a crash and had no end to it, other than a tarpaulin. This was in a breakers yard for old commercial vehicles. He was employed to cut them up. At the time of my visit he was cutting up old dust carts from the local council. I loved helping but it was just too far for me to cycle to visit again. Sleeping over in the caravan was so spooky with the only light being from oil lamps and the rain coming in through the sides of the tarpaulin. Through all this I was the only person in the world that he knew. He would expect me to undertake any task, however dangerous, and scream and shout if it wasn't good enough. He was every inch from a bygone age. We would sit for hours, in the gloom in his shop and when he was not singing would be talking about his time building roads, riding the rodeos etc. He treated me as an equal, never touched me, hugged or said anything nice to me but guarded me with a passion if anyone was to comment on our friendship and made sure that we both ate. The food was ghastly however, slices of bread with oily fingerprints and tins of beans.

Another experience, another friend. An ex-member of the royal household staff, living in a grace and favour apartment, a truly kind and caring friend, whom I worked with, wanting to groom me in etiquette, teach me social skills, cut my hair and ensure I was eating properly when we met. Okay, he did want to caress and cuddle me with wandering hands but it was with no fear on my part, and never did he go further. I always believed it was in true love for me and not lust - well, maybe a bit of both. Sadly he died when I was visiting one evening, which led me onto another adventure…

I would fight free if and when anyone wanted me to touch them or show me their private parts. Just to look at them was horrific. It was a time when one could never reveal to anyone. The guilt was overwhelming. Many times, I would lay in bed, trying to hold my breath and hope to die and never wake up. Since then, of course, I have never accepted gifts, presents and never sold anything even from family and friends. There is always a price to pay.

Until just two months ago and seeing these hunter sites appear on Facebook around 98 of them in the UK, it has been like a drug. I am addicted to them, enjoying watching the predators squirm, hilarious excuses and more when they try to run and fight to get away. I love it! Now I am 76 and just realised the real reason that I don't like sex or seeing anyone near me naked. I could not bear the thoughts after my experiences of anyone wheezing, smelly and overweight, eyes staring and mouth drooling and seeing these posts. Even more horrific is that most are perverse to the extreme with revolting predilections.

I have had a long life filled with many adventures, met many people around the world but always with a full sense of propriety, even prudery. However, it has not stopped me enjoying the activities and joyful participation of young people, be it teaching or adventures, rock climbing, trekking etc. I am not unaware of what goes on. I have indeed written a comedic book of gay sexual activities, some from witnessing and some researched online. Maybe that is what keeps me happy and sane, plus being knowing the foibles of sexuality and the many various degrees that make up the sex drive.

I had a partner for twenty-six years and another for fifteen but I have never liked physical sex or seeing people naked. These were wonderful years where I never slept in the same bed or room, unless for a cuddle and comfort. I rambled a bit there but am pleased to have done so. Only now do I realise why I am regarded as strange and eccentric, but also funny and entertaining at the same time. Thanks to you all, you predator hunters for what you do!

As a child in the fifties, most were unaware of the dangers of being on the street, caught a few times but mostly it was down to being unable to run faster and that was my bad luck. When one was caught you thought it was one of those things that happens and blamed yourself and told absolutely no one.

Whilst being abused in the family, when I was quizzed as to why I did not have a girlfriend and saying I did not like girls, I was ostracized and then went off to sea. Another story, but I did stay safe. Almost!

Wow, I must have been gorgeous looking, for it never stopped. I have been invited to parties in the best places in London. Film stars, etc. However much I declined attention, I did attend some auspicious, secretive events and gatherings, but managing to slip away before the hosts or others got too amorous. I have had some wonderful offers nevertheless, always declined for good reason. Fortunately, with age and slower reactions and many wrinkles, sadly, the chasing no longer happens. Were it to, I can now escape in my mobility scooter. On the other hand, should I want to stalk someone, I can keep up with them!

On a much more serious note, grooming now of minors, has come along as an epidemic from the development of the internet and the lack of control by the servers as to who has access. I really don't understand that anyone can have multiple Facebook accounts. I could understand two, one personal and one for work verified by ID, but what checks are there from these companies?

You should not be able to register with a mobile phone without a social security number or ID and any provider of these services stopping more than one telephone number unless one is a work phone. Similarly, sites like Facebook or all the other apps should by law have the same restrictions. I hold these social networks equally to blame. Perhaps every phone, tablet, laptop, desktop should have fingerprint recognition by law and only then could anyone access the web and apps with each having to prove their identity.

WAITING FOR SPRING

Desperate for Covid freedom and warmer weather!

Today, early, I dressed in my arctic clothing for a monthly trip out for urgent supplies. Grabbing my shopping trolley to place near the gate through the path I had cleared, a wheel promptly fell off, the clip securing it had fallen off into the snow. Luckily, I was able to find it, but my trip had to be cancelled until urgent repairs were made. Maybe it was my fault in overloading it, not only with shopping but also, removing the bag and using the wheels, like a sack barrow, to transport packs of briquettes, 4 packs at a time from my shed to my hall every week. Just one pack is heavy enough, so to shift so many at a time is a boon and gets full value from the shopping trolley's double purpose.

So now my shopping trip will take place tomorrow, going by taxi. As always, I try to maximise my trips to double purpose them for maximum value. First trip will be to the Covid Atta centre in Riga, just to see if they will be able to, as last time, print off my covid certificate to include the booster that I had a couple of months ago. I did read today that it would cease operation for Covid business as of the 16th of February. Important for me to get a print now because otherwise I would not know how to get one.

I could do it online if I had the app on my mobile phone to download and print myself, but it seems impossible to make it work. My friend has tried without success and given up. I have tried many times on the health departments web page, supposedly in English, which after a couple of pages of questions reverts to Latvian and then goes into a never-ending loop. Another friend tried for me, could not understand and also gave up.

In spite of having a residency ID, a health certificate, a local native suggested that it was because I did not have a Latvian bank account. Surely there must be many Latvians that don't actually have a bank account, so I don't think that is the reason. I do have a bank account with Revolut that is supposed to be recognized by Latvia, with a sterling and euro account. I used to pay directly for the rubbish collection, my phone top-up, Bolt and of course my pension payments from the UK. Certainly, I do not want or need another bank in Latvia and the charges in addition to what I already have. However, I would open one if I had confidence in the Latvian banking system but there are reports of corruption and fines they seem to regularly acquire.

Back to Covid. It is great to see so many countries relaxing the rules as the virus and variants are no longer swamping hospitals. A natural immunity is becoming prevalent. Indeed, the figures for infection are now higher in the inoculated than those that aren't, which to me seems to imply that the testing now is reporting positives because of the covid antibodies from inoculation.

That being said, the death rate amongst the elderly tips the other way, mostly from those not inoculated. Testing now en-masse, I believe, can be dropped.

Whilst I was and am in favour of inoculation, especially amongst the elderly, I welcome the dropping of all other constraints for the population at large and hope to see all industries back to normal. Proud that at least I did my bit during the peak of the pandemic not to exacerbate it. If I don't need ever again to have a certificate in the future, no efforts made to this date were wasted.

I seriously look forward to the ease of travel once again.

Have a wonderful weekend everyone!

WHERE DID I GET TO?

Where did I get to yesterday?

As planned, I was up early for me these days and by 11.30 I was boarding a taxi to take me to the Atta Centre to see if someone there would, as before, print off my Covid certificate with the all-important block of black and white things (ed. QR Codes) used to scan to prove stuff before being allowed entry to anywhere. More importantly, to travel, should I wish for a vacation when it gets warmer, to the Seychelles or the Ukraine.

Entering the Atta Centre, before, long lines of people outside, soldiers at the doors directing as one entered. Thirty or more manned desks, a receptionist to check paperwork at each before moving forward to another desk to be asked a lot of questions, such as does one suffer from any ailments, has one recently had a brain operation, suffer from scurvy, is pregnant or suicidal. Then on to another where a doctor views the replies and lastly to the person giving the jabs.

Today it is such a huge space, empty, save for one soldier at the entrance, who asked me what I was there for, got bored or confused with my rambling and just waved me to go in. Just one of the reception desks manned, one person to ask the medical questions and one person to give the jabs. The sum total of all those operating that I could see throughout the entire complex, just four.

I had been before following my first and second jabs to get a print off as proof. Easy, quick and so efficient. This time, the staff explained that none of them had the authority to access the health database. They tried, they telephoned their bosses, conferred with each other and decided I would have to go elsewhere in the city centre that was set up for issuing certificates.

Why could I not get the app onto my mobile phone to download my own certificate, I asked. They each looked perplexed until one asked to see my ID card. He said, "Your residency card is temporary, only for five years, and that is why you cannot get recognised in the health systems computer," even though I have, and always carry a letter, complete with all my registration details, from the health department assuring me of equal health and other services in Latvia, or any other EU country.

Such a nice group of people, friendly, helpful, even telephoning the place I should now go to, making an appointment and be met later in the day. Brilliant! Then it was another taxi to go shopping at the Plaza Centre.

With my regime of buying enough food and other supplies for a month on each visit, once again my trolley full to bursting, a large carrier bag and backpack too, it was another taxi back home.

Arriving home, drat! My lovely landlady is pummelling the ice on the pavement outside with a large, solid iron pole, the kind of implement you would use to make a hole in the brickwork behind a bank.

It is never easy for me to exit a car. My hips, knees and joints in general don't allow for an elegant exit, more a stumble onto the pavement. Worse this time, with the height of the snow to climb over, dragging my shopping from the boot of the car and over the mountain of snow.

My landlady has seen me and rushes to help me carry it all to my gate. How embarrassing. My portrayal of being superhuman, dashed. Just time now to unload and put away all my shopping, my empty bookcases now looking like a corner shop. Light my log burner, call another taxi an hour later for the trip to get my certificate.

Went like a dream. In the centre of Riga, ten minutes later, not one but two copies. I had thought of walking around for a while to look at the shops, however by now I was getting cold and tired, so just one more taxi home.

Now I am pleased with myself, ample stocks for a month again, certificate in hand, should I need to keep in front of any Russian advance. After all, if they do gain the whole of the Ukraine, what's to stop them carrying on? Anyway, that was yesterday and today I seriously overslept.

A DREAM

Something quite different from my normal bubbly, playful self. As always, my posts of experiences and adventures are real. Luckily, I see the funny side. That helps not to dwell on any situation. The following is an honest account of a recent dream of mine. Make of it what you will. I am not religious, nor saintly, nor deluded.

I find myself, alone, walking slowly atop a brick wall, just one brick wide, how high I cannot ascertain. When I look down, there seems to be no end, but I view through the mists much of life from many centuries ago, seeing slowly as I walk what happened, is happening to this day. I see sometimes if I peer hard all the way to the bottom, closer still to recognise people, sometimes they look up and wave. Can they really see me? I don't know, but I do cautiously wave back, just in case. Every day is the same. Weather calm, not even a breeze, like an overcast day, never dark, never sunny, never stopping, just walking and walking, slowly and steadfastly, do not run, do not slip, do not stop, it seems forever.

If I look to the left of the wall, the cloud is thick, I cannot peer through, who knows what is down there, is it safe or not. Similarly, to my right, that I am observing, as one period of time morphs into another, my glances reveal all peoples, lands, mountains and seas, yet still I can just stare and look as closely as I wish.

The wall appears to have an infinite height, is smooth, no handholds, no ladders, I feel if I sit down on it, I could slowly slide down without danger to the bottom, but I will be trapped and not able to climb back up if I did not like what I had landed amongst.

No, I must continue to walk, walk, walk, never stopping to sleep or rest. I don't seem ever to get tired. I don't need or want to eat or drink, I don't know how to smile or laugh or even cry. I think and try, screw my eyes up, make a sad mouth, but nothing comes. What happened to emotions? I care, but do not love. I feel, but not pain. I want to help but no one sees me.

Yet I feel for all the sadness I see as I traverse through time along my wall, unable to interject. Just an emotionless calmness as I continue walking. Sometimes slower to see another waving up - to me or what? Who is that? Is it me? Can't be. Am I seeing, I ponder, a person? I have known so few that are truly ones that I would be part of their heart. I admired them, without them ever knowing, for honesty, caring of all humanity and wish to envelope them in my dreams or them to envelope me in their arms, to never wake up. I tell myself not to be foolish. After all, I have no sex or feelings, no parts even, nothing to hide, except I do have some rough sort of grey smock that I feel comfortable in. But no, I must keep walking and walking and walking.

Looking behind me, I can never see how far I have walked or for how long. The clouds obscure everything in the distance, as indeed looking ahead of me. Will I ever reach the end? Do I want to? What is there if there is an end? I am not sure if I should walk further, but I do, I feel I must!

Maybe soon, the cloud on the left of the wall will clear enough for me to see down and know if it is better that side of the wall than on the right. It seems to be obscured deliberately to put me off sliding or dropping down. The only way is forward, walking, walking, walking, never stopping.

Then a slow realisation that I am observing sunlight, finding a chink at the edge of my curtains. Time to leave my dream and wake up fully. A new day is beckoning here at the bottom of the wall.

I did tell you, that I was not a full shilling or a sandwich short of a picnic. Happy days everyone.

A WORKING LIFE

From leaving school in 1961, a chronological history of every job, business to this day, or until I retired at 75 to come to Riga, almost penniless, homeless, wearing just a small back-pack and no luggage, my worldly possessions after a lifetime of adventures.

I am doing this weekly, focussing on one job adventure at a time. The list is long and for that reason I will number them in order, "Brian's work life, chapter 1" and so on. This will alert you to know if you have already read or search through my posts for the next chapter.

The ramblings of an elderly man, with the ogres of senility, bad health, lunacy, following me trying desperately to catch me up, I through much prompting by my Facebook friends have finally agreed to write more whilst still young. Maybe sparking memories of specific place to those ex-pats from the UK.

I am not clever or inventive enough to write a book so this is the only way I can retell my life through my posts. In particular, every job, location, even the dates and salaries, contracts etc. that I had kept throughout my life, I recorded to Google and copied to three friends, two in Latvia and one in England. So, every detail can be verified by anyone.

Arriving here in Riga with just two pairs of clothes and shoes, I had to leave twenty or so box files with all my records, even business accounts to have now been consigned to a skip after my former business and property are auctioned off, on behalf of the person I had gifted to, sadly to pass away, six months later.

So, on with the first chapter.

WORK HISTORY

Brian's working history 1: The Post Office

1961, Fifteen years old. An interview for the position of a young postman in London, hoping to be a telegram boy and get a red post office bicycle or better still a small red motorcycle, delivering urgent telegrams. First a full medical examination, stripped completely and prodded, fondled and every orifice carefully looked into, just so hugely embarrassing, standing naked in an office the doctor was given for the day, window open to the world and no lock on the door, praying no one would come in, but I did pass with flying colours.

Next to another room where three austere looking men sat behind a boardroom desk. I was told to take a chair in front of them whilst they seemed to take an age, not looking up but quietly whispering to each other, they then shuffled their papers, looked up and down at me, each asked questions about my hobbies, what I liked about school etc.

The last person then asked, "Why do you want to become a young postman in her majesty's postal service?" I replied that I would want to work all my life and one day be the holder of a position as important as theirs before I retired. In unison, they all chuckled and laughed. I didn't think it was so funny an answer then! However, they thanked me for coming and to expect a letter in the mail within a day or two.

The letter arrived informing me I was successful. The work would be forty hours per week and the wages £4/19s/6d per week, around 6 euros, plus luncheon vouchers, and I would report to personnel the following week for the position of an internal messenger for the next three years. The offices being the headquarters of the post office engineering department, numbers 2 to 12 Gresham St, London EC4.

Amazingly, I was required to go to Brixton day college one full day a week for the next three years for general education, exactly the same as at school, including sports, which I hated. Standing around in the winter in shorts on a football pitch was never my idea of fun. At my secondary modern school, St Marys, Newington Butts, next to a huge Rowton House for the tramps and homeless, where the cheapest stay was literally on a line – a strong rope in a huge room, strung from one side to the other. They had to sleep leaning over it. On sports day, a coach would take us from the Elephant and Castle to the sports fields in Morden, the end of the northern line. Here, everyone would alight, go to the changing rooms to don shorts and then a football or a run around the park. Mostly, I would just keep running home. The sports master got used to it in the end. The worst part of those days was, if I could not escape, it was hot showers to finish the day. I so hated having to take all my clothes off to shower amongst a whole class, but at least I did not need to have a bath those weeks. Somewhere on my Facebook are the school reports for those three years. I still "know nothing"!

Although I never ate or drank anything other than water at home my father insisted I give him £2/10s/0d for my keep, which left me little for myself to pay for food, travel to work and clothes. For now, I had to wear a clean shirt every day with the stiff paper collars and studs, although you could keep them for two days by turning them inside out. I was earning ten shillings a week at the off licence, C.H Wightman and son in Vassall Road. I had been working there since the age of 11 years in the evenings and weekends. The owner encouraged me to go to night school twice a week when he could manage without me. Now a young man, he felt I should make friends and have other interests, not be working all the time. That is what I did, one night learning metal work, another jazz appreciation. I really enjoyed both. It was he who gave me my first car, a 1932 Austin with running boards and a glass thermometer that screwed directly on to the radiator and could be seen by the driver. The windscreen wiper was manual. You had to turn it one way and then the other from the driver's seat.

My money - no different now, I think, for a youth to manage. I sometimes did not have enough for my tube fare to work so ran instead, five miles. However, I was a fast runner, by necessity. Going at full pelt, I could at times beat the bus or train, even a few times, running over the bonnets of cars at junctions in my way. The roads then as now grid-locked in the rush hours. Brixton Road, past Oval Station, Kennington Road, Newington Butts, over the roundabout at the Elephant and Castle, up Borough Road and High St to London Bridge and then to the Bank and just one street left to my office. The northern line tube was always a crush, rammed full, ever more people joining at London Bridge Station from the mainline. At least I was never ever late.

I never took days off sick until after a year had passed and I was summoned to the Chief of Messenger Services office. He castigated me for not going sick. He told me that everyone was allowed six separate days sick leave and I had to catch up because I would spoil what was a right that had to be taken. So, I did from then on. The boss was happy.

Ten floors of offices looking after the UK's postal service, each of the hundreds or more of postmen around the country, having a unique number and a brass chest badge. Latterly one of my duties was to refer to huge ledgers along with the latest list of those leaving or dying, crossing the name from the register with a red line. Their numbers were to be re-issued, but these ledgers were not to record individual numbers but to move every single postman up a seniority list. You could see those at the top with a lifetime of service down to me, nearly at the bottom.

The same offices had a research and development department managing science in communications and postal systems. One day, a huge machine appeared in the reception area of the offices, thirty metres long, three metres high and three metres wide, full of belts and stuff. With a great fanfare they started it up. A real beast, with a man at one end feeding bunches of letters into its hopper as fast as he could, the machine whizzing all of them around wheels and channels, reading the addresses and sorting them as well as franking the stamps. It was the first after developing the post code system. Soon after, the whole country was given a postcode. From here it was adopted around the world, including Latvia, eventually, over the next decade. How bad anyone's writing was, it was of no matter. If it was addressed with a post code, it would read it and direct anywhere in the UK.

Also developing, were experiments with colour television at its engineering works in Bermondsey. Top secret. I was sent there whenever the guard had a day off or holidays. Nothing to do except allow no one to enter that was not expected. It was at the end of a grubby road of warehouses and such, but there was a cafe a few doors away that made the most beautiful ham rolls, thick cut ham half an inch and I have never had such since.

Secretly, I was invited into an experimental laboratory one day to see the first colour TV experiments. All the scientists, so excited to watch for the first time, the words 'OXO' flickering hazy colours. Very important, they told me not to reveal what I had seen. It was still top secret. I felt honoured and told no one until colour televisions came along.

Also within the offices were the administration and control of the UK's telephone network, the hundreds of telephone exchanges manned by an army of women at huge exchanges in every town who deftly plugged the long leads from one doll's eye flashing on an exchange board with hundreds of calls coming in, to another, pulling a small lever for each to connect, keep waiting or end the call. At one of these, just visiting for a day or two, I learned how to operate them. You could talk and listen into anyone's conversation through your headset, and if you did not like the caller or they were offensive or rude being kept waiting for the line to be free, you just pulled their plug out.

From government ministers to the window cleaner wanting to know when to come around to Mrs Brown's when the husband would be at work. For this reason, I and anyone in the post office was required to sign the official secrets. Until I left the UK to come to Riga, I still had my signed copy.

Back to my office just a couple of hundred yards from King Edwards Building, the headquarters of the British Post Office, the biggest in the UK, where I would later stand sentry as an army cadet for poppy day. There are many other government buildings around the area, all linked by underground tunnels, plus of course, the post office underground railway system for mail and parcels on driverless trains. The carriages were more akin to coal trucks, no passengers or staff allowed, although I did manage it by just leaping in and lying flat. It was possible to travel across London to other major post offices, just climb out unseen, exit, look around and return the same way. No one ever stopped me because I melted into the post office staff in my uniform.

The railway still exists in part. A section is now a museum. Mostly, the rest are a forest of wires and cables feeding London's network and a secure backup of landlines for if ever the internet goes down or satellites were to be attacked by a foreign power.

However, back to my offices which also encompassed the Maritime department and the laying of undersea cables around the world. A fleet of deep-sea cable laying ships, HMTS, Her Majesty's Telegraph Ship. Much more on these later as I was to be on the flag ship, The Monarch, to the far east.

So where was I?

Oh yes, back in my office, issued with two uniforms, dark blue with matching greatcoat and hat, standard postmen style, another light tan one for summer, everyone being told on the day throughout the UK when to switch from winter to summer uniforms. A shiny brass badge with your unique number on a black background on your lapel, a row of brass buttons with the Queen's portcullis on them and a button stick and a tin of brass cleaning wadding. You were expected to polish all your brass, including your cap badge, every day. Five luncheon vouchers for the week, every week thereafter one for each day to use anywhere that had the luncheon voucher blue round logo. Value: one shilling.

On the top floor of my office was the canteen, seating for around a hundred at a time. Help yourself and pay or give your luncheon voucher to the lady on the cash register. If you had taken two jam rolly-pollies or anything else that exceeded a shilling, they would, if you smiled sweetly and looked hungry, take your voucher and wave you on.

Every three floors in this building was an office for the messengers who looked after those floors. Every hour, the six messengers in each of those offices, all like me between the ages of 15 and 18, looked after usually by an ageing long serving postman in a divided section at his desk, always trying not to fall asleep or shouting for us to be quiet. He answered the phone and would call out your name, perhaps to take an urgent letter to another building or do the rounds of six other buildings delivering and collecting internal mail. This took place every hour, all of us on a rota. Each hour one of us would take a huge trolley with twelve pigeon holes or open boxes, travelling the three floors, collecting mail from each office, each person's desk and the tray marked 'Out-Tray', then from your trolley taking mail for that same person and dropping into their 'In-Tray'. An hour later, you have visited every person over three floors, distributing post, collecting post, to return to the ground floor where there was a mini-post office sorting office with huge racks where one man would take all your collected stuff and sort it into where it should be going within the building. Along with a dozen or so canvas mailbags for post going outside or around the world.

Then, collecting posts for your three floors, back up for the next messenger to take over, sorting out his trolley first. Mostly one could dash around and get it done in 35 or 40 minutes, so we would meet each other for a sneaky cigarette break in the cleaners' cupboards on the emergency stairs.

There were always two of us in the messenger's room, doing nothing, waiting for a call to deliver or collect somewhere. With a lot of spare time, we sat around a big shiny desk and played table football, using our combs and pennies. At times, all six of us would be in the room, chattering, playing on the table, arguing whose turn next to go and deliver post to another building, in the rain.

I always liked to get out. I sometimes could use the underground staff pedestrian tunnels from the King Edward Building, but mostly walking around the city of London was just so fascinating. Watching this huge tract of land and what was left of its prestigious buildings and streets where I used to play following the bombing of London in the Second World War. Now it was a forest of cranes and diggers creating a whole new area known now as The Barbican. Huge office blocks, theatres, shopping centres and housing for the super-rich.

Weekends before starting in the off licence, I would cycle every street in London, pick a start point and logically move to the next area another day and so on. Sometimes I would buy a Red Rover ticket for the day, ten shillings, and access any bus, any journey. I made it a challenge to travel every route, hundreds of routes throughout London. Similarly, I would do the same on London's underground network, travelling to every station and popping out to look around, then back down to continue to the next one. Eventually, I had travelled and seen every station and street outside on every line.

These walks, delivering post, that I loved so much, took me into dark alleyways and cobbled narrow streets, which is why I love Riga. Horrendous for me to walk over with arthritis in my feet, and my electric mobility chair feels as if it will break up rattling and banging over the cobbles. Still, I like them and hope that Riga does not go the route London did, tearing them up to be replaced by tarmac.

I remember a cafe in one such alley, itself dark and dingy, aged plastic tablecloths, old tables and chairs. The boiler was always going, standing forlornly at the end of the counter, steam rising from it, as it had done for many years. An elderly rotund foreign lady, dressed in a grubby dress and scarf on head would shuffle to serve you at the counter, cigarette in mouth, no smile, no interest, but it was somehow nice to drop out of everything. Plus, she did have the radio always set on Radio One. I had never seen another customer there, unless with one of my other messengers showing them the route. Stopping for a cup of instant coffee. Decadence would be having two slices of toast as well.

At lunch times, I would go to look around St Paul's Cathedral or into the Old Bailey where I'd walk up the stairs into a corridor. Left and right were different courts, maybe a dozen. You could open a door, any door, peer in and see and hear a court case, slide in, sit down, like being on a balcony in the cinema or theatre. You peered down at it all taking place twelve feet below. Sometimes, a murder trial, the judges all in their robes of ermine, an usher in his symbolic dress and staff, announcing all rise for his lordship and other stuff he said that I cannot remember. So many different courts to choose from, if you slid into one and found the trial boring, you just quietly slid out again and tried another door. Sometimes I caught the end of a trial, sometimes the beginning or the middle but never enough time to see it all. These days, you cannot walk in unless you have been scanned, searched and left your mobile phone in the cafe opposite for a small fee.

My lunch times used to fly by and often had to run the half mile back to Gresham Street.

Occasionally, a walk along Cheapside, which a hundred or more years ago lived up to its name. No longer. Most shops had disappeared or been bombed. Some special ancient shops remained, the tobacco shop with a window and shelves filled with open barrels of pipe tobacco, filling the air with pungent aromas. An outfitters here, a hatter or bespoke tailor there. Walk down Cheapside, turn left and along again to Gresham Street, but if you crossed the road, you went into the Guildhall of London, another place that then I could walk into and roam around.

To get to work from Brixton, in fact halfway between the Oval, Gosling Way, a huge pre-war estate, is where I lived. I could walk to the Northern Line tube, The Oval Kennington, and stay until Bank Station, a hundred yards to walk to Gresham Street. Bank Station, being the Bank of England, now also has a fantastic museum that they don't appear to advertise. See the counting sticks for your bank balance, a groove cut out every time you made a withdrawal, safes, locks from three hundred or more years ago to the present time, bank notes, printing plates and coins. See it if you can; it was free, too.

On the other side of my office was Goldsmiths Hall, where gold items, jewellery mostly, would be sent or brought for the purity to be assessed and the items stamped with the British hallmark.

Back to my job. One of the duties of all messengers every six weeks was to come into work on a Saturday morning from 7.30 to 1pm. This is when you would up-date the registers, maybe half an hour or so's work. Your primary function was to listen for the telephone to ring. If it should, and fortunately it never did, the voice on the other end would say, "War has been declared", and hang up, no name, no other words.

You then had to call a special number and say exactly the same, no conversation, no names. They, whoever they might have been, did the same and so on. It was an early, early warning system and that was the only reason to be in on a Saturday. Being young and bold, I would take my moped into work, the only time I did. I took it up in the lift to the third floor; after all, I was, in theory, apart from security on the ground floor, the only person in the building. The offices for general staff on any floor were all open plan, so opening the doors at each end and the middle, I would pass the time riding around on my moped, swerving between desks in and out of the doors, hoping I would hear if the telephone rang.

Whilst being a messenger, I joined the Post Office's own army cadet force which they were proud to have. They gave generous support to it - equipment, armaments, vehicles, they would all be there. No aged army vans to go away in but real army lorries sent from Finsbury Barracks. For me, it was like going on holiday every few months, and still being paid! Plus, once a month, I would don my army uniform and accompany an officer to go on a recruiting drive to other offices in the city. Camps for a week at a time, Pirbright, Thetford and Oakhampton where each section was given map coordinates for a hill or Tor on Dartmoor. We were to walk to, take and hold it. The first section to reach it were the winners. We took the Tor, no one else there; great! We waited and waited, but no one came. The leader suggested we walk to another Tor on the horizon, trudging through streams and brooks, bogs and hillocks. No luck. Soon the Dartmoor mist descended. Zero visibility. The dark of the night, freezing cold, joining two waterproof capes together to make tents for two. By then it was heavy rain, no food, not even our bars of chocolate which had been consumed hours ago.

Early the next morning, before light and before the mist had lifted, on the horizon could be seen a line of lorries and Land Rovers, obviously looking for us. A few rounds of blanks fired by us and we were saved, but still we had to walk to them, such is the nature of Dartmoor topography.

An enquiry ensued which decided that it was the fault of a lieutenant giving out the wrong map references. But it was fun. Salisbury, Aldershot, midnight manoeuvres, treks and joining the real army for a day or two, watching tank battles, chasing us or vice versa through the terrain, never a shortage of blanks for the rifles, the Post Office covered every expense.

I had to be saved trying to swim across the Thames. The captain had ordered all of us to swim to the other side. No excuses about not being able to swim. At Wallingford, The Thames is not nearly as wide here as in London and we were camped in a field alongside. I just made it across and was told to swim back. Halfway over, I could not swim anymore and started to sink, until the captain came up behind me and kept shoving me hard in the back to the other side. Wow! I think he was more relieved than I was. I never did like swimming and could only swim a short distance anyway.

The Post Office had links to The Royal Engineers, and the main barracks were in Finsbury Square, a mile away. You'd get the tube to Moorgate and walk up the road half a mile. It was at these barracks that I was chosen to go for an examination on fieldcraft, map-reading, drill weapon dismantling and assembly. It came to cleaning a rifle. Take the four by two which looked like a bandage. You tore off a piece, used a small bottle of oil and a two-metre length of string with a weight on the bottom, all this being stored in the butt of a rifle. The string had a loop at the top in which you oiled your four by two, folded it carefully and fed it half-way, through the loop of your string, appropriately called a pull-through. After this, remove the bolt in your rifle, feed the weight on the end of your string down the barrel until it appears at the bolt end. The important part, to clean the rifle barrel and not get the other end of the string jammed halfway down. It needed a rigorous rapid tug, as hard as you can.

I did it, with great success, in and out at such speed that the weight flew off and through the captain's window. Glass everywhere! I thought I would be in real trouble but no, he congratulated me on my enthusiasm, not a bit worried about his window.

Amongst all this I learned how to speak in public, or voice projection, by having to stand at one end of a parade ground and bark orders to a section of men at the other end. If they did what you wanted, you had made it.

I returned to my unit in King Edwards Building. The officer, a captain, congratulated me profusely for coming 3rd out of 50 others from many different units sending their best cadets. I did get a stripe as a reward. Incidentally, in the basement of the same building was an army cadet unit with rifle range, weapons store etc, plus a motorsport club, gymnasium and the Post Office railway. This vast network of tunnels were wartime shelters used to maintain communication links from and to the seat of government.

I was chosen to be the one each morning and afternoon to make tea for a group of secretaries who looked after the number two Postmaster General. As with all civil service establishments, there is only one tea or dinner service colour, green. It was hallowed ground to enter these offices. Quietly, in a corner, you brewed and poured the tea, serving it to them at their desks with the obligatory biscuits, whilst one of them would take him, who must be obeyed, his tea and biscuits. Two biscuits per person, then to quietly leave. Who did the washing up, I never knew, but they did insist that they only wanted the nice messenger, me, to serve them. It was good because on the way back to the messenger's room there was time for another cigarette in the cleaner's cupboard.

In the offices of the maritime unit, where I delivered and collected post, I noticed one day pictures of ships on a desk. One, the flagship of the fleet, HMTS Monarch, along with HMTS Arial and ten other smaller ships that went around the UK waters laying and repairing undersea cables. The Arial was confined to go around the North Atlantic in circles, year in, year out. The seamen spent their time chipping away ice from the sides to stop it sinking under the weight. Any seaman causing a problem on any other ship of the fleet was transferred to the Arial or left the service.

I saw the man every day, almost every few hours, collecting his post, so I smiled and asked, when I noticed he was in a good mood,

"Sir, how does one get to go on a ship?"

"Come back when you are 18 and I will put you on HMTS Monarch under Commander Bates."

Wow, such excitement! I am only fifteen. I have three years to wait. Will he remember? Will he still be at his desk? I never spoke to him again, not my place, but two weeks before my 18th birthday, I asked again.

"Sir, you said to come and tell you when I was 18 and you said you could arrange for me to go on one of the ships."

"Yes," he said, "I did. Come back in three days and I will issue you with authority to get a seaman's card. You will not be a seaman but a postman on detached duties. You will be an officer's steward. In two weeks, report to HMTS Monarch. It's currently moored midstream at Greenwich where it will be for a month, taking on undersea cable directly from the factory over the buildings and into the ship's hold. Destination, Singapore, to lay cables from there to Jesselton, Borneo, for the great Far East link up with America."

And I did!

Next episode, my life for a year on the ship.

BUSINESS CREDENTIALS

My friend B... suggested that I might list my business credentials here, should anyone want advice or just someone to talk to about anything in general. Not sure where they would fit in on the site but the following lists my businesses, employed work etc. A varied list, always I strived to do something completely different. Just for the fun of it.

My first job - behind a bar

- Cellar boy, off licence, from 11 years to 18. Nights/weekends 40 hrs a week 10 shillings.
- Messenger, the post office.
- Seaman, still a postman but on detached duties to Borneo.
- Second hand bookshop manager.
- London underground porter
- Window cleaner.
- Patent roof glazier, jobs like stations and factories.
- Indesit, company customer engineer
- Super drug, trainee branch manager.

- Progress chaser, Decca Navigator.
- Grocery shop owner, Dorking.
- Grocery shop owner, Woking.
- Milkman.
- Lighting shop owner.
- Mallorca bar owner.
- Mallorca, second hand furniture and commercial owner with four shops in prime locations.
- Sign company estimator for government contracts.
- Batchelor soups quality control and testing.
- Builder maintenance business proprietor.
- Removal services.
- Training manager, ICL reported to by 7 other specialist units with a budget of 1.5 million. Working on an allowed 90k loss within a year turned it into a 90k profit for my own operations.
- Rubber factory labourer and then leading hand.
- Security guard, sgt, inspector, chief inspector, superintendent, vault controller for all of the uk and commonwealth countries.
- Night porter in hotels
- Concierge in others.
- Texeco night manager.
- Grolier international, Encyclopedia salesman.None sold.
- Double Glazing salesman. Non Sold.
- Psychiatric support, secure assessment unit.
- Guest house proprietor.

That is as much as I can remember, although I always had a yen for road sweeping with my own wheelbarrow and broom.

BRIAN'S WORK HISTORY 2: ALL AT SEA

The day came to join my ship, HMTS Monarch, the Master, Commander Bates RN, fifty officers and roughly the same number of other ranks. The number of officers was by far several times more than would be expected on a ship of this size but two thirds were post office engineers, a radio communications team that even now I cannot reveal the purpose of because of the official secrets act.

There were also weather analysts who sent back everyday weather information to the meteorological office in London. The top deck was top secret. No one except those whose duties took them there were allowed access. This whole deck was added a couple of years earlier and counterbalanced to stop the ship turning turtle in a storm by adding 500 tons of pig iron into the hull. Experienced seamen were convinced that that was exactly what would happen in a rough sea. The top of this added deck bristled with a small forest of different sized aerials, radar dishes and radar deflectors, the flagship of the Post Office, 11,000 tons, yet small by today's standards. To me, it was a towering monster. Moored in the middle of the Thames at Erith, it could not moor closer because of the depth of its hull under water. Built the year I was born, the fourth ship bearing that name HMTS Monarch, she was the largest cable ship in the world.

HMTS Monarch

Four cylindrical cable tanks thirty feet deep into the hold, each forty-one feet in diameter, each with a capacity of 125,000 cubic feet combined to hold enough deep-sea telephone cable for 2500 nautical miles. Except for a few cabins on each side of the main deck, such as the purser's office and the chief steward's office, the whole deck was a mass of giant machinery for unwinding the cable.

Dover to America, Australia, New Zealand and Asia. Unlike normal merchant ships that would, other than tramp steamers, go the same routes every time. Plus, when docked, it would stay for a week or two, lauded by local governments and the press, with garden parties on the deck for their members and diplomats.

Paying out the cable was a scene of much shouting, orders being barked out and bells warning all hands to the deck. The ship continued at just a few miles an hour as the cable was paid out, never stopping for weeks on end. Every hour, this could be heard all over the ship, warning one to stand clear, except for the rush of sailors to manhandle the repeaters, the size of torpedoes, holding them apart from going through the winding machinery, carrying and guiding them to the stern, gently allowing them to drop into the ocean. A small parachute, the size of an umbrella, would then open as they hit the water, allowing them to fall gently to the seabed, as much as, or more, than seven miles deep.

The cable would loop every twenty miles or so to the aft deck where banks of these repeaters were stored high, refrigerated to the temperature of the sea, connected in line to the cable, produced at the factory, conveyed directly from production line to the warehouses and into the hold where they were wound around the tanks.

An engineer proudly told me that this single cable could carry two hundred telephone conversations across the globe at the same time on what was a single, two inch heavily armoured copper wire, and these conversations could be separated at the other end.

Also on the foredeck was a swimming pool, made of canvas, five feet deep, fifty feet long and twenty feet wide. So much fun to swim in when the sea had a swell as the water would make great waves within it. Surrounded by piles of high repeaters, machinery, ropes and chains, it was not the prettiest place.

When the ship moored in foreign ports, a huge rope net would be lowered over the side from the derricks into the sea for the crew to swim in, safe from sharks. I did swim once outside of the net in the Suez Canal, at the midway passing point. On reaching the end scrambling over the razor sharp coral onto the blistering sand, hopping about, from out of nowhere up came a group of Arabs, rifles, aimed at me, barking,

"Get back into the water or we will shoot."

I was happy to oblige, if only to get off the burning sand.

I was told by the man in the London office where I worked as a messenger to remember to shout as loudly as possible over to the ship and a lighterman would come to fetch me from the shore. By the way, there were no interviews for the seaman's job, I was just asked if I could swim. Technically, it was just a transfer. I was to arrive at any time on the day. The ship wasn't going anywhere for at least six weeks. No need to pack a bag. I was wearing most of the clothes that I owned on the several bus journeys through Camberwell Green, Lewisham, Catford, Woolwich and Erith. A walk then down to the Thames foreshore, through winding, cobbled alleyways, between sheds and warehouses, dark and dank, until reaching the shore.

Here, in all its magnificence, the first sighting of the ship that took my breath away. Scared and apprehensive, I walked along the foreshore on a path, past dozens of old Thames barges, all resting on the black mud, at obtuse angles. The tide was out and men in torn, dirty black overalls were bobbing about, from one to the other, some chipping away rust, others painting, panels being welded to others over their rusted hulks. Tugboats with long lines of barges, sometimes two abreast, were to be seen coming and going into the Pool of London between London Bridge and Tower Bridge where ships from all over the world would be unloading into the East India Company dock warehouses. Many ships, boats of all sizes, tugs and barges all vying for space.

The ship was sold for scrap eventually in 1977. Now the space is a permanent mooring for HMS Belfast, a battleship, a museum, moored opposite The Tower of London. To get there, take the train to London Bridge Station and walk down Tooley Street, past what once were all the cobbled tunnels under the railway arches lined with wine and spirit bottles, always dark or dimly lit.

It was in one of these arches that my grandmother worked until she was 90 years old. She had started working here after the First World War, the same tasks, the same spot, cobbled unevenly through many decades of wear, sometimes sticking labels on bottles, sometimes operating a hand corking machine or bottle cap covers, smelly and gloomy. This was a time when the normal lighting anywhere was the incandescent bulb, mostly 50 watts, spread far apart, a dull yellowish light. On my grandmother's 90th birthday, she was retired against her will. They told her that no one had realised how old she was.

This had been her whole life. After sitting in her flat at Snowfields, Bermondsey, a few hundred yards from St Thomas's hospital, at the foot of London Bridge, she died within a year, lonely, with no other activity but climbing onto a chair with a match to light the gas lamp hanging down from the ceiling, taking great care not to touch the silk sock, the size of your thumb, as it would fall apart like ash to the floor. To replace it, you had to fit it over the gas pipe, turn the gas on and light it with a match, watch it glow yellow, burn, then shrivel up and turn white. Job done. Light the coal fire, do some washing in the stone sink shared by the other flats on that floor, as was the toilet. No baths here, you did everything at the sink.

It was possible to walk through all these narrow, winding, gloomy, cobbled streets, between all the warehouses on both sides, at times connected to each other on the other side by walkways high up, from London Bridge all the way to Woolwich. I did this walk when I was younger; on a Sunday you rarely would see anyone.

The real fun part to end this walk was to get on the Woolwich free ferry, cars and pedestrians carried across the Thames every half an hour, sneaking down to look at the massive engine, throbbing away. The only other way at this part of the Thames to cross, other than a Victorian pedestrian tunnel at Greenwich, deep down a spiral stair. Again, rare to see anyone, a long walk, this tunnel devoid of colour or interest other than the smooth white, with a green line in the middle separating the tiles. Now there is a lift but you pay, too. You can still walk down the sixty plus feet on the original spiral staircase.

I reached a point opposite my ship and yelled across to it. There was a man at the top of the ladder which reached down to the water. He shouted back and down the ladder he clambered, into a small motorboat that could hold perhaps a dozen men, the engine chugging across and collecting me. The four of us were charged with going from the ship to shore to collect food stocks. On reaching the shore, a crane lowered into the middle of the boat, a pallet piled high with all the boxes, sacks of sugar, flour, vegetables etc. The boat sank low in the water.

The lighterman proceeded to head over to the ship, each of us spaced out either side to help keep the boat stable. The Thames at times does get wavy and rough. One wave managed to tip the pallet over and the boat with it. Some of the goods sank, some floated away and all of us, especially me, panicking to swim to grab the side of the boat which, once it dumped us and the stock, righted itself.

The river was highly polluted then, so a long shower and a warning to visit the ship's doctor if feeling unwell in the following few days. As scary as it was, I loved it.

"Joining the ship are you, sonny?"

"Yes," I replied. "Are you one of the sailors?"

"No lad, I'm the lighterman, here to take people back and forth. Me and my mate cover 24 hours, so if you come late at night back to the ship, just keep shouting. We will hear you, eventually."

The lightermen on the Thames are a respected profession, just like taxi drivers, years of knowledge, theirs of the tides, navigating channel paths in thick smog, not fog but smog, a mixture of smoke from every home's coal and coke fires in London's many belching factory chimneys. This fog was so dense and choking, it filled your room. During this time, thousands of people died from emphysema and bronchitis; mainly the elderly.

On the street, it was possible to stand back just four feet from someone else and completely disappear. Cars, if any dared to be out in it, would crawl along, peering not for what was in front of them, but down at the edge of the pavement to see when it ran out at a road junction, attempt to keep going straight, hoping to reach the start of the pavement on the other side of the junction. The headlights were completely useless other than for seeing the pavement.

Once, a friend and I took the dustbins from outside some houses and placed them across the middle of a junction in a line, then waited to hear a car coming, the headlights a yellow glow, the driver looking down at the pavement. Losing sight of it, he would bump into the dustbins. With no pavement in view, he would reverse a bit, turn a bit and hit another dustbin. Cruel, but funny.

The certification for the lighterman came from the Thames Port Authority at Billingsgate, site of the then fish market for fish landed from all corners of the world. The lightermen worked driving the tugboats in, along and to the pool of London from as far away as the Thames estuary at Southend, some twenty-five miles away. Now they mostly have jobs on the tour boats, sharing knowledge of sites along the Thames on the tannoy/speakers. A joy to listen to their rich cockney or South London accents, just like a friend of mine called B....

When Billingsgate closed, demolished and located elsewhere, it took up to seven years for the permafrost below to melt, just metres from the Tower of London. This was where, as a child, I would walk. Within The Tower's grounds was the cobbled road from one end to the other, next to and parallel with the river, twelve feet below. Looking over the side, down to the water, at Traitors Gate, the tunnel from The Tower was used for many centuries to take prisoners to and fro, often to their death. However, as a child, you could walk down a metal staircase to a beach area. Londoners would come here to play with their children on the sand, sit on deckchairs, knotted handkerchiefs on their heads, the Daily Mirror or Racing Post over their faces, a pint of Guinness, happily settled, outstretched on a deckchair. Maybe for the foolhardy, they'd roll up their trouser bottoms, the women tucking the hems of their skirts up the legs of their knickers, providing they had any, and have a paddle in the dirty dark water, if they dared, and if lucky, whilst there, see the bascules of Tower Bridge raised to let another cargo ship through. Not many years later, this beach closed as being too dangerous, the sand left to wash away.

There is, above the Tower Bridge roadway another walkway between the two towers. This was closed, my father remembering in the late 1800s, because too many Londoners chose it as a suitable spot to commit suicide.

Not many years ago it was reopened to the public but glazed in. Now, you get fabulous views of the Port of London, The Tower, HMS Bulwark and more. Descend into the bowels of the towers and you can see the engines that lift and lower the bascules, now all electric, plus the original coal boilers that once provided the power, all restored, a veritable deep and cavernous dungeon, beautifully lit, high arched and curved brickwork that supports the tower above it.

It's interesting to remember that so many buildings in London I used to sneak through doors and gaps to look around secretly are now all beautifully restored for visitors to see - for a decent admission price, and following health and safety rules etc.

As we drew closer to the ship, he said, "Look up. Those staring over the side at you are the ship's stewards. They can't wait for you to get on board."

He said this with a wry smile. That was so nice, but a bit scary, too.

Up the ladder, maybe forty feet from the water's edge, met at the top by a gaggle of those stewards.

"Are you the new steward? How old are you? Where you from? We'll take you to the Purser's Office."

And with that, I was duly escorted there.

In a miniscule way, it was like the bank that I had been into with the off licence owner. I had never heard of or knew what a purser was or what he might do to me. He was, in fact, the whole ship's office routine master, a senior officer, kept the payroll, ordered the ship's supplies, arranged shipping documents plus the personnel functions. If it was recorded on paper, he did it.

Even organising me to collect my seaman's ticket.

"Young C.....," he said, "I guess you have come to join us. We have all your details from London HQ. On this ship you are a civil servant, in Her Majesty's employ. Keep away from the ratings, they can be a rough lot and are all merchant seamen. They did one trip mostly and then on to another ship at the end of that voyage. Some of the stewards have come from your direction. They were former young postmen, also now on detached duties. On board you will be an officer's steward, mine, as it happens. Don't be late with my tea in the mornings, nor the chief engineer, the second officer and the navigator. They're all sharing you," he said.

He was nice, with a kind smile. He reminds me now of John Le Mesurier, explaining that I would get paid directly into a bank account, as of my choosing.

The next day off, I went to Loughborough Junction, Brixton, to open an account. No problem, as I had told the manager my wages were to be paid directly into it by the Post Office. When the next weekend came around, I went home again to find a chequebook that had been posted to me. My parents were eager for me to open the envelope. The only letters that normally came were from the Labour Exchange where my father took me with him twice every week, having to attend, join a long queue, eventually reaching the window. There, they asked if my father had found a job yet. If not, they would look at their card index and maybe suggest one. The answer was always no. They recorded his visit and next time he collected his dole money, around £2/10s/0d for the week. Fail to attend, no money.

Returning home via the Atlantic Pub on the corner of Atlantic Road for a quick pint, whilst I waited outside. The best part was walking past the butchers which only sold horse meat. My mother occasionally, as a special treat, bought a joint here, too. It's a ghastly taste to me. Onwards a few doors and the treat was going into the Pie and Mash Shop, always busy, benches all the way down inside, with high solid continuous backs with a simple bench table in the middle. Reaching a counter that came up to my eyes, my father would order pie and mash with liquor, a thick green pea gunge, which would be poured over the mash, and a plate of jellied eels for himself.

Instantly served from a deep tray of baking hot pies behind her, replenished every few minutes, as was a large cauldron of mash potatoes and another of the liquor. Plates in hand and shuffle along the counter where on the end was a box of cutlery, one side dinner spoon, the other forks, take one of each and turn to see if there was room for two on one of the benches. I loved this outing, firstly to get some hot food, which was great, but also the noise of people coming and going, the clanging and banging of pots from the kitchen as the lady behind the counter shouted out for more pies or mash, always, always busy.

The labour exchange was next to the large covered, Atlantic Market and the Sunlight Laundry in Acre Lane, Brixton where, at times, I watched the man on the live eel stall, customers choosing from a large box the eels wriggling around, dozens of them. He would grab one, chop off its head, slit it lengthways and deftly scrape out all its innards, the heads chucked in a box as waste. He would let me take half a dozen, getting them home to play with on the doorstep, their mouths still opening and closing an hour later, eventually giving them to the cat.

Awe as I showed my chequebook to them with my name printed on every cheque. No one in my family had ever had such a thing. The only other person I had known with one was the owner of the off licence where I'd worked. Apart from ten shillings each week for cigarettes, whilst at sea everything went into my bank. Many seamen did this so that wives back home could get the money, or people like me who did not drink, but at the end of a trip have a healthy sum of money to go home to. I could have four tins of beer every day or a slug of rum free at 4p.m. and purchase cigarettes - Senior Service or Players - that came in tins of fifty over a half door along the corridor, one deck below, always a long line, open for half an hour only. Spirits or anything else, you had to bring aboard yourself and hide it. Anything other than a few beers, not allowed. I did get my beers each day and then sold them or exchanged them for cigarettes with the seamen who, when off duty, always seemed to be drunk and smelly.

With that, the purser summoned the steward's chief petty officer to show me my quarters and explain my duties fully. I never got to see the chief steward but once, on instruction from the commander. I later learned that he was disliked by crew and officers. He never appeared in the officers mess or bar. I was told the reason being that the former HMTS Monarch had sunk, he being one of the first into the lifeboat, abandoning his crew. Still, such excitement as the steward's petty officer, an older man, slim and wiry, a fearsome face with a pencil moustache. I never saw him smile once all the time I was aboard. He would snarl any instructions. He led me down below decks to a cabin in a long corridor, one of four cabins, each containing three bunks. Some of the stewards in these cabins were ordinary merchant seamen looking after the crew. My cabin had only officer stewards, so that was nice.

The cabin was six feet wide, two bunks on one side and on the other a single bunk, a porthole, a tall slim cupboard for each and a chest of three drawers, one drawer for each officer, plus a bench seat, beneath the porthole. Standard thick linoleum and a small shelf above each bunk for books and personal items, also a curtain to pull across for privacy. The bedding sheets, with the government arrow in the corner, and the counterpane, a beautiful blue design with the crown in the middle and expansive scrolls, standard issue on all royal navy ships. This alone distinguished its position.

Laundry would need to be taken to the laundry room once a week in exchange for stiff, starched stewards' jackets and trousers plus one sheet. The other sheet would be for the following week. The rule being, you turned one sheet over each week, then the next week took it to the laundry with your uniform.

Personal clothing, which for everyone was socks and underwear, you took to the showers or heads as they were called, rows of sinks, toilets and showers for all to see. Here you did your dhobying (washing) in the sinks, being careful not to go for a shower when too many seamen were there, and certainly not to drop the soap.

Apart from all that, I loved my cabin, so clean, as much of it was covered with Formica. I did not see the others in my cabin a great deal as they, like young men do, would either be in their bunks sleeping, or in the sailors' mess, drinking. Some of the other stewards definitely had the hots for me, but truly I stayed away in spite of all the chasing and groping in gangways and kitchens.

The chief petty officer had taken me to the officers' mess, (dining room) with seats for the fifty officers aboard. I was given two tables of four. When meal times came, a plinking, plonking from a small xylophone over the tannoy signalled all to come. A stream of officers would arrive en-masse except for those steering the boat or looking after the engine room. They took their allotted seats at their allotted tables. The routine was, you had to take all four dinner choices on each table at the same time. They chose from a selection of three options for each course. You were not allowed to write anything down, only to remember what each had ordered, course by course.

This was the hardest part for me, remembering when I had turned to go to the server behind a wooden partition to the counter where I would join the queue of other stewards doing the same thing. When it came to your turn, you had to be quick in asking the man behind the counter for what you wanted or he would skip and go on to the next steward's orders. Having told him my wants, he would turn and shout to the team of galley staff. Soon, four plates would appear with the main course on and three silver dishes with the vegetables.

You had to take all four plates in one go, deliver to your table and race back to collect the vegetable dishes. It was silver service and strict. It took a few meals for me not to fumble with a spoon and fork dishing out the vegetables without throwing some over officers' laps. They were forgiving, however. Then on to your other table with the same routine. Mostly, I remembered who wanted the lamb or the beef, roast potatoes or none. Only when all four officers had placed their cutlery down were you allowed to take orders for the next course. No one started eating until the commander had taken his seat.

At the end of each service, they left as quickly as they had come. Now it was to strip all the tables, change the heavily starched tablecloths and lay out the silver cutlery for the following meal, dinner or breakfast. Once a fortnight you had to polish the silver, and there seemed to be mountains of it, but it was taken in turns by all the stewards.

Getting up at 6.30 a.m. every day for months at sea was a chore. You could not take a day off here if you weren't awake, and even if you were, the petty office would bang hard on each door for a response. Then it was up to my officers on the top deck, into a small galley/utility cabin to make the tea for my officers to be delivered to their bedside at 7 a.m. one at a time, cup and saucer in hand, knock gently on the door and enter, putting the tea on their bunk side table.

"Good morning, sir, your tea," whilst swooshing the curtain open over their porthole.

The nice chief purser would always be sitting up waiting for me in his pyjamas.

"Thank you, steward," with a smile.

One other would turn over and go back to sleep, that was the chief engineer, a Scotsman with such a broad accent, he mostly had to repeat everything for me to understand, but still friendly enough. The radio officer thanked me but did not smile.

That over with, it was down to the officers' mess to prepare for breakfast, precisely at 8 a.m. called again by the xylophone. Put out the jugs of orange juice and water, a single menu this time. They chose as many items as they wished. Grapefruit, which one had already prepared, cut in half, gently cutting into quarters inside the peel, and a maraschino cherry on top. Kippers, boiled, soft or hard eggs, scrambled eggs, fried eggs, kidneys, bacon, sausages, baked beans, toast, cereals, again, having to remember, four officers orders at the same time.

When that was over, lay up in the dining room for lunch. Being a steward in the officers' mess meant never having to eat in the seaman's mess. A raucous area, at any time.

The time between breakfast and lunch was cleaning your officers' cabins, making up their bunks, changing their bedding once a week, cleaning the brass port hole, scrubbing the floor in each cabin, scrubbing your bit of the corridor with wire wool to get out the scuff marks left by shoes.

All this done and a leisurely cup of tea in their utility area with another steward on the same deck of officers. He looked like the singer, Freddie from Freddie and the Dreamers. Shorter than me, jet black hair and hands everywhere, he would trap me up against the sink behind me and it was all I could do to wriggle out free every time. I liked him, though. He was lively and great fun. But I remained largely un-sullied all the time I was on the ship. I was gay but dared not ever reveal that, never denying nor ever confirming. Sometimes I think of him still to this day.

Backdown to the officers' mess for lunch. When it was all over, we prepared again for the evening. It was four hours off duty. Most went to the cabins for a snooze, others to the seamen's quarters. I preferred to go to the prow of the ship where a sort of gang plank of steel but with handrails, jutted out some twelve feet over the sea. This was for an observer to stand and look back down to check the deep-sea cable, when being laid, did not snag the ship as it slowly drove forward. Here I would sit at the end, legs hanging over, looking down at the sea, serene, the noise of the engines muffled and far behind, watching flying fish or porpoises or dolphins, swimming below in perfect formation in front, some would break off, dive under the bow of the ship and come up the other side.

No one ever came up onto the foredeck. It was full of capstans which were used for wrapping rope around and winding them up, such as mooring ropes. Also there was the machinery for operating the derricks, a ships crane, used to lift buoys in and out of the water. These marked where a cable had run out, the boils being fifteen feet high and four feet wide, full of batteries to last six months, keeping a beacon flashing on the top and finished off with a radar reflector, the purpose being to allow operators time to return with joining cables.

The ship had a grappling iron that could go down seven miles to drag the sea bed, looking for the end of a cable, circling for days, around and around. The foredeck was all my territory, unbeknown to me, the commander, high up on the bridge behind me, had watched me over the months, sitting astride the gangplank for my four-hour break virtually every day at sea and never seemingly associating with anyone other than the ship's photographer.

He spent all his time photographing everything, including me, one day dressed as a fireman with an axe in my hand, another day dressed as a seaman starting a capstan engine, another in overalls, deep down in the cable tanks pretending to watch them as the cable fed out. These photographs he developed in the official dark room on the ship. They were sent to the commander who, if approving, would then send them back to the office where I first started as a messenger for the Post Office to use in publicity.

I learned from someone that I could be seen life size in different poses around the bottom of the Post Office Tower. It was new then and all part of explaining the advancement in telephone technology, here in the darkroom. Whilst fending off my teacher's hands, I learned developing and printing, the downside being, he had to lock the door and turn the main lights off for a low wattage green light to come on when developing, so more wandering hands and no escape. He was asked by the commander why it was the same person in all the photographs, but he approved them anyway, telling the photographer to not have me wearing long socks in all the pictures.

One day the chief steward, miffed, called me to his cabin to tell me the commander did not like that I was a steward and going nowhere. He asked if I wanted to transfer to the permanent ships company and be trained in all things to do with seamanship and navigation. The day came after weeks of being moored in The Thames whilst the cable and repeaters were being fed into the ship. We were to set sail in the afternoon. I can't express the sheer excitement, lots of shouting and activity by the sailors and the sudden rumble of the engines being started which you felt beneath your feet. Ropes were hauled in, two tugboats appearing to slowly and gently guide and pull the ship to the widest part of the river where it bends at Greenwich. Midstream, the tugs manoeuvre the ship around 360 degrees to face down river, the tugboats releasing the lines.

Standing on the foredeck, when the ships engines powered up more, we were soon slowly and quietly heading towards The Thames estuary and the English Channel, passing factories, right and left, spewing plumes of smoke. The foreshore was busy with barges being loaded and unloaded, and oil depots with tankers disgorging their loads. Awed at seeing London in a way I'd never seen before, I leaned on the rail for an hour or two, transfixed by the slow, smooth progress.

Dusk was upon us as we rounded Gravesend and out then to pass close by Southend Pier. The longest pier in the country, or the world, over a mile with its own railway to take day trippers to the end where there were amusements, penny machine arcades and theatres.

SOUTHEND PIER

My parents never celebrated Christmas other than go to pub parties. On Christmas Day, the trains were still running so instead of watching my neighbours children and my friends parading around with their presents, I would take the tube to Fenchurch Street Station and get a day return ticket for Southend on Sea. Surprisingly enough, it was always busy. An hour later and I was walking along the front. Even in midwinter, there was always one huge amusement arcade open, spending an hour with a big pile of pennies, playing all the machines. Instead of the hundreds of holidaymakers there during the summer, now there were just a few.

I liked the machines, or rather the tableaux. One was a scene of people under the guillotine having their heads chopped off. There was also a model of a castle with ghosts appearing. Walking along the seafront to the Kursal, outside was the laughing policeman, a full size model, that if you put a penny in, he would laugh loudly with his hands on his hips, rocking from side to side.

A huge complex could be accessed free through the gates. The first thing to see was the Kursal radio station, sat in a large, round, plain glass windowed building. As you entered, there would be a radio presenter sitting behind his control box playing records, dedications for visitors, the weather for the day and new and exciting rides to go on. It was almost entirely empty of visitors on Christmas Day, but a chance to go on some of the rides that were still open.

In the summer, with the mile of promenade ablaze with lights and tacky gift shops, rows of stalls selling small bowls of whelks, mussels, winkles and cockles to eat where you stood and a bottle of vinegar on the counter to use. Or buy a jar-full to take down onto the beach with your milk stout.

This was every bit a mirror of Blackpool that served the North of the country. There, they would have 'wakes' or weeks, the majority of factories closing for a week for all the staff to go on holiday at the same time, thousands and thousands of them filling special trains to Blackpool. Similarly, on the East Coast there was Scarborough and

Great Yarmouth.

An hour or two in the Kursal before returning along the seafront for a ride along the pier on the green train, looking much like an underground train in London. It was a strange feeling to be on this train and see the sea on both sides, as the promenade behind appeared smaller and smaller the further the train moved to the end of the pier. Alighting the other end, to more amusements and penny arcades.

I had some money with me, from working at the off-licence. My day here was planned and saved for, my money carefully hidden in the room I shared with, first, my step-brother, later my father. At times, they knew I had money and would search for it but never found it.

Finishing off my day at the seaside, it was time for fish and chips. By now it was dark, returning on the pier train and back to the main station for the train home. This return journey, unlike the morning's outward one, was now busy, and at times rowdy with drinkers who had been to Southend for the afternoon and were now thoroughly drunk. Back home to quietly pull the string from the letterbox with the key on the end and sneak into bed.

ALL AT SEA (CONTINUED)

My ship passed by and out into the sea. Time to serve the officers their evening meal, all now present, getting to know new ones who had just joined the ship, everyone with a feeling of relief to be sailing once again.

After the meal it was back out to the foredeck once again to spend another hour just watching as the ship, now full speed, 11 knots, which was slow actually, around eighteen miles an hour, cutting its way through the bow wave, the silence of the night, the swishing of the sea. Magical.

We were on this, my first trip. I was told that this was a short sea proving journey to Spain, just two weeks, in preparation for the main voyage a couple of weeks later. This was to ensure everything worked as it should.

The next day, sailing into the Bay of Biscay, as the ship progressed the swell of the sea became larger, pitching the ship up ten feet and down again in every swell. We and the other stewards in their two cabins decided amongst ourselves to see who would be brave enough in each cabin to lean their head out of the portholes and be the last to draw back in, rapidly shutting the porthole, dropping the deadbolt to hold it against the sea. It was to be me in my cabin, with great glee and bravado from everyone. Lean out, watch the waves, ten feet or more below, as the ebb and flow of the swell of the sea would sink to twenty feet, then rise up to almost port hole level, holding one's nerve, not to slam it shut yet. A real game of dare. When you thought the swell was coming up too quickly, pull in your head and slam the porthole shut a second before you see the sea rise above it. Phew! Some close calls. This went on until another cabin misjudged it and their cabin ended up awash with a mountain of sea water.

My cabin, until now all mine, had another two occupants for the other bunks. We all got on well, sharing a small space, none of us taking a lead or making demands, respectful of each other but also sharing the camaraderie. No danger either. We retired to our respective bunks, having turned out the main cabin light, drawing our curtains and switching on the little light above the pillow and sleeping soundly until being woken by the nasty petty officer hammering on the cabin door at 6.30 a.m. until he had a response from one of us.

I had chosen the top bunk, because of the small grill (the size of an extractor fan you get in a shower room) which in the winter would push out warm air and in hot climates cold air for the cabin. It was more like a whisper than a whoosh, no control as it fed all the cabins, never warm enough nor cold enough, but I at least had the first breeze from it, the sound quietly comforting. Getting used to the vibration and the noise from the engine took a little longer, however.

We were in the cabin together mostly at bedtime or the four- hour breaks in the afternoon. One might be reading a book on his bunk, another sorting his locker. At times, I and the steward in the bunk below would be talking, sitting together on the bench seat under the porthole, just engaging in jibber jabber.

The guy sitting next to me, about 26 years old, was greatly looking forward to getting to Vigo in Spain where he'd heard that a female prostitute for the night was really cheap. He had teamed up with another two of the crew to go out on the hunt together with the hope of finding a couple of girls so that all three could share at the same time. The other guy in the cabin, perhaps a year older than me, was quiet, but he did have a friend somewhere on the ship.

When I had first boarded the ship, one of the stewards was a kitchen porter who did all the washing up in two stainless steel sinks, underneath a porthole. He was in his mid-twenties, good looking, fit, funny and lively. Once the Petty officer had shown me my duties, the last being where I got the food for the officers' mess, around a partition at the end of the saloon, he disappeared, leaving me free to explore. This lad I described said, "Come around and meet everyone." To do that, I had to leave the saloon and go down to another door into this galley. They all laughed and beckoned me in. They were just so friendly, standing amongst them all as they laughed, joked and made ribald remarks. The kitchen porter looked at a particularly dirty burnt pan, tossing it out of the porthole into the river.

"Are you supposed to do that?" I asked.

"Yes," he answered, amongst the laughter. "If the chef can't cook and burns the pans, he can come and clean them himself or out the porthole they go."

It was great amongst his joyous hubbub, until for me, horror! The kitchen porter jumped on someone who had their back to him, arms around his waist, wrestling him to lean over, another holding his arms out. Amongst all the screaming, laughter and shouting, he pulled the guys pants down. The victim, seemingly enjoying and going along willingly. Next, he turned to me, wrestling me to the deck and saying,

"You want some?" with a big wide grin.

"No!" I said. "I can't breathe with you sitting on me. I have to go."

Thank goodness, he got off me, patted me on the back and said,

"You'll do, don't worry. Just having fun kid."

Amidst much mirth, I was up and out of there. I never went around to that side of the counter again. From then on, I kept myself to myself, never daring to talk to even those that I liked, apart from those in my own cabin. No one really knew if I was Arthur or Martha.

After such a first day, I never walked on the accommodation deck, fore or aft. The stairs were near my cabin, straight up to the main deck and safe. If I ever was not sure about someone walking behind me, I could go up another flight to one of the officers' decks. No one would dare go up there.

The only other area that scared me was the heads - the toilets, sinks for washing yourself and clothes, fortunately just socks and underwear (dhobying) and the open showers for all of us below decks on the starboard side, as was the seaman's mess, my cabin being midships on the portside. I learned to choose my times carefully along a safer section of hallway. I never took a towel with me, even for a shower, that way on entering, if it looked busy or I did not like what was happening. I could just about turn, as if I had lost my way, but not before someone had shouted, "Come in and scrub my back." When all the seamen were out working is when I would make a dash for it, shower quickly and be out again, still soaking wet.

One night, I was hungry. I thought it would be safe to get something to eat, like cheese or corn beef sandwich. Always in this one mess, for seamen working through the night, you could get a large lump of cheese and corned beef, a dinner plate with equally large butter on it. I cut a thick slice of corned beef, buttered two slices of bread, baked in the ship's galley, then returned to my cabin and enjoyed it. This was when we were in tropical heat. Waking up hours later with serious cramps in my stomach. I won't go into detail, but I could not get off of my bunk for two days, doubled up in pain. The nasty petty officer had been told by one of the others in my cabin. He came along and said I would be excused from duties for a few days.

"If it gets worse or lasts longer, go and see the doc," he said.

I did not do that and managed to recover enough to continue working again.

The ship had its own hospital with surgery for life threatening operations but mostly broken legs, gashes and drunken falls, VD or gonorrhoea.

Spread over what would be the size of three cabins put together, inside there were two hospital beds chained to the deck, the sort you would find in any army barracks, iron bedsteads, a desk and an array of cabinets around the bulkhead walls. These contained bone saws, scalpels, drills and other surgical equipment that looked as if they had come from the Victorian times and equally dirty. Having been told that the doctors on these types of ships were usually at the end of their careers or could not get a practice anywhere else, ours was an elderly alcoholic, confused, affable, if a little unsteady. The crew lived in apprehension should they ever have to be treated by him.

We are on our way to Vigo in Spain for sea trials, through rough seas in the Bay of Biscay, knowing nothing of the country, then a dictatorship ruled by Franco with an iron fist. After the evening meal, we would all be going to explore this port town. Four of us. It was nearly dark when we left on foot from the docks, none of us speaking a word of Spanish. A cursory check of our seamen's cards at the gates and a stroll through the market square, everything closed, mostly boarded up. The only shop not closed was a butchers, meat still in the windows and dogs skinned and hanging.

It became chilly and started to drizzle. The other three were eager to find where the ladies of the night might be. At this point, I made my way back to the ship alone, wary when passing a police station and seeing two officers outside, black hats, green uniforms and, over their capes, rifles. They looked as if they meant business. I made my way back to the ship, relieved, my impression of Spain a bit bleak.

In the morning, I asked the steward on the bunk below me how he got on with the others finding the ladies. They had walked around for hours, afraid to attempt to ask anyone. When they eventually did meet a prostitute and made their proposition, she would not agree and so they went in one by one, arguing about the price after. They had to just pay up.

The ship was only in Vigo to bunker, take on more fuel and any supplies required. We set sail for home the second night, returning through the rough seas of the Bay of Biscay.

The sea trials were successful and within a couple of weeks it was off, this time to Singapore, to connect it to Borneo by cable. At 11 knots an hour at maximum speed, it took months. Every day the same routine and every few days having to change our watches through all the date lines, losing an hour of sleep every time. When we eventually returned, changing them back again every few days was grand for the extra few hours lie-in.

Always, I took my time off, sitting on the gangplank at the bow. The weather grew warmer once past and through the Straits of Gibraltar and the Mediterranean, stopping at Port Said where we took on an Arab dhow, lifting it directly onto the foredeck along with four Arabs who were to be our pilots through the Suez Canal, only recently reopened to shipping after the war there.

On 26 July 1956, Nasser nationalised the Suez Canal Company, which prior to that was owned primarily by British and French shareholders. On 29 October, Israel invaded the Egyptian Sinai. Britain and France issued a joint ultimatum to cease fire, which was ignored. On 5 November, Britain and France landed soldiers along the Suez Canal. Before the Egyptian forces were defeated, they had blocked the canal to all shipping by sinking forty ships in the canal.

Such a fabulous experience, looking over to the desert and low white buildings, camels standing around, the Arab dhow being raised high by our derricks and made secure on deck. The Arabs were to be on board through the canal, living and sleeping on their own boat.

We fed them, after the ship's crew had eaten. The galley porters would carry out cauldrons containing all that was left of ours, the contents of which were exactly as would have been tipped over the side after meals. Mixed together were all the plate scrapings, leftover meats, vegetables, soup, puddings, bread, fruit, everything. We gasped, watching them happily sitting under the hull of their Dhow on our deck, seemingly ravishing this concoction with their hands, most grateful.

The ship had to wait a couple of days in Port Said until enough other ships formed a long enough convoy. Halfway through the Suez, which was only one ship in width, we coordinated with the port at the other end, so that convoys should start at the same time from either end. From Port side, it would reach a lay-by canal midway. All ships in that convoy took a rest for four to eight hours whilst the convoy coming the other way passed by. Then our convoy continued. It was at this stopping point, having gone for a swim, I was forced back into the water at gunpoint.

At Port Said, prior to leaving, around the ship on all sides, was a veritable flotilla of dhows and wooden punts, anything that floated, mostly having flip-flops arranged for sale and other tat, dirty postcards, the lot. The Arabs would be screaming for money, soap, cigarettes and more in exchange. They looked grubby, some with loin clothes and torn clothes, desperately poor.

Should any of our crew want anything, they would throw down whatever was to be exchanged and a long pole from the dhow with the goods on for you to take. The noise of all this going on, shouting, cursing, insulting was an experience and quite sad. Some of the sailors had lifted a heavy cement block and tossed it down onto a dhow; it went straight through it, such was the chaos.

Soon, a police flat motorboat arrived, three or four officers with long canes, thrashing those on the Dhows with them as they joined the melee. The flotilla of small boats and dhows escaped as fast as they could in any direction.

Here in this assembly point were many ships that had been sunk in the war, masts sticking out of the water on the smaller ones, some on their sides, some with bomb and fire damage. An incredible sight. Once we were on our way again, it was back to my position on the gangplank, now looking at the stern of the ship in front as we sailed to the passing point.

Whilst waiting here, we looked across the desert on each side at endless sand dunes, as far as the eye could see. Nothing, no buildings, the occasional camel train in the distance.

But wait! Suddenly, there was a long line of ships, seemingly slowly sailing across the sand. It was the ships passing us as we rested in this mega lay-by. As the last ship passed, we continued to the other end where we stopped whilst the Arab Dhow on deck was lifted back into the water.

Another bevy of dhows surrounded the ship, the crews in cleaner clothes, the wares including cameras, radios, binoculars and a whole raft of goods, in total contrast to those at Port Said. From here it was on to Singapore.

Some weeks later, seeing nothing but sea, day in day out, would we ever see land again, one asked oneself. The same routine, every day, some of the crew, those time-served sailors and stokers from deep down in the engine room, were allowed to string hammocks along the outside of the main deck. Here they would sleep, drink and party, some choosing to stay naked. A place to be seriously avoided.

I did, one day, open a door from the deck, and look inside. It was the stairway to the engine room, looking down into the gloom, the engine noise now loud. I ventured down this iron staircase, level by level. All around were pipes going in all directions, getting hotter and hotter the further I went, until deep in the bowels of the ship, huge boilers, the stokers, some naked, some with just underpants, twiddling a pipe here, a valve there, greasing the massive moving parts, the shaft to the propeller turning, the noise and heat almost unbearable.

An officer asked what I was doing there. I told him just to look around. I wanted to know how it all worked. He explained the boilers and pipes and the amount of oil burnt every day, but better than that, I was in an area about three metre square, standing on the gratings, in the middles of which was a brass telegraph, the one the captain pulls the lever around that points to full ahead, full astern, slow, stop etc. Well bless my soul, I had thought the captain was driving it, like the throttle on a car. Now I learned that when he turns it one way and then the other to rest on one of those points and the bell rings, this one in the engine room does the same. The officer telling me all this was an engineer. When that happened, there would be a flurry of activities as everyone turned something or adjusted something. He confirms by turning his handle for the one on the bridge to also turn, acknowledging the order.

Happy to tell my cabin mates where I had been, they were impressed as in reality it was forbidden territory for anyone but grease monkeys, stokers and engineers.

It was around this time that the ship's photographer spotted me and asked if he could take my picture, sitting on the gangplank of the prow. I said yes. A day later he sought me out with a foolscap picture of me. Wow, how did he do that! There's no chemist for thousands of miles. He wanted more pictures of me mimicking what some of the sailors do around the ship. In return, he would show me how to develop and enlarge print film in the ship's darkroom. Plus, he had an old reporter's camera, a micro-flex twin lens reflex that he would give me. He would teach me all the settings, plus give me some film, as much as I would want from his stores. In the evenings, off I would go to the darkroom, developing, printing, hanging negatives on the line to dry; it was great. Taking my camera around the ship, photographing whatever, later to return to the darkroom to develop and print them.

We would sit in the darkroom on a bench and talk about stuff. He told me he lived in Northampton, alone in his own house. He was really a rating on the ship who had been given the photographer's job because of his keen interest and expertise. When he was not taking pictures around the ship, he could be seen along with the other ratings, painting the rails, scraping rust from rusty places, on a bosun's chair lowered over the side with a bucket of paint and a brush.

He was to me an older man, about forty, nice, kind and fun in a way. This continued for the next few months until his hands started to rest where they shouldn't when leaning over my shoulder to see if I had set the enlarger correctly. I would ignore it. I'd already had experience of this and, providing it stayed gentle and unintrusive, I could live with it, for now. There is more that I won't elaborate on, except to say that the friendship had to come to an end. I made my excuses. We were on a ship so there was no point in creating a drama. It all ended amicably, and I remained impenetrable. I had learned a lot in my childhood.

STILL AT SEA

1964. Continuing my journey towards Singapore on HMTS Monarch. Returning from Vigo in Spain we went to Southampton for a week or two where it took on board more cable, watching it go over the roads and buildings into the cable tanks.

Having so much time to ourselves whenever the ship took on cable, most of the crew would go home at nights and or weekends, leaving only half the number of officers to serve.

I was often alone, so I could continue exploring Erith and Southampton in my time off duty. Only now, in hindsight, do I realise why I was a loner, affable, happy, joining in the fun and camaraderie, but never getting close to anyone for fear of what happened so often in my childhood.

Having sailed through the Suez Canal, we continued on to the next big event - approaching Ceylon, but not before two legal and important drills. The first, abandon ship!

If a number of blasts were heard on the tannoy and ship's horn, I forget how many, it was everyman to rush and get their life vests on and report to their dedicated lifeboat. We knew roughly when this would happen. When it did, it was a mad dash for me and the other stewards to our cabins to collect ours and report up on deck. Easy, but not so for those in lower decks or indeed the engine room, which would be first to take on water if the hull had been breached.

On each level of the boat, in the walkways, at regular distances, are watertight doors that are slammed shut with levers all around, turned to stop the ingress of the sea from a flooded compartment. On all ships now, most passengers would not notice.

It was the duty of every petty officer to ensure his crew were accounted for and to close the doors. Those in the engine room had to run and climb fast up all the gangways before the doors might be slammed shut and they be sealed into their fate. Most everyone has a duty to perform, the commander looking on, timing everyone. All went well, everyone at their lifeboat station.

Part of the drill was the lowering of one of these lifeboats into the sea, Sailors playing with the ropes and pulleys, the boat going down one side and the other getting stuck, the rust in the gearing holding it firm until the man with the big hammer freed it and down it would go. The commander's launch lowered, only to find the engine would not start.

On the day of sailing from Southampton, fully loaded, the ship's plimsoll line, a line on all vessels around the hull to indicate overload, was several inches below the water line. This was remarked on by experienced seamen, wondering why the ship was allowed to sail.

A couple of days later was the fire drill. This was like something from the Keystone Cops. Another number of blasts on the horn and crew to positions. Much shouting, with sailors running around the deck holding buckets and axes, unrolling fire hoses then connecting them to a hydrant on the nearest deck.

But wait! This hose won't reach! Rush to get another. Damn, it got tangled up. Connect it to the hydrant. Who's got the spanner? All connected, everyone in their correct positions, a sailor on the end of each hose, hand on the lever to let the water spurt out. Turn on the water, someone shouts. What now? The rest of us started to laugh at this unfolding chaos. Then the hose fills, expanding and taught, the sailor on the end looks into the end of the hose to see if he can see the water, others shouting to him to turn the fucking lever. He does, but still peering into it. He's knocked back onto the deck, losing control of the hose now spewing out water at great pressure, the hose flailing about, soaking everyone. The sailor regains control and with that the fire drill was over. It was just like going to the theatre.

I was relaxed and happy with my duties when suddenly a warning came loud over the tannoy.

"Within the next two hours we will be passing the tip of Ceylon where extremely rough seas are expected from a typhoon. All crew are to ensure everything is battened down, portholes closed and sea doors to the decks secured shut. Now!"

As I had not left the officers mess as yet, someone told me to secure the chains under each table and every chair to the deck and put up the boards, about four inches high, that ran around all four sides of the tables. These boards being on hinges, I had never noticed them before. Plus, when returning prior to lunch, the crisp white tablecloths were to be folded to sit within these boards, thoroughly soaked with water to stop plates and cutlery from sliding off in the pitch and roll to come.

Looking out at the sea, it was beautifully calm, a bright, hot sunny day. Never mind, I did what I was told and then proceeded up to clean my officers' four cabins on the top deck. Usual routine, beds made, portholes polished, decks scrubbed, all looked beautiful, cabin doors pinned open to allow fresh air. I never ever had a complaint. Then scrubbed the passageway with my ball of wire wool. Looking out to sea, the tip of India lay to the left and the tip of Ceylon to the right.

I stood up and looked back admiringly at it all being neat, tidy and pristine.

As we passed through a channel and out into the open sea, an incredible crash of waves and wind hit the ship, making it keel over at an alarming angle. Everything in the officer's cabins now lay in a heap in the passageway. I turned and headed down. After all, I had done my duties. Who would know that I wasn't on my way down when it happened?

Down below, it was bedlam. Sailors were locking everything down. The gun doors, the size of warehouse doors at the end of the main deck, had not been secured before taking on water like a whale with its mouth wide open. Sea water rushed inside the whole deck from forward to aft where now there was a two-foot wave swishing backwards and forwards, side to side. Fortunately, not too much flooded below decks because of the steel step at the bottom of the doorway. Everyone running around, bells clanging. Down I went into the main galley below decks where all the cooking was done. A huge ranges of cookers with chefs and staff screaming at each other as sea water sprayed over the whole ship, crashing down the ventilation funnels - the white ones you often see on a ship - catching the air or expelling the heat from the galleys below.

All the gimbals up around the cookers. Huge pots of soup and vegetables, sliding around on top, the contents with their own waves, spilling over. The deck awash here with soup, the staff slipping and sliding, pots and pans, knives and ladles that had not been secured, clanging around. Still it was incredibly hot.

I had decided after my first experience in the officers' galley that I would never enter again. But, passing it and looking in at the open door, I just could not resist.

It really was mayhem. However, the food had to be cooked, the bread baked. No one noticed me peering in or attempting to walk along a passageway, like climbing a hill, holding on tight to the handrails. Quick as a flash you were running down, tossed into the bulkhead, one side and then the other. Not a touch or a nudge but a full body blow each time. A mind-blowing experience.

Looking into the officers' saloon where I was tasked to cover for its own bar steward when required. A big saloon to accommodate fifty officers, plush carpets, armchairs and a television for when in a port. The full uniform had to be worn by all the officers, on duty or not. The easiest bar I ever worked in, I already knew all the drinks and spirits from my early years in the off-licence. They would just amble over, "Johnny Walker, please, steward, a medium sherry, steward," etc. You deftly dispensed and wrote on a notepad what they had. They signed and that was that. No one would talk to you or tell you their problems in this kind of bar and it was "Yes, sir, thank you sir," only.

This saloon now was a disaster zone. All the furniture was in a gigantic heap at one end. The television lay smashed on the floor, along with lamps, ashtrays and other knick-knacks that decorated the bar.

We were in the eye of a typhoon and stayed in it for the next week as it tracked slowly on our course, the commander refusing to turn into the waves, trying to keep the deadline for reaching Singapore, the welcome of ambassadors and dignitaries, plus of course the deadline for laying the cable to Borneo.

After a day of this pummelling and a porthole somewhere on the ship being smashed through (I was told that these portholes would take a ten-thousand ton wave to smash), the order was given that all deadlights, which swing down over the portholes and are thick steel, should be bolted down on all decks below the main deck. Every crew member wears a life jacket twenty-four hours a day, meaning sleeping in it too. Sleeping in them was almost impossible, as they were those bulbous cork-filled types, designed to stay afloat a couple of days before becoming completely water-logged. They were fitted with a whistle for attracting attention, a red light and a glorified rear bicycle lamp, the batteries lasting just a few days. You had to lie on your bunk with one of these attached, akin to a full small backpack on your back and front, the pitch of the ship pulling your skin and your hair one way and the other.

Along the edge of the bunk were bed-boards, about six inches high to stop you being tossed onto the floor, but even with this, one sailor was thrown over. The doors were solid metal plate from the inner main deck and the gun doors had to be welded all the way around against the power of the sea.

Four experienced sailors were summoned to have eyes on the sea. A ship eight hours ahead of us had put out an emergency call for ours to keep a lookout for one of their own sailors. He had fallen overboard and it was deemed pointless and risky for that ship to attempt to stop and search. They had thrown a lifebelt to him but had seen him drift away. By the time we passed the same point, the sailor, if he was still alive, would have been miles away. Davy Jones got that poor soul down into the depths of the ocean. After this, all doors were ordered to be welded shut. No one but no one was allowed out onto the decks.

Talk then of a mutiny from the sailors if the commander did not head into the waves hitting the ship with such force as to turn it turtle. He would not budge. Below decks, no sign of daylight from any cabins or portholes with all the deadlights down. My escape was still carrying out my duties on the top deck where, as you were thrown about in each cabin, you could hang onto the rail below the portholes, some hundred feet above the water line. The higher you are on a ship, the further the swing in the waves. One moment literally hanging as if from a ceiling as the ship lunges over to the port and then pushing yourself away from the bulkhead as it lunges back to starboard. I would make my way along to the forward cabin, the commanders, and the lookout of his forward windows, watching the bow of the ship, where I usually would sit on my gangplank, rise up, lifting the ship at an angle, like an aeroplane taking off, to crash down with the bow disappearing deep into the sea. The stern was now out of the water and the whole ship shook, like an overloaded washing machine on full spin. The mighty propeller rises up out of the water, shaking the ship before plunging back down again.

The dark black waves rapidly followed each other, each up to a hundred and fifty feet high. You watched as the next one towered above the ship, riding up and under, lifting it high before the ship slid down the other side with an almighty thud, then you'd have to wait until the next one did the same. Every so often this momentum would change and the ship being at the bottom of one of these waves would be completely enveloped in the next one, crashing down on top of it.

On our arrival in Singapore, my modelling was in great demand by the photographer. The commander wanted detailed photographs of all the damage. The long gangplank disappeared in the storm, lifeboats with holes in them damaged beyond repair, the ship's rails all around the deck buckled and bent over, the swimming pool gone. The ship, white all over now, looked like most of the paint had been stripped off by the waves. A large contingent of sailors left the ship here, convinced the ship was jinxed.

In the midst of all this, I was one of the few that did not get seasick, so was able to savour all the chaos and drama. I would, as usual, be serving the meals in the officers' mess, laying tablecloths inside the gimbals and then throwing a bowl of water over them before adorning them with the cutlery and the condiments.

I played a tune on the xylophone before each meal, summoning everyone. I had to take this to the ship's tannoy system and plink plonk on it a few times and it was done. Bored with the monotony of this plinking and plonking, I learned to play, over a few days, a nice melodic tune, praised by many, until word came from the commander via the chief steward, via the petty officer that he appreciated my efforts, but could I not play, "Come to the cookhouse, dear boys"?

The officers, or those who turned up, less than half, mainly out of sheer hunger, looking green around the gills, occasionally leaped up to dash out, retching. There I would stand, leaning to stay upright against their table, taking their orders whilst the chains under the chairs went taut. In the middle of these chains, by the way, was a screw adjustment to avoid any slack. Nevertheless, seats would tend to swing around, the officers hastily grabbing the table to stop themselves doing a full circle.

Orders taken, it was about dashing into the servery, judging the roll of the ship, lurching in the right direction, side to side. This is what is meant by sea legs. Returning to your table with plates firmly grasped, waiting for the right moment to jettison oneself over to it. Slamming each plate in front of an officer, at the same time he would grasp it with both hands to stop it whooshing away. Such fun. Vegetables would roll off their plates and go backwards and forwards on the table whilst the officers did their best to cup their arms and hands around the plates to stop losing any more of their food.

On one occasion the nasty petty officer stood guard by the servery watching with his back firmly planted against the bulkhead, the only occasion he did, he was not of a rank to eat with the officers, but to

A sip of rum in Jamaica

ensure the smooth running of the ship. The steward before me had his soup slosh over the edges of the plate in all these waves, onto the deck. Out of the servery I came, dashing to the table, but I slid, my arms up in the air, throwing these plates of soup up and behind me, to land all over him. In a hardly held back rage, he stepped forward leaving his outline in soup over the bulkhead. He glared at me, saying through gritted teeth,

"C....., I will get you for this!" and stormed out of the mess.

The officers erupted into laughter, so I just knew he would not dare do anything to me and never appeared again in the officers' mess.

The only other time I saw him, I was the bar steward one evening. I had run short of glasses which meant a long dash below decks to get more from the stores. One tray held about twenty glasses. It was either three trips, one tray each trip or, one trip with three trays stacked high. I had chosen the latter and on climbing the companionway, tripped, stumbled and down they all went with an almighty crash of glass at the nasty petty officer's feet. Once again, he glowered at me and this time shouted,

"C....., you will pay for them," but I never did and was never asked to. I guess he thought better of it.

No one liked him. He was the same to everyone. A sailor behind me said, "Ignore him, everyone else does." I think he spent all his time in his cabin drinking.

Actually, I did see him once more. He came to my cabin, waving my timesheet in his hands, saying,

"C....., what's the meaning of this? It's not good enough, do it again."

"What's wrong with it?" I asked. "All my hours are correct."

He shouted, "Not the point! You haven't claimed your bicycle cleaning allowance. Ten shillings a week. Do it now, and don't forget it again either."

I did politely remind him it was a ship, so just who has a bike on board?

"You are still a postman and entitled to it," he barked. "We all claim it."

Who was I to argue. What a great perk!

The other perk for me was trading my four beer allowance every day with a seaman petty officer from the day I had boarded. He had invited, nay insisted, I visit him to thank me for trading my beer only with him. Although he looked like a real bruiser of a man, roughly shaven, deep guttural voice and with many years' experience, I did go, albeit nervously. He seemed genuinely thankful and caring in a strange sort of way for my well-being.

As a petty officer, he had his own cabin, lots of pictures of him as a boxer, cups and medals as well as a champion's belt, all proudly displayed. He talked to me about his story, his boxing career etc. Now much too old for boxing, it was his bit of history and as with so many others aboard, an alcoholic. A pleasant and strange visit, but at least I had someone looking after my back, the rough sailors under his charge all being afraid of him.

SHIP CINEMA NIGHTS

Below the foredeck, also called the poop deck, was a cavernous space that went down deep to the hull. A door led into it from three decks below. Here was where the anchor chains were kept, connected to the anchors, hanging each side of the bow, the links being the size of one's forearm; mountains, it seemed, of rusting chains. When the anchors were dropped there was an horrendous noise as they rapidly fed up and out, creating a cloud of rust dust. Also in this cavernous space were stored the giant buoys, used to tie to the end of the telephone cable when it had come to the end. These and a wide assortment of machines and engine spares.

Above all this heavy duty iron were half a dozen long planks of wood, precariously balanced across and on the junk tied to hooks above and below. These were the seating for the cinema nights, once a week. The whole space was lit by a single light bulb. The cinema was under the deck and the shape of the hull sweeping in, a shiny white bow outside, a rusting hulk inside.

I went just once, a scrawled A4 notice outside, declaring it to be the cinema. I went for the feature film, something with lots of music and women. The film had started, the projector flickering away through the haze of smoke in the gloom, just a respite when the roll of film had run out to a chorus of shouts and swearing. The beam of light from the projector that had been cutting through the smoke went out whilst a new reel of film was fed through the projector making the whole place even more dark and forbidding.

The planks accommodated a few sailors on each, although they could have taken three times as many as some were sitting on the anchor chains or machinery around.

The noise from them shouting at each other, beers being downed and ribald jests at the characters on the screen was too much. Half an hour of this and I quietly slipped away. I definitely would not want to be caught in the back row there.

After a week under a typhoon, both the ship and it going slowly in the same direction, it passed over. We could assess the damage, make repairs as far as possible, then full steam ahead to Singapore. After weeks of not seeing any land at all, to see the island appear on the skyline, lush and green, was sheer joy.

Slowly the ship approached its docking place. The first time for me to see Asia, mesmerised by the row of bamboo shacks, built up on stilts, just a hundred yards from us. I'd seen only pictures in magazines of these Asian peoples, now seeing them for real, fishing, cooking - and the cacophony of many transistor radios, some blaring out Chinese radio stations and music, some western music. Listening to the local news in English, there were reports of many dying and going blind in these shacks from brewing their own hooch.

It was late afternoon when we arrived, after the evening meal. I sat in my usual position again on my gangplank overlooking all the activity. The photographer later asked me if I wanted him to show me around during the following day's four hour break. He then asked my nasty petty officer if I could miss that evening's meal to accompany him on his photographic brief from the commander. He could not say no, although the reason the photographer gave was complete hogwash, knowing the petty officer would not dare to check.

So difficult to sleep that night, the heat, the humidity, the sheets wringing wet with perspiration, the whisper hardly noticeable from the air conditioning vent above my head. The overpowering noise of the crickets, millions of them, that never stopped. How, I wondered could anyone live through it all? Plus, the excitement of tomorrow's outing.

The routine in the officers' mess the following day was to be much quieter, as some of the officers had chosen to stay in Singapore with friends or in the Officers' Club in town, just like an old colonial club. I asked another steward in the officers' mess who served two tables near mine, if he could cover for me for the day, as so few officers were going to be around, if I covered for him the following day. He was happy to have a day off. After months stuck on the ship, it was a delight.

Morning duly came, white trousers and white shirts were soon bouncing down a gangway borrowed from the dock side, I guess, as ours had been destroyed in the typhoon. The photographer with a large, all singing and dancing Japanese camera that he had bought abroad. This was kept in the commander's safe when in the UK to avoid tax. It cost many hundreds of pounds at that time. With the microflex camera he had given me slung around my neck, both of us looked much like news reporters. Off the dock and into a taxi. First stop, Tiger Balm Gardens, like a park, but not that tidy, on undulating land in the centre of town. Going in under the high arch, at the time I did not realise that Tiger Balm was an ointment, a cure for most anything, like Germoline on steroids.

Not only being a slice of the jungle in town, it had almost a plague of monkeys bouncing around everywhere.

A walk around the area. Singapore had few buildings higher than two floors, some in the centre and that was it. Shops and markets under the colonnades along the high street.

Back in a taxi to see Raffles. Everyone knows Raffles. We did not wait long as we were to have tea in the officers' club, we were just waved in. A large lounge and bar, all armchairs, panelled walls, the fans gently whirring around overhead, people sitting smoking cigars or reading The Times. The steward came to take our orders, pink gins, sipping them leisurely, trying to catch snippets of hushed conversations. The most salubrious environment that I had ever been in, having to stop myself shrieking out when looking at the wall in an odd corner that led to the garden. Chameleons were scrambling all around. I soon surmised that this was normal as no one else felt the urge to climb up on the table.

An hour here, yet another taxi to Princes Hotel, a smart modern hotel, not to be confused with Princess Hotel. We were to have lunch here. Immediately on entering after coming off the street and the stifling humidity, it felt instantly cold. The sweat of our shirts and trousers giving an uncomfortable chill. The concierge reminded us that it was a strict dress code - black jacket and tie to enter, but no problem, he had rails full, to fit the largest to the smallest person and no charge, soon we were attired and allowed entry to the dining room. It was the size of a tennis court with low lighting, potted palms and again the dark panelling everywhere. To the front of this large restaurant was a complete orchestra on a stage, playing requests for patrons' requests discreetly delivered by the waiters, immaculately turned out.

By this time I was a bit nervous about what this was going to cost. After all, I only had ten bob.

"Don't worry," the photographer said to me, "I have an American Express card. It only costs some…" (alarming, figure to me…) "for annual membership, and there is no limit how much I spend".

I had never heard of such a thing. He must be rich, I decided. He ordered five or six courses. I thought it would never end. Such was the grandeur of this place, our table had two waiters, exclusively for just our table. They stood discreetly in the background, watching every move, impeccable in their white gloves, gliding over to light our cigarettes between courses. As soon as the cigarette end touched the ashtrays they were immediately changed for clean ones. At the end of each course, our cutlery placed down, they would clear the table whilst we chatted and watched the orchestra play, everything deftly lifted away, a clean white tablecloth laid and I swear that sometimes one did not even notice it happening. Wine to accompany the different courses.

Someone from the orchestra came over to the table to ask if we had a request that they might play for us. The photographer asked me to suggest something for them. All I could think of was Rock Around The Clock or Tchaikovsky's 1812 Overture. I chose the latter and without turning a hair, he made his way back to the stage and that is exactly what they played. In modern parlance, I was gobsmacked.

I needed to have a pee, leaving the table for the toilets. Before I reached the door, one of our waiters rushed to open it for me. A beautifully tiled area, sparkling clean, gold taps, piles of monogrammed towels and flannels, a vase of flowers on the shelf where one could preen oneself whilst the attendant wore a uniform much like mine. Pristine white with a row of brass buttons, except I did not have the white gloves. A bit embarrassing having someone discreetly watching me have a pee.

As soon as I finished, he leapt over, beating me to turn the taps on, hand me the soap, then a towel, help me on with my jacket and then brushing the collar and shoulders. All the time with a broad smile and utter deference. I come from Brixton, South London, the poshest place I had ever been to was the pie and mash shop!

I knew I had to give him something. The only money I had was a ten bob note, my whole week's allowance. I thanked him and thrust it in his hands. He clasped his palms together and bowed, thanking me profusely, then again ran to the door to open it for me. The waiter, still waiting outside to guide me back to my seat.

The photographer asked me if I'd tipped the attendant and how much?

"Ten shillings, it's all I had."

"Good God, he will be happy. That's a whole week's wage to him, at least," he replied.

We had been having this lunch for five hours. Had I suddenly become a king?

Leaving and handing back the jackets and ties, stepping outside was like entering a sauna. The doorman waved a waiting taxi over for us. Where now, I wondered? Before the photographer could say, the taxi driver wanted to know if we wanted girls or boys or both. My jaw dropped. Did I hear right? The photographer asked me to choose. I went red with embarrassment but kept my cool and said he will have to decide.

"Girls, then, driver," he said.

"Do not worry, sirs. I will take you to a special place. I know you are gentlemen from the restaurant," he said.

It was a long ride, maybe half an hour. Out of the bright lights and into a posh suburb with elegant houses and large gardens. One might well be in Surrey.

He pulled over to one such house and led us through the tall drive gates to the entrance, rang the bell and a Chinese lady answered, guiding us to a chaise longue in an equally elegant hall with a sweeping staircase to the upper floor. The photographer spoke to her, out of my earshot, my attention being distracted admiring the architecture - truly, it was.

He came back to sit with me and asked me to choose one from a line of six girls to spend the night with. My angst and worry as to what to do! I had never been with a girl and certainly had no interest ever. The only girls I had seen were on the top shelf of back street newsagents, even then only breasts and corsets. I just had to brazen it out! In a way, I was almost relieved that he had chosen girls in the taxi, which took away my first fear. He must only want women so I would be safe.

The girls duly walked in to stand a few feet in front of us, smiling and wiggling their assets demurely. I had to choose first. I looked hard at each. Big full bodied ones, slight ones, pert figures. I chose the least threatening - slim, shy, I thought, and petite with short black hair, Chinese.

Singapore is made up of three populations almost equally, at least then - Malay, Chinese and Japanese. Now Indians have replaced the Japanese. The photographer chose his woman but my thoughts were only on what would happen next. The hostess led us up the stairs, not before asking what time we wanted the taxi in the morning. Oh no! My heart sank. My plan was to pretend I was much too tired and hopefully be out in half an hour.

The girls led us to our respective rooms, the photographer bidding me a fun filled night prior to closing our doors. What to do now? I sat down on the bed, my woman taking her dress off and jabbering at me in broken English,

"Take clothes off now, mister."

I averted my eyes and lay down with my first plan. I was too tired, too drunk or both, whichever would work. I turned to the wall, still clothed and pretended to be sleeping. She would have none of it, jumping on the bed alongside me, taking my hand and rubbing it on her breasts. Yuk! I pulled it back quickly. She would not give up, fighting me to get my trousers and shirt off whilst I pulled and tugged at the sheets to keep my modesty. A while of this tussle, she then resorted to playing with my bits, forcing her hand under the sheets I had wrapped, I thought tightly around me. Absolutely no joy for her.

"Why is it asleep?" she shouted angrily. "You no like Chinese?" She gave up and lay alongside me, muttering occasionally in Chinese. Best I did not know what!

About two in the morning, a Malay girl comes into the room. They have a heated argument. The Chinese girl orders the Malay girl out of the room. They have a tussle, shouting and fighting by the door. The Malay girl shouts to me,

"Chinese girls no good. You want Malay mister," and with that they both disappeared, thank goodness. Perhaps now I could sleep, but not without worrying that either of them would bounce back in.

A long time just lying there, staring at the wall opposite, where a cockroach is skirting the edges, slowly making its way in my direction. I had never seen one before and it was huge. I threw a match at it, hoping it would run away, but no, the matchstick landed in front of it. It stopped, picked up the matchstick, tossed it to the side and continued walking towards me. The perfect day had turned into a horror story!

I crept off my bed with my shoe in one hand intending to bash it to death. But I couldn't. It would probably squish everywhere or make a crunching noise, or worse, attack me. I returned to bed, leaving the light on, and eventually fell asleep.

At 7 a.m. the photographer knocks on the door to announce the taxi has arrived to take us back to the ship. With great relief and happiness, clothes on, racing down to reception, out of the door and into the taxi, barely looking back, not even having the courage to say goodbye to the madam.

The photographer asked me how I had got on.

"Yeah, great!" I said.

"What did you do?" he asked.

As it happens, certainly with a girl, I would not know what to do. I had no idea then and no idea now. I can only imagine, not having seen all parts of the female anatomy nor wishing to.

"Actually, I was so drunk and tired, I can't remember a thing! It was great though, thank you for a wonderful day and especially last night," I responded with glee and a broad smile, thanking him profusely again. Phew, a great inward sigh of relief on my part.

Back to the normal routine, not sitting so much on my gang plank in the afternoons but foraging around the shops ashore. Being followed almost constantly by the tri-shaws and rickshaws wanting to take me somewhere - anywhere. I got used to ignoring them but they never seemed to give up.

In the evenings, after dinner, I was in the darkroom with the photographer developing our films. He did not appear to take umbrage at still not knowing if I was Arthur or Martha.

One day, it was announced that a garden party was to take place on the foredeck. It being cleared of any extraneous clutter and freshly painted, a marquee without sides was erected. Buffet tables, white tablecloths, silver platters, heaps of wine, sherry glasses and champagne flutes.

The ship was dressed with bunting from stem to stern going high up into and over the masts. A military band will soon arrive to welcome the British High Commissioner and other important dignitaries. The ship's photographer buzzed about taking pictures along with the local press of the comings and goings, speeches and everyone in their finest uniforms, including me, a royal navy dark blue officer's one with cap and brass buttons. Even the sailors, or at least some, in their Royal Navy kit. Now the ship represents Her Majesty and the British Government. The local radio reported events.

A few days later, any crew that had abandoned the ship were replaced with new ones and we were once again setting sail for Jesselton in Borneo. Along the way, I realised that we were going in ever decreasing circles, leaving what looked like a giant pond in the sea. We were grappling the seabed for the other end of the cable that had been laid a year earlier. The buoy that had been left with its radar reflector and flashing light on top – gone, apparently stolen by fishermen for the huge amounts of batteries, plus a ton of scrap metal.

When eventually this cable was found, the grappling iron being able to clamp over it automatically, it was wound up to the deck using the large capstans. The next day, on the way to my usual position sitting on the end of the gangplank, a long black cable led from the cable tanks to a man sitting with his feet, on the aft deck. I kid you not. Down a manhole cover, two of these undersea cable ends clamped whilst he spliced them together. Brassier was going to heat his soldering iron, the standard barrier around him, the hole and the green tent, exactly as you would see in any high street when the Post Office was fixing telephone lines. It seemed so incongruous here, deep in the ocean. Worse, I had lost my gangplank because it was now surrounded by sailors working with machinery of one kind or another. The cable disappeared over a great stern wheel, mounted on the end of a gangplank similar to the one at the bow. Now, that cable from the deep was joined to the new one.

More weeks of steaming along slowly, the relentless noise of bells clanging and ringing twenty-four hours a day as the cable was fed out from the tanks and over the sides.

At last, Jesselton. The ship continued its course, straight towards the shore. I was on the top deck at the time and just finished my cabins.

The second officer asked me if I wanted to go on the bridge to watch the ship's arrival, another normally forbidden place. He would ask the commander for permission. Yes, I could, but told to keep quiet in one place without moving. Officers moving around, the commander giving orders, shouting out, slow, dead slow, ten degrees to the right or left as the sailor standing in front of his steering wheel repeated every order. Steady ahead, as he blasted out many times the ships horn, for below, around and in front, were many fishing boats going hither and thither, some with nets out.

"If they don't get out of the way, we will run them down," he told the officers on the bridge. The ship could not veer out of the way or stop, the cable still being paid out over the aft. Boats altered course at the last minute, their horns and whistles blowing as our huge ship would not alter its course.

Almost when it seemed that we would crash into the beach ahead, the ship stopped.

The commander turned his signal one way, then the other, slow, dead, slow, stop, slow astern, stop - whilst also on the phone to the engineer deep down in the engine room, confirming the instructions as well as turning his signal device, acknowledging. I had been down there myself, so I knew and could visualise exactly what was going on.

On the beach, great activity with gangs of native workmen. We had stopped near a tugboat and other boats with workmen aboard. More orders.

"Drop anchor!" the commander's mate yelled out.

With a crescendo of noise, the anchors on each side crashed down into the sea. The sailors on the foredeck, standing clear as the chains came out, the noise heard all over the ship. What a privilege to be on the bridge watching all this in awe!

The barge moved closer as the line being paid out was cut and dropped, to be hauled on board where the workman and engineers spliced a cable coming across the sand into the sea onto the trawler.

A full day we sat in this position and watched. Job done. The anchors were raised and we headed to dock in the port. Whilst there, the net was lowered into the sea.

In Singapore, I had bought a pair of flippers as I was not a strong swimmer. So, donning them, I climbed out of the net and into the open bay, ships moored all around. I was able to swim easily in the warm waters, and with goggles on I could look into the water. Fish of every size coming towards me, the larger ones I shut my eyes to, hoping they would swim past. When I bobbed up, treading water, to look around this huge port in the bay, on every ship were sailors, all waving, and I cheerily waved back at them before returning to my ship, thoroughly happy with my new flippers.

Getting onto the deck, a seaman said,

"Did you not see all the other ships waving to me to get out of the water? It's heavily shark infested! That's why we use the net!"

Oops.

Another place to eagerly explore. I arranged for a day off. After all, we were to be here for a week, bunkering up prior to returning to Singapore. A day later, having asked other stewards if they wanted to come with me, my plan was to get on any bus and go to the end of the line into the jungle, the city consisting of one long street, hotels and banks, offices and shops on one side only, the other side the sea. When you looked up the side of these buildings, the streets ended, just jungle.

Everyone declined to come for fear of their lives. Not thwarted, that is what I did, walking six hundred yards to the end of this capital city's streets which opened into a dirt-filled area, the bus station and amusement park. One ride, no shops, just shacks on the edge of the jungle. They surrounded the bus terminus and all other buildings, save for this single fairground feature, a circular railway track around fifty metres in diameter, and a diesel engine pulling enough open wooden carriages to fill the circumference.

It was packed with children and parents, all whooping with glee as this thing went around and around in circles. No bus stops, just unmarked places where groups of people would be standing, waiting, all seemingly carrying crates of chickens or holding one in their arms, all alive of course, some with goats on string, sacks of vegetables, all manner of things. The bus, clapped out and battered, a windowless and doorless heap, pulled up. Everyone waiting to fight each other for a seat.

I had no idea where it might be going. I gave the driver some local money and I was on. Standing, packed in tight amongst the passengers, all gabbling away at the same time, looking at me. Animals and chickens on laps, some hanging out where the windows would have been. The bumpy dirt road through the jungle adding to the sense of adventure.

An hour later, we had arrived as I was propelled out by everyone getting off as they'd got on, all at once. No idea where I was. It seemed like a jungle village. I dared not leave the vicinity of the bus which was taking on new passengers, apparently for the return journey. No way was I going to risk it being the only bus of the day or even the week. Half an hour later, it was ready to move off. I clambered on.

Back in Jesselton, safe and sound for a slow walk back to the ship. Unlike Singapore, no one bothered you, almost no motorised traffic. The people were pleasant, all smiled and acknowledged my wave. They were mostly thin and their clothes mostly rags. No distinguishable shops but wooden huts with produce out on the floor in front. A fabulous day for me, envied by my colleagues aboard.

The crew would leave the ship and head to the nearest bar or whorehouses normally and this place was no exception. Although I never went there myself, one in particular was mentioned. Whatever time of day or night, it was open. One especially grubby sailor spent the whole week there, not leaving it, sleeping on the benches inside, totally paralytic, only returning to the ship on the day of sailing.

The seaman's petty officer who I'd exchanged beers for cigarettes with, prior to the first port, had advised me not to go ashore without two or three mates, stick together, take condoms and not go too far away. If you itch or your willy is leaking, see the doc in the morning. Not much use to me. I did know what a condom was, let alone how to use one, and I did not drink so I would be the last invited to a party. In Singapore, after the garden party on deck, the steward on the bunk below me, following a night out to meet local girls, said in the morning that his willie was not right and he would see the doc. Apparently, it was normal for a number of crew to be doing this after a night out in every port. The doc would give them an injection and medication after examining their offending appendages.

The commander, the day after, wanted to know from the doc the names of all crew who had been to see him and had them sent back home immediately, including the guy on the bunk below. That happened only on this one occasion because of the importance of the visit to our government.

A week later, sailing back to Singapore via the South China Sea, lookouts were posted on the bow to check for Russian submarines. A reported Russian sub had fired a torpedo on an American destroyer in this area around the time of the Cuban crisis. President Kennedy gave orders that if it was to happen again, they should return the compliment. The world was on high alert fearing World War Three. Everyone on board was fearful that things might escalate as we were right in the middle of any intended hostilities. All was well, however.

When we reached Singapore this time, instead of docking in port, we moored in the bay, having to go ashore in a ferry boat assigned to the ship from the dockyard. This was like the ferry at Greenwich. Every hour it would leave the docks to the ship or make the return journey.

At the time, President Sukarno from Indonesia was threatening to overthrow Singapore and claim it as theirs. A day later, whilst walking around the shops, ashore in Singapore, it was announced with immediate effect that there was to be a twenty-three-and-a-half-hour curfegypt

ew each day until further notice, lifted only for half an hour. Anyone on the streets would be shot.

People were rushing everywhere. Panic ensued, a rickshaw owner trying to hurry me to get back to the dock and my ferry to the ship. It had started. Later that evening, the sailor on watch reported armed boarders attempting to climb up onto the ship throwing up grappling hooks; they were repelled. A message on the tannoy:

"All weapons trained seamen report to the armoury."

Rifles were issued, sailors patrolling the decks all night and into the next day. Drat! No more trips to the shops and streets of Singapore.

A day later, HMS Bulwark, now a museum in the Pool of London, then a battleship, arrived in the bay to escort us out of danger to dock in Jakarta to take us back to the UK. Not far out, a day's sailing away, lay the American Sixth Fleet including an enormous aircraft carrier with thousands of sailors aboard. Warships, battleships, thousands of soldiers in this mega dock, many brought here for rest and recuperation after fighting in the jungles of Vietnam.

Our ship's crew were invited to a short tour of this aircraft carrier whose name I cannot remember. The size of it, moored along from us, made ours look like a bathtub boat. The main deck resembled an airport runway. The visit finished in their crew's messroom, hundreds and hundreds of American sailors, all at long benches, all seemingly drunk, some fighting, some dancing on the benches, others singing, some naked or being stripped for the fun of it. A hellishly noisy, gloomy environment filled with smoke hanging in the air like a dark cloud, the stench of beer being consumed and benches were awash with it. Pop songs were blaring out. It made our sailors look like angels in comparison.

A day or two later, the long journey back home began. Peace at last, and back once more to the steady routine broken only by a visit from a fuel tanker at sea to refuel. Somewhere on route, sharks were spotted and announced over the tannoy: "Sharks starboard side!" Many of us rushed to the main deck to look for them. I stood up on the middle rail and leaned over, peering at this fin, slowly and gracefully coming closer and closer until it was alongside us. Gradually it raised itself, the fin now growing larger and larger to reveal the true size of this shark, in excess of twenty feet, black and with a coldly menacing mouth. I carefully lowered myself back down to the deck again.

Some of the seamen, with the permission of the officers and the

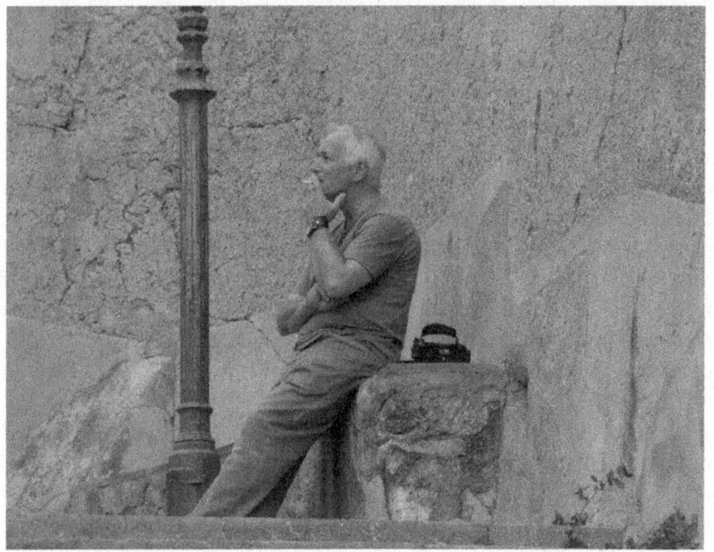

Somewhere in Egypt

galley quartermaster, brought up a whole side of beef and hooked it onto one of the derricks, a crane, hoisted into the air and over the sea and lowered, like a giant fishing rod. Very soon, one of these giants was caught, hoisted up onto the deck and left hanging in the air whilst sailors would stand alongside for photographs. Too gruesome for me, I went below again where I was told that a chef had come to get some best cuts from it for the galley before it was ditched back into the waves.

Days, weeks before stopping in Aden, prior to going through the Suez canal again. A couple of days here whilst taking on stores and fuel. Looking at a map, a thin sliver of land and the Yemen behind. Many British soldiers are in the bars along the main strip. This time, I went with a few others to a hotel that had a roof terrace and bar which looked out over the sea, dozens of ships at anchor in the distance. This would be the only chance after dinner to see Aden.

My interest was the view. Conversant with all the camera settings, I took some startling pictures at dusk with the lights of the ships and cabins on, standing the camera on the roof edge and setting the timer, aperture, exposure etc. My colleagues called me over, offered me a beer, which, as I did not drink anyway, turned out to be bitter and horrible, but at least it was a long, cool drink in the heat, even at dusk. Then another, then a gin and tonic. All around the soldiers were, talking avidly, about wives, women and killing.

When the time came to return to the ship with my colleagues, I stood up and immediately fell down. There I stayed, completely sozzled. I could not stand. I was carried back to the ship, briefly carried over the gangplank to my bunk. At this point, I fell out with the photographer. He had come a little later to check that I was okay, proceeded to strip me and then… as hard he might try, he could not. I might have been paralytic, but not so that I couldn't keep myself tightly clenched. I looked at him through squinty eyes when he was fumbling at my bunk side to see him take his false teeth out. After his complete and humiliating failure, he did not stay long and I was able to sleep in peace.

Off we sailed again, the photographer asking me if I had remembered anything from the night before.

"No, not after I fell down at the bar. Nothing until I was woken by the petty officer in the morning. I don't even remember getting undressed," I said.

So that was that, another drama saved.

Through the Suez again, in reverse and sailing straight through this time, into the Mediterranean and on until Gibraltar came into view. This was shortly before serving lunch in the officers' mess. Grand. I managed to look whilst serving to see the rock getting closer and closer. An officer came rushing over to the commander's seat and whispered something. The commander jumped up, shouting at the officer who was running back to his post.

"Hoist the black balls!" the commander shouted, then stormed out with half of the other officers following.

The engines are thrown into full astern from full ahead. This does not happen immediately because the tonnage of the ship takes it a mile to slow down before slowly building up to full astern.

Watching from the officers' mess as the rock approached, pleased because my officers had abandoned the meal, although not before telling me that the ship had lost all control of the steering! The black balls were two big, round black baskets, hoisted high up the mast to warn other shipping, 'Ship out of control."

Just like in a movie where the girl is strapped to the train tracks but the train miraculously stops, we did too.

Sadly, no opportunity to go ashore. Anchor dropped and over. The next day, the problem was sorted and off we went. Now, just the Bay of Biscay which, after everything that had happened before, was not so threatening. We would soon see the white cliffs of Dover come into view looking greener atop, so verdant and beautiful.

Expecting the ship to go up the Thames Estuary to Greenwich but no, it carried on and went around the east coast, past Southend on Sea and up. Had the skipper got lost? No, I was told we were going up to Newcastle and along the Tyne to Hebburn and the dry docks for essential repairs and refits. We would be there for at least a month.

One of the officers on my table asked what I would be doing during this time. I told him that I would stay in my cabin if I was allowed.

"You can", he said, "but all the seamen will be either home on leave or finding another ship. There will be just a few officers during the days. The ship will be full of dock workers. It will be noisy and there'll be no heating in the cabins."

He then asked if I wanted to stay at the Officers Seamen's Mission in Hebburn.

"Would I be allowed?" I asked.

"Yes, don't worry. I will radio ahead and arrange it for you." What a really nice man!

He did as he said, and I made my way to the mission the day after we had floated into the massive dry dock, watching the gates close astern and the water pumped out. The next morning, looking out of my porthole far down to the bottom of the ship with great beams holding it upright, stem to stern. Walking off the ship to find my way to the dock gates, bits of ships everywhere, piles of timbers, chains, machines to find your way around. Hundreds of men in black and blue boiler suits, all hauling something around or hammering hell out of it.

Leaving the dock gates, I headed into a wide, cobbled square with a long line of buses parked up. A loud siren blasted for a few seconds, then out of nowhere, it seemed, came a throng, a dense crowd of workers, some running, followed by dozens and dozens of men on bicycles peddling like fury. They were all heading for the buses that started their engines and drove closer to the entrance gates seconds before the first one had filled, at which moment they all moved up.

The whole area was a throng of people going hither and thither.

Standing and watching all this was mesmerising. Five minutes later, out came cars, honking at the pedestrians to get out of the way. A car pulled up to me and a man asked me where I was going.

"To the officers' seamen's mission," I replied.

"I know it," he said. "Jump in. I saw you leave the Monarch and guessed you'd be lost," and with that, off we went.

Arriving at the mission, an austere looking building, double doors and a bell to ring. A man in uniform answered. I told him who I was, signed the register and he proceeded to take me upstairs to my room.

"Dining Room is midships on the lower deck at six bells," he said.

Who would know what time that was? Not me.

My room was plush, for me, bigger and better appointed than the officers' cabins on my ship. A comfortable double bed, the first that I had ever slept in. Panelled walls and pictures of sailing ships. A bit nervous to explore the rest of the building in case they might discover that I was not an officer and throw me out. Similarly, I did not stay for breakfast.

At 7 a.m. I was woken sharply by a man with a large ship's bell coming up the stairs. What a racket as he swung the bell back and forth, shouting, "Six bells! Six bells!"

Up, dressed and out.

It was late November and cold. I had to find somewhere to eat first and get warm again. I had not eaten for two days as, on arriving at the docks, there was no more food or service. I returned to the ship in its dry dock, boarding the man at the top of the gangplank, now a foreman of the dock workers.

"Morning, sir," touching his forelock. "Take care, it's only emergency lighting now."

Down I went to my cabin, passing more dock workers scrabbling around. My cabin looked like a lonely place, no other crew on board. I put together what little clothes I had in a bag, sat on the lower bunk and thought what to do next.

The officers' mission was great as far as accommodation went, but I could not stay there any longer than two nights, it was too expensive. The commander, months earlier, had offered to transfer me to the proper seaman's side where I would be trained, including navigation. Sextants, triangular measurements, protractors, mathematics; I knew I was not bright enough. Plus, having seen a year of what seamen were like en masse, I could not envisage morphing into one of them.

When we had docked a couple of days ago, the customs officers came aboard, sat down at tables placed on the main deck and every member of the ship's crew had to, before leaving the ship, present themselves to declare anything they had bought overseas and if necessary pay the customs duty. Not before they had searched the ship, high and low, every nook and cranny, even divers under the hull, looking for anything that might have been lowered into the water. Then into every cabin with a torch and mirrors on long sticks into the air vents, even unscrewing the bulk headboard behind the bench seat. They did not discover however that the seamen had stored contraband inside the huge buoys, the steel access panels bolted down all the way around. Then a lick of paint to mask any sign. Stored in the dirty, rusty chain locker where we had the cinema nights.

I came to the decision that I would find some cheaper accommodation and stay here for a couple of weeks, using up some of my leave, then return to the Post Office as a postman.

With that, I said goodbye to the ship for good and headed to a cafe outside the dock gates, entering into heat and a rich smell of bacon, eggs and sausages, ashtrays almost full, cups and saucers yet to be cleared. I had arrived after the breakfast rush for the dock workers. The woman at the counter, looking like Nora Batty, scarf tied tight over her head, apron and long socks like mine, but hers had fallen around her ankles. A full breakfast, warm and cosy again. She had written down the name of a hotel, supposedly cheap, not too far away. Next plan, check out of the Officers' Seamans' Mission and head for Jarrow, across the Tyne, at the time lined with shipyards, shipbuilders, ships half built towering high above the rows of terraced houses in grimy cobbled streets, to cross the river on the chain ferry.

The ferry went back and forth by its own power, but chains fed up and around wheels so that it could not be pulled off course by the strong currents. A noisy crossing.

Walking around, I came across the hotel, maybe five floors high and stretched between two roads at a junction. I cannot remember the name of it, although it was announced on a wide board across the front, followed by, 'All rooms centrally heated, hot showers and baths.' A grand entrance into a tiled reception hall. Looked just fine. The price was something like ten shillings a night; three nights twenty-five shillings and seven nights thirty shillings. What a bargain. I thought I would stay just the three nights initially, but it would be silly not to stay the week at these prices.

With my receipt in hand, never having stayed in a hotel before, I bounded up the stairs to the first floor. Dramatically, the plush entrance had belied the reality upstairs. Long corridors, shabby paint work and no floor coverings. My room opened to the tiniest room ever. Six foot long and three feet wide. No window, and the central heating was a two-inch pipe from one side to the other. An iron bed and iffy bedding.

It was a place to sleep, a tad cold and quiet, apart from the people on either side of the wooden walls, coughing and retching all night.

In the morning, venturing out to find signs of a hot shower and bathroom, I came across a large room, door open, tiled, grubby, broken with shower heads dangling from the ceiling. A line of cracked sinks, some missing taps and the toilets missing doors or with holes where they had been punched through, no locks (obviously) nor toilet paper. A few old men, coughing and retching. This was evidently a place for tramps. One was having a shower, his pile of clothes on the floor on the side. A quick pee into a pan that had not been cleaned in years and I was out of there.

I wandered about and in the afternoon visited the cinema, something grandly named The Ritz in South Shields. Wherever you were in those days, you could walk into a cinema at any time. There were always two films, a main attraction and a B film. During the intermission, the ice cream lady appeared with a tray slung around her neck, whilst Pathe News played followed by adverts for Charlie's fish and chip shop or the hairdressers around the corner. At any time of the day or evening, you bought a ticket, sat where you liked and could stay and watch the films three times over, mostly not bothering about the start time. You would probably be watching the last half of a film, but no matter, after that and the intermission, you'd watch the other movie and then the first part of the one you'd missed. You got used to it.

The woman in the kiosk was also the woman that tore your ticket in half who sold the ice creams in the intermission and changed the reel of film when it ran out. We used to call them flea pits. The one in Brixton was The Classic.

One more night at the 'hotel' then left and caught a coach back to London and home.

This is probably the longest chapter of my haphazard memoir. I had to mention things that ordinarily I would not want to, but they were what added to this job, the thoughts and emotions, the experiences that could not be forgotten or avoided by going home each day. My earlier life as a child all the way up to this point made me who I am and would stay with me for the rest of my life.

BRIAN'S WORK HISTORY: 1964

Leaving the Post Office

Having left the ship, I was transferred as a postman to Victoria Post distribution building for the whole of south London. It was a few days' training first before being let loose in the sorting offices.

I already had four years seniority behind me, but still had to join the new recruits who needed to pass the training before being employed. This made it something of a conundrum for the tutors, as for all the rest of the recruits, if they did not pass this training, then they would not be offered a job. So, I was issued with an armband for the time being until I was once again given a postman's uniform.

The new postcode machine that I had seen in its experimental stage a year earlier in the headquarters of the Post Office's engineering department was not yet fully operational. Always wanting to know how things worked, it was interesting, if rather simple. One day, how to tie a bunch of letters together before leaving the sorting office. No elastic bands but string. How in detail to tie and knot each bundle across and side to side. This seemed to take hours whilst everyone in the class, around twenty, had to practise one at a time.

With everyone in a tight circle around him, the instructor showed us how to tackle the famous red street letter box. He laboriously gave detailed instruction how to open, scoop out the mail into a sack, change the collection metal slide for the next collection time, ensure the scoop was pushed back inside and slam the door closed before removing the key. Whilst doing this, it is vital and against the rules to accept posts from anyone rushing up to add letters. You were not allowed to accept or allow it to be put into your sack. Rules were rules. Only when you had shut the door, could they put letters into the slot again for the next collection hours later. Instruction, how to stand whilst scooping out the mail, how to slam the door shut without trapping your fingers and everyone, one by one, practising. Mind-bendingly boring.

The next time it was practising how to sort letters into the sorting frames. Each of us was given a pile of letters to sort into these frames, street by street, town by town, city by city, county by county, country by country. Speed being the test, sixty letters a minute. Rows of sacks behind to sort, others behind.

It was nearing Christmas when many thousands of students joined the Post Office for the period as temporary postmen. Mountains of post and parcels to deal with all day and every day.

I was given an inkpad and instructions to stamp all the postage on parcels stacked into a huge pile, towering above my head, completely filling a large room. Standing in the middle of them, I was to stamp away, without sorting, all the packages I could reach. I would arrive in the morning, collect equipment, check the date, see no one all day, just stamp everything in sight. No tea breaks, no lunch breaks, nothing.

A few days of this and it was enough for me. Posting my letter of resignation and dumpiong my arm band into the nearest letter box, it was off to seek another job.

Roof glazier's mate

My two step-brothers both worked as roof glaziers and wanted me to join them to make up a team of their own, Faulkner Greens, Marshalsea Street, London SE1, a company specialising in glazing factory roofs, station roofs, even on Dungeness nuclear power station where I was sent one day with to replace breakages. The sides of Dungeness were around two hundred feet, a huge building glazed all around. A number of previous glaziers had been literally blown off the roof by not letting go of the glass under their arms in the most ferocious winds. I was sent to replace the breakages – five thousand of them. Watching a cradle lowered down the side, being picked up by the wind and thrown into the side, smashing another twenty sheets.

The Dungeness power station was out on the coast, miles from anywhere and always windy. The builders, of which there were hundreds, mainly from Ireland, all lived on the site in a sort of shanty town. Rows of wooden huts, dormitories, kitchens, a bar, shops, much like a western cowboy town. Many of these workers, here for years, would drive around in old cars with no doors, maybe no windows, fronts and rears smashed in, some without bonnets. No policing or security, it was everyone for themselves. I had no choice but to stay there too, after all it was a long drive back to Brixton and I did not even have a driving licence.

At first, I was reluctant, the nearest stepbrother being some eleven years older than me, the second five or six years older than him. As a child, they hated my mother and consequently she and I were mostly ignored, except once. Many violent confrontations broke out. On this occasion, a carving knife was thrown, whizzing through the air. One of the stepbrothers picked her up and threw her out of the top half of a sash window.

The other brother was a professional boxer, later professional heavyweight wrestler for Dale Martins Promotions in Brixton Road.

Another was a gangster. His team would come around to the house at times looking shifty with things hidden under overcoats, hushed tones. They were part of his protection racket in Soho, sometimes targeting gays by being friendly, inviting them back to their accommodation then beating them up and robbing them.

He was released from the army after spending a couple of years in Shepton Mallet Military Prison and being dishonourably discharged. Diagnosed as a schizophrenic who, on being called up for his national service, insisted on being in the tommy gun regiment. Told there wasn't such a unit, he was forced to do military training. During the first leave, after twelve weeks, he threw his kit, uniform and rifle over Westminster Bridge.

My father had taught all his sons to box, giving up on me when, at age five or six, the boxing gloves weighed down my arms. I shook them off and refused point blank to fight. A beating and swearing made no difference, I would not and never did. I was virtually disowned then, him saying that even at that age I must be a homosexual. No more hugs, it was time I grew up.

My older stepbrother never owned a car but would steal one to go where he wanted and steal another to return home. One day, a radio programme was interrupted with a live report of a gunman being chased by the police from the west end of London, through the streets, via Kennington, only to hear a screech of brakes outside our front door. It was him. He jumped out and climbed on the top of the air-raid shelters, lying flat whilst the police looked for him, climbing down when they had given up left.

Our house was raided from time to time by the police searching for him and stolen property. I remember once being forced out of bed and made to stand by the coal box in the kitchen, a large box that would hold two hundredweight of coal, next to the gas cooker. Standing there with a police dog, his nose coming up to mine and quietly growling should I attempt to move.

My father would fence (sell) any stolen property from break-ins to shops, doing so quickly but always keeping some of the money back to pay for a good lawyer should my stepbrother be caught. One particularly cold night, the stepbrother came home to see myself, mother and father huddled around a coal fire. He promptly threw some live bullets into the fire saying,

"These should warm you up."

We dived for the floor as they exploded and whizzed around the room. He tied my hands behind my back and walked me to see his girlfriend and mother who lived in blocks of flats opposite the Oval cricket ground. His mother went mad and screamed at him for being so cruel.

One sport of his was, if he caught me, to hold my hands up my back to see how long it took me to cry.

When I was a boy, I had a teddy as a friend, constantly talking to it in bed. Sometimes, my father or mother would shout from the living room,

"Stop talking to that fucking teddy bear!"

I would instantly go under the covers, under a blanket and army overcoat to whisper to it. My first brother sometime later, coming into the room, grabbed it with one hand and, holding me by the neck dragged me to the front room in a rage where he threw my teddy bear onto the coal fire and held me there to watch it burn. Even now, I can't reveal what else happened. Suffice to say that he used to sleep in the same room as me.

Before becoming a roof glazier, my second stepbrother, had just come out of prison for the last time after robbing a fire station and serving seven years in Winchester. He had by this time served half of his thirty-nine years, carried a gun, and had been shot a number of times, on one occasion in Brixton by a rival. His picture, on a hospital trolley, was all over the Daily Mirror national newspaper on the front page.

Like I said, he was a professional boxer. I remember my father listening to him fight in the Royal Albert Hall on the radio, winning an all-England heavyweight championship.

I wanted a job to earn some money to pay for my keep and feed myself. My stepbrothers promised good money, now also believing that I had grown into a man and never pressing me about girlfriends. We had a reasonable working relationship.

As the third member of the team my primary role was to carry up the glass, delivered in crates from Pilkington's in Lancashire, two sheets at a time, across muddy building sites. I would place them on the roof from where they would be picked up and laid onto the glazing bars which had earlier been put across the purlins, along with rolls of lead, to seal the apex and sides of the roof.

Every one of the workers making up a team acted independently. Travelling all over the country from factory to factory, building site to building site, new warehouses being erected etc. The pay was calculated on how much square feet of glass was laid. Three pence per square foot. Speed was the essence. The sheets of glass, two feet by five, wired Georgian glass each weighing around twelve kilos. These you would carry on your arm, across your wrist and resting on your head, the other arm holding the top. The wire cast through this Georgian squared glass would protrude a little at the edges, digging into your arm. It helped by not allowing it to slip and cut but grip by sticking it into your arm. If your arm became too bloody, you would carry it tight up in your armpit, resting on the tips of your fingers, but again the wire protrusions would dig into them.

They were heavy, two sheets at a time, carried up scaffolding high to the roof. You needed to be quick as the weight of this glass on your fingertips would gradually force your fingers straight when the only option was to let go. Needless to say, it was excruciating doing this all day, in the winter, the glass frozen in the wooden grates needing to be gently forced apart, tramping through mud and climbing ridiculously high walls where scaffolding may have been already dismantled or not yet arrived. This was the only nod to health and safety. If using a ladder, it had to be a wooden pole ladder, from top to bottom, sometimes forty feet high with no joins. As you climbed the ladder, the glass would sway in and out and the wind would buffet you as you climbed, trying to get to the top before dropping it. There were moments when you had to decide whether to let it go or risk being blown off the ladder.

I was useful to my stepbrothers, being small and slim but strong. We used to leave home around 4 a.m. to drive perhaps two hundred miles into Wales or the north of England, arriving before a building site was operational, climbing over the gates or fence to start work. Once there, we had to look around for a pile of glazing bars along with nuts and bolts and rolls of lead. One day, the site manager had locked the nuts and bolts into the site office where there was only a small window in the middle of the door. My oldest stepbrother was not daunted as work had to commence. The window was smashed and they lifted me up, pushing and shoving me through the hole to unlock the door from the inside. Working non-stop, we would leave for home around 3 p.m. to return at the same time the following morning.

The money was good, earning around twenty pounds a week, the most I had ever earned.

My oldest stepbrother insisted that I take a turn driving early in the mornings when there was little traffic, pushing me to go faster and faster each day, fifty or sixty miles an hour through towns and villages. I did not have a driving licence. Once, driving at speed, I hit a high grass roundabout, not noticing it until too late, so driving up and over it to the other side. My stepbrothers, who had been fast asleep, bounced up from their seats, cracking their heads on the roof. The oldest praised me for keeping control.

At the end of each job, which rarely took longer than a few days to complete, there would always be a lot of aluminium glazing bars left over. These would be put inside the car, squashing us all together and making it difficult to see out. The boot of the car filled with rolls of left over lead, weighed the back of the car down onto its springs. All to be taken to a scrap metal yard and sold. A sort of bonus.

This was a six-day job. Too tired on a Sunday to do much except sleep and recover from the aches and pains before the same again on the Monday.

A few years later I was visited at home by a policeman to tell me that my oldest stepbrother, just 39 years old and working alone in Harlow New Town, had fallen from a scaffold tower and been killed. The tower was ten feet high and four feet square, but it was set on rough ground. As he walked across the top of it, he leaned over to place the glass. This caused the tower to tilt and a wheel at the bottom, not being secured properly, dropped out. On returning to the other side, the tower toppled and he landed on his head. He'd died instantly.

By then, I had bought my ex-prison bus, collecting my nearest brother from the Guinness Buildings at Vauxhall to drive to Harlow and identify him.

Vauxhall, near Vauxhall Bridge on the south side of the river, was a dirty, grubby area. Here were vehicles feeding a huge coal depot, with lorries, horses and carts all arriving to buy coal and coke from great heaps, delivered by trains tipping their loads from the Kent coalfields. And there was me with my half-sister, pushing a pram to buy a hundredweight of coal, fed from hoppers measuring the exact weight as it tumbled down into the pram. Then the long walk back to Brixton and home. It was cheaper to buy from here than the coalman delivering to the flat on his horse and cart.

The only other time I remember this pram was being pushed in it by my half-sisters to Camberwell Green, taking my father's suit to the pawnbrokers in exchange for a few shillings. These places took anything for money. If you paid it back, with interest, within a month you got back whatever it was; if not, it was sold. Always a queue, people pawning a suit or dress one week, the next collecting it again, if they had the money. I never saw my father wear the suit; it was just kept for this one purpose.

I was on the Dungeness job with another guy. He pulled the car up outside a shop with lines of washing machines whilst I waited in the car, telling me that he wouldn't be long. He put on a blue overall, promptly picked one up and heaved it into the boot, telling me to drive off fast with the boot still open. He said that he got all his appliances this way as most members of the public assumed he was a delivery driver. The following Saturday afternoon, he drove into a building site with the gates still open and no one around. It was to be a school. Piles of window glass around, he lifted about fifty sheets to the end of the bench and instructed me to cut them to a precise measurement, which I did. After loading them into the car, I said that I didn't know we were going to do this. He agreed, but added,

"I am building a greenhouse for someone. Save me buying the glass."

He already had the glazing bars, stolen from another job. He was just so brazen and casual!

At that point, I decided to leave.

I bought a copy of the South London Press, a thick tabloid with lots of local news. At that time, if it wasn't something my older stepbrother had been involved in, it was who was to appear in court or sentences handed out. The crimes of choice in south London mostly breaking open gas and electricity prepayment meters, shop break-ins or some garage assistant running away with the daily takings. They would mostly be caught in a few days, having gone to Southend or Margate, booking into a hotel for a few nights before the money ran out.

I get to be a milkman

Listed in the paper was a vacancy for a milkman in Croxted Road depot, not far from Brockwell Park where my father worked for a time as a groundsman, painting white lines, before he had to have a leg off. He had been working in the London docks during the war where ships were unloaded. He was unfortunate to have a large crate of goods fall onto his foot, breaking his toes. Being an ARP warden and a St. John's ambulance medic, he set his toes himself with rough splints and bandages, no NHS at that time. He was too old for the Second World War but had served in France during the First, being born around 1896. Twenty years after the accident in the docks he got gangrene in the foot. It was removed, only for the gangrene to return a few months later when he had his leg amputated up to the knee. The doctors said that he would be unlikely to live after both operations, but he did.

Brockwell Park had an international sized swimming pool. My stepbrother, according to my father, was a strong swimmer and was entered into a swimming competition here. The chief of police and the mayor were in attendance. My brother won and was invited up to receive the medal.

"Is that all I fucking get, no money?" he'd said, and promptly threw the medal into the swimming pool in front of the assembled dignitaries and audience. A police sergeant had said to my father that he needed a good thrashing. My father said he was more than welcome to visit our home if the police sergeant felt he could do that, as a challenge. A couple of days later three police officers arrived, only to leave soon after, my stepbrother easily dispatching them.

My stepbrother added insult to injury by stealing all the lead off of Brixton police station's roof one night, reported in the South London Press. They did not know until a few days later when it rained, nor that it was him.

So, to the milk depot.

I went, had an interview, the hardest part being asked to add columns of figures. So many pints of pasteurised, homogenised and sterilised milk (the latter produced during and after the war because it stayed drinkable for months), gold full cream from Jersey, tea and eggs, butter and bacon. All these were carried by the milkman on his float in a little locked cupboard.

I passed.

I guess it was from serving at the counter in the off licence from 11 to 18. The following week I was to start at 7 a.m. and accompany another milkman for a week to learn the job.

The depot on Croxted Road, approaching Crystal Palace, was a huge area, the site of the great exhibition of 1851. You could still see the footings of some of the buildings, a dinosaur area around a boating lake and a huge radio and television transmitter for the whole of South London at the top.

The rules and regulations of being a milkman included how to look after your horse, not to race it, give it proper breaks by fitting its nosebag and stopping at the roadside horse troughs for it to drink etc. Sadly, I knew that most horses had been replaced a few years earlier. The stables were now a parking and charging place for the new wishbone electric milk floats. Not a steering wheel but a wishbone, looking like a great steel bow, which you swung from side to side to steer. No doors nor sides save for a couple of panels that read, 'United Dairies'. Where the sides would have been, and along the back, was a chain which swept across to stop milk crates falling into the road when hitting potholes or bumping over manhole covers.

The lever to start it you just turned one way forward and the other way to reverse. No dials or other switches, only a windscreen wiper and lights. If you did not change direction by allowing it to stop first whilst going at full speed, about ten miles an hour, and instead swished the handle the other direction, it would almost stand on its head before turning. Not allowed of course.

I spent a week with this experienced milkman who had been doing the job for years. We had around five hundred customers each. He knew them all, remembered what they had each day, rarely needing to look at the milkman's book, just occasionally writing in 'Mrs Jones at 48 cancelled her milk for the day', or 'wanted half a dozen eggs' or 'a bottle of orange juice' as he went from house to house.

Normally you would finish your round by 1 or 2 p.m. return the float back to the depot, plug it in, drag all your empty bottles and crates onto the loading bay, plug in its charger and off you went. Only Fridays and Saturdays you worked until the evening when you had to knock on every door for the past week's payments. The money was emptied from your cash bag around your shoulders onto the counter in the office where they would count and record it. On Saturday evening you would get the total cost for all the milk you had taken out that week. If you'd paid too much (sometimes gratuities were thrown into the bag with the other money) you got it back; if you were short, you paid them.

Less than a week later, I had to take a driving test for a milk float. The government examiner came along, sat beside me and told me to drive along this road, that road, turn right, turn left, do an emergency stop and wave my arms out the open door to signal other traffic. All was going well until I ran over a drain hole cover set low into the road. The float, having only three wheels, lurched to one side. The examiner, marking his paperwork, was immediately thrown out of the float onto the pavement. Getting up bruised and shaken said, much to my relief, that I had passed, it being his fault for not paying attention. My first ever driving licence - milk floats, powered grass cutting machines and road rollers! I was proud to be legal, at least for these.

I used to start at 5 a.m. opening the depot as I was the first to arrive. In the loading bay, doors opened onto a large refrigerator room. The afternoon before leaving, I made a list of all the milk I wanted for the next day - twenty crates of pasteurised, seven of homogenised and so on. These would all be piled up together inside the refrigerator room for me to drag out and put on my milk float, sometimes so many that I would have to hang hooks on the back of the float to carry more. Out

I would go to the first street, often some distance away. All the metal crates filled with glass bottles clanging in unison as I went over every bump in the road. Driving to the start of the round was always slow and often cold or wet with the wind and rain blowing through the cab. Dark, too, in the winter.

It took a couple of weeks to remember, without looking at your book, what street to go down next or what most people would have. East Dulwich and Dulwich Village was my route, the latter including posh houses, the Dulwich Art Gallery and Dulwich College, an expensive, private school. The off-licence owner's son had gone there. Some famous film and radio stars from the war years lived here too, such as Anne Shelton, who would always invite me in for a cup of tea and a chat.

The downside to these posh areas were the long paths to the front doors. In poorer areas, the path was much shorter and, mostly, you could take milk to two or three houses at a time by climbing over fences or just leaning over.

It became relatively easy, a seven day a week job. I enjoyed it, especially in the summer, finishing early sometimes. I would drive around on the float, miles off route, to return slower and slower as the battery began to run down, barely making it back. On some days, I deliberately left empty bottles, just for the fun of picking up twice as many the next day, hanging crates off the roof and on side hooks, seeing how many I could carry. It really rattled along then.

Occasionally, for the fun of it, I headed to the top of Crystal Palace, a seven in one steep hill about a mile long. I'd turn around at the roundabout at the top to come down at full pelt, thirty or forty miles an hour, the single front wheel bouncing around, taking care not to tip it over on a bend.

My home between Brixton and The Oval was quite a distance to the depot. I had two ancient mopeds that I used to get there. One day, the manager said there was a vacancy for a wholesale milkman in Balham High Street and asked whether I'd like it as it would be nearer my home. I jumped at the chance, not only because of the above but also because it had the latest super speed, larger float. It was still open on all sides with no doors but reached speeds of twenty or twenty-five miles an hour. It meant starting at 4 a.m. loading dozens and dozens of school milk bottles and orange juice. These bottles are a third of the size of a pint bottle. They were delivered in bulk to all the schools in the area, long before they opened. Great, no money to collect at weekends either, no tips or gratuities either but I did not mind that.

Long rides between schools and later to return to the depot and collect milk for sale in a series of United Dairy Shops on various high streets where I would be invited in to have tea with the female staff. Some were rather keen to cuddle me and make lewd suggestions, but all were good fun. I really enjoyed it.

Six months later, having worked from the age of 11 years old, maybe because of my age or loneliness, I wanted some time off to share with my friends, just hanging around with them or repairing old cars or sitting around listening to records.

So, I left being a milkman. I knew how it all worked, had seen everything, and wanted to do something different. This was a time when you could go to a company you fancied working at, ask the manager if there were any vacancies and if he liked you, the job was yours.

I tried a few - a rubber factory at Streatham, a second-hand bookshop in Fulham, the London Underground and Decca Navigator. In another section I will briefly describe them, but not necessarily in the right order, after all it's a lot to remember. I do have everything documented of course, having kept all my contracts of employment. These are all up on my Facebook page and some are included in this exciting book.

GETTING OLDER

A realism of the practicalities of age and the best way to quietly merge into the shadows, seeing only from a distance. Enjoying the seasons, the peace and solitude, promising nothing and doing even less. Musing to myself about getting older and of ever decreasing value to anyone, however hard I try, my age fights against me in so many ways.

Interestingly, this is the best time of my life. No work, no major responsibilities, waking later every day, enjoying the warmth and comfort of my rented home, planning how to use my pension to fit my lifestyle and still be able to smoke, have a beer or two and even help someone in need.

Following a full and at times dramatic life, I find myself in Latvia, a resident, if only temporary, for five years at least. How I managed it, I don't really know but I did. I haven't sorted out a doctor yet or my id number and I still only speak one word, "paldies" (thank you) that seems to work for everything, so long as it is said with a smile.

I have made some friends and acquaintances on Facebook. One in particular helped me fix a lock to my gate, put a registration plate on my mobile scooter, donated a power saw and tool set for my mobile scooter, visited a couple of times and even donated a garden bench set. Another couple threw their home open to me to stay over whenever I might want. The latter have a completely different lifestyle to mine, eating exotic foods, drinking copious amounts of wine, many foreign holidays (to which they have kindly invited me but which I always decline), regular concert and opera visits, pillars of the ex-pat community and executives of businesses here in Riga. So different to my own working life. They are great company and have even donated a crock-pot, allowing me to wean myself off pot-noodles. The downside to the latter is that I now eat every day and have got fatter. My clothes mostly don't fit any longer, limiting what I am able to wear, with the rest looking decidedly threadbare.

My landlady and family watch over me, bringing me presents at Christmas and birthdays, something no one else has ever done. The only way to repay is to attempt repairs, without tools, or mow the grass. Alas, as I get older, my skills are diminishing as is my energy to the point of mowing the flower beds or cutting down bushes, which doesn't endear me to them. I expect at any time to get a month's notice. My policy is to keep my head down and stay out of trouble.

I take an interest in monitoring myself as I get older, wondering why I forget everyone's names or where I live - I do know really, just that I can't always remember the exact address. Fortunately, I have an almost photographic memory for visual recognition of places, street signs, buildings, even brick walls, so I never get lost anywhere in the world. Once I have seen a location and every step along the way, I remember it. Recently, on a tram at night in the sleet with all the windows misted up, I was able to recognise, through the open doors, a blank brick wall and knew when to jump off. This is the reason that I love my mobile scooter, discovering new streets, footpaths and shortcuts.

As the months roll by, I find new ways to get dressed. I learn how to lay one's underwear on the floor then step into them, holding the arm of a chair to gently lean forward, grab one side and yank them up without falling over. The same with trousers. As for socks, is it best to lean forward or lift one's leg up to a chair? Mostly, if I don't have to go out, I just wear shorts and a tee-shirt.

My eyesight is slowly diminishing. I now have to wear glasses all the time and change them if I want to read anything. Annoying going into shops, constantly switching them over to see prices or sizes.

I used to cut my own hair with electric clippers, but now I'm struggling to reach behind me, much less seeing what I am doing. I end up looking like a coconut. A day ago, on my jaunt with my scooter, I looked for a barber's shop, but I don't know what it might look like from the outside in Latvia. I can't read any of the signage. But if I'd found one, what to ask for and how much would it cost? Looks like I will have to use the clippers again and clip all over, but I don't want to be bald.

During my time here in Latvia, I have acclimatised myself to being alone, living isolated from people and traffic, looking out onto my beautiful garden in peace and serenity. If I need to talk, and I do quite often, it's to my furniture or Doris the microwave. Actually, I do manage to fill every minute of my waking day doing something. I find my concentration lapses and I'm reading the same paragraph twice, wondering how I got to post a picture on my mobile phone last time and putting my electricity consumption reading on Facebook instead of sending it to my landlady. If I attempt a task, it sometimes can be arduous. Suppose I need something off a high shelf, I must find a chair to stand on, hang on the shelf edge and hope the chair doesn't collapse under me. Perhaps leave it for another day that may never come.

Riding around on my mobile chair is always an adventure. Riga's old town has completely cobbled streets and pavements, shaking the life out of my machine and me. I keep to the narrow routes, stopping to move another e-scooter out of the way, trying to nudge past bicycles padlocked to a drain pipe. When I reach the end of the street, I find a steep drop, impossible to navigate. Either I slowly attempt the descent without damaging my chair or, if too steep, slowly reverse all the way back.

The worst part of the journey are the roads around and to the main station. The road that leads down to the bridge over the river is four lanes wide - each side. A steep kerb and traffic moving at high speeds both ways with no central reservation. The area is well catered for with underground pedestrian passes but alas the wheelchair ramps, which are simply metal shutes, are just an inch too narrow for me. I must find a spot to drop off the pavement, bite my lip and chance crossing eight lanes of traffic, horns honking, lights flashing.

Riga is fantastic for cycle paths, safe along the riverside and over the bridges which are smooth and clearly marked. You soon get to know the ways around junctions and roundabouts, the only requirement is to work out what side of the road you need to be on.

Beautiful to be able to stop, admire the views, have a cigarette and sometimes talk to a pedestrian enquiring about my machine. I drive slowly around the open market, looking at all the wares. This week I purchased a pair of shorts and some braces, now all I need is the trousers.

Once I return home, I recharge my scooter before putting it in its garage, taking anything up to nine hours on a slow trickle charge, ready at any time to hit the roads again.

Mostly at home I watch the world news from many different sources or play with Open TTD building new worlds and ever more complex rail and road systems. Facebook Watch is my prime source for amusing videos.

I follow avidly and give all my support to Ukraine. As appalling as it is, after a lifetime of witnessing wars around the globe, the horrors, always thinking it could not happen again, it does. Too old to do anything meaningful but to let it play out. Maybe this is hell and the next life will be better. I know for sure that I would not want to live my life over again.

In my soul, peace reigns for the moment. Who knows what might disturb it next. I am not too bothered, just plodding on enjoying the sun and the birds singing.

I met an impressive young man who helped shore up my fence and cut back a tree lolloping over my roof. Now he is outside in the garden with my landlady's family, cutting back dead branches. So nice to see, but I am keeping a low profile. I don't want to disturb them in case a branch falls on their heads.

Someone asked me how I manage to survive on just a basic government old age pension in Latvia. Well, it is quite easy. Compared to Latvian pensions, it is generous. I do not purchase anything that I can do without and that goes for clothes, food, gadgets and furnishings, unless from a charity shop, and even then only if it's absolutely necessary. Pork is cheap as are chicken wings. My only luxury is cigarettes and a can of beer every day, sometimes two. Maybe every two months a bottle of gin.

Electricity amounts to just two euros a day at most. I only open the doors to my small and efficient fridge/freezer for a few seconds every two days for food for those days, or to put in stuff I've bought, enough for the next fortnight, mainly crinkle cut chips and pork joints that I cut into chops and dice for my crock-pot. My milk is long life. I don't buy bread or butter or cheese or cooked meats or cakes and rarely sweets, so my shopping is cheap.

My bathroom, or cupboard, is small. Every time I go to the loo, I pop under the shower, quick and efficient without wasting hot water and never having to purchase loo paper. Other than the shower, every other day I don't use hot water at all. My washing up is one plate and a knife and fork. As regards my washing machine, it takes several weeks to build up a sufficient load worth washing, then on a low temperature. Dried on the washing line in the garden.

My home is small enough not to need more than one light of twenty watts in each of the two rooms, then only switch on when it is too dark to see. Plus, a two-watt security lamp in the window.

I belong to no clubs and have only been into a pub with some friends of mine three times. I never eat out. This allows me to sometimes have fifty to a hundred euros left over from my budget at the end of the month which I either spend or give away, trying to do something with it that might help someone else. I have some money put by for a holiday but am still not sure if I should just blow it.

I realise my shortcomings and am trying not to post my rubbish and jaundiced life views on Facebook so often. I have had my turn, it is now for others to fill that gap.

In short, I still love you all madly but am experiencing what it's like to be a hermit.

I do still have a book to finish which will take ages. No worries, however, because it is for publication after I expire, and any rewards go to a charity of the publisher's choosing. At least I can write what I want to and not worry about being sued later.

Have a lovely weekend everyone.

GOOD FENCES MAKE GOOD NEIGHBOURS

There is a fence between the school and my home. The children play on it and it's in danger of falling. My landlady and I, have been trying to meet with the head teacher. This is the letter I wrote to the school a few days ago:

Good day to you and thank you for agreeing to see me today!

Knowing just how busy you are, I outline what I wanted to say in person but fear it might take longer than the time you can afford, so at least you will be able to refer to it at your leisure.

I would like to clear any misunderstanding arising from my visit to see you on Monday last.

The previous Friday afternoon I had called and spoke to a lady appearing to be tidying up the playground. I had asked her if it was possible to see the principal or arrange a meeting, to express my concerns regarding the dangerous condition of the fence and the storage of school waste against my property wall.

She did go in to see if you were available but returned saying you had already left.

She suggested that I return Monday at 13.30 when you would be available, in parting I asked and it was confirmed that she would advise you of my intended visit. Clearly that had been forgotten, hence your ire at seeing me, un-announced.

Over the past 18 months, this had been my third attempt at seeing you, always met by one of your staff, I suspect the same person busying around the garden/playground.

The first time was when hearing and coming across three children climbing along the top of the wall, who quickly jumped back down into the playground. I used my steps to peer over the wall and could see below the school's rubbish piled against the wall that they had used to climb up.

I asked that perhaps another location would be better to avoid any accidents, as on my side of the wall, it is dangerous should any attempt to walk on the outbuilding roof or fall down amongst all the detritus around, perhaps in attempting to retrieve a ball, which when I do find any in my garden, I throw back over.

The lady that I had spoken to agreed to speak to someone seeing the problem and sympathising.

I had also asked if it was possible to meet with you or whoever was the principal/head at the time but had no further response.

During last Autumn, the fence between us had deteriorated to such a degree that it had collapsed at the far end and it was possible to climb through in various places from missing boards. I gathered it was in excess of thirty years old and received no maintenance at all in that time. I set about attempting to replace missing boards, securing all the others and putting battens on my side along the whole length, at the same time screwing back from your side.

Whilst, because the fence rails are your side, which indicates it is actually your fence and responsibility, and knowing how tough managing any business is at the moment, I was happy to make superficial repairs.

The winter gales and winds took their toll and the whole fence started to collapse from the prevailing winds into my side. I have, on my own (not inconsiderable) expenses shored up in several places along the whole fence line.

To my horror last week, I discovered that the bottom of one section had been completely destroyed from what I originally thought might have been the children playing ball against it, but now think, on seeing your side of it last Monday, it may well have been an over enthusiastic strimmer operator of yours, who has made a great improvement, (from when I had climbed through to attempt to stabilize the fence from your side last Autumn), now your play area coming right up to the fence and looking so much nicer.

So this was one of my objectives in wanting to meet you and perhaps showing you the other side, my side, of your property.

To see if we could come to some mutual understanding and shared ideas for resolving or mitigating any future problems.

I hope that that is still achievable.

Please rest assured that I do not have a problem with any amount of noise from children playing and am not wanting you to restrict their activities in any way. My concern is for their safety and our mutual security.

Regards, Brian

UKRAINE

Ukraine will win this war. The west cannot afford not to let it win. This is more than about one country, it's about calling a halt to Putin's scheming to expand his sphere of influence. Ukraine happens to be the catalyst to achieve this with a strong, fresh and popular leader aware of his and his country's role in bringing Russia to heal. Ss long as Ukraine holds its nerve, its own future, and consequently that of the EU and NATO, will emerge stronger and safer, just as long as no one or organisation gets too greedy or over ambitious.

We are moving quickly to the end game as far as Russia is concerned. Putin is strangled financially, militarily and soon by his own people, apart from speculation as to his health. The political upheaval might result in a civil war. The exodus will grow from a dribble to a flood with money being hived and hidden as we speak.

TROUBLED MINDS

Now what was it I did this weekend?

My first cinema visit, pub crawl and meeting the crowd with my guide and a day later, a garden party with some other close friends. Following a year and a half in Latvia throughout Covid, seeing little, meeting few people, but at least having my beautiful home and garden, at last a chance to see everything come to life.

Saturday May 28th 2022 was a trip to the cinema, escorted by a new friend. It all started a few weeks ago when the howling gales over the winter had almost collapsed my fence completely. My landlady's daughter, Marta, hearing of my plight, had asked a local young man, Kristaps, if he could help me. He is a roofer in the summer months, also a builder and all around handyman, but his real forte is as a skier, skater and surfboarder, a sort of James Bond figure. He organised these extreme sports both here and abroad.

My luck was in, and on visits to his parents over a couple of days, he did a marvellous job on the fence, including clambering over my roof to cut back branches from a tree that were in danger of breaking through.

A week ago, he had posted to me, now a friend on my Facebook, a recommendation to see a film, "Troubled Minds", in Riga. I had not been to a cinema for more years than I could remember and this cinema, Kino Bize, through their own web page, looked particularly interesting. Hosting films and events, not just of an artistic nature but those with thought provoking subjects, produced by and starring local talented young people either in or wanting to be in the film industry.

With their help, I was able to master the art of booking a seat online in Latvian. It had been suggested that the booking team would appear a bit casual but they were most helpful. I messaged my thanks to Kristaps and he messaged me back to say that a friend of his, Peter, an artist who could make something stunning out of two bits of wood and a pot of paint, or weld a vacuum cleaner to a teapot, would meet me there. Perhaps we could have a drink afterwards. That sounded great. I would not get lost or bored on my own. By the way, Peter showed me on his phone pictures of one of his creations, that of his car covered completely to look like it had been bombed by flocks of seagulls. This drew a lot of attention from passers-by. He apparently had heard about me and wanted to meet this strange Englishman. He also wanted to see the film again.

So exciting for me, having planned my route, a bus from my home to Riga Station then changing to a tram for the second half of the journey and a short walk to the cinema. Kristaps asked me to call him when I got to the station, to ensure that I hadn't ended up in another town.

"Wait there," he replied when I arrived at the bus stop. "I'm not far away, on my bicycle. I will meet you and we can walk together, even have a drink on the way."

In minutes, he arrived. He led the way through the old town, cobbled streets, and cobbled pavements - not easy for me to walk over but I would not want them to change. It was great to see the shops, more open now after Covid and a feeling that the town was coming to life, something I had yet to really experience. He pointed out a huge charity shop, one that I would remember when I next come into Riga as I am down to a single pair of tatty jeans.

We visited a bar on the corner of a junction, a large yellow building with coats of arms covering the end gable wall. We went in a round stone tower, perhaps once some kind of gunpowder store. Down into the bar, drinks ordered and a pleasant and warm seat outside in the sun. We still had forty-five minutes to waste, so it was sit down for another, Kristaps using the facilities and talking to customers at the bar. An elderly couple from Portugal wanted to know if they had to pay for their drinks before going upstairs! Yes, of course, I said, as they might run away without paying. As always, a conversation ensued. They were here for the Tango dance competition, staying the weekend. They asked where I was from so I told them that I had cycled from London for the weekend and that was my bicycle locked to the post by the table upstairs.

Another pleasant half hour, sitting watching people coming and going, a few falling over Kristaps' bike as they tried to go between our table and it, me jokingly accusing them of trying to steal it.

Time to continue our walk to the cinema, past the Russian Embassy, where I was happy to shout out Viva Ukraine, fortunately without getting us arrested but smiles from the local policemen. Up this street, down this road, up this road, down this street - now it started to rain! My guide checked the route only to discover that we had walked the wrong way after the last junction. Drat. Now we had to walk faster and arrived at the cinema wet and a few minutes late. After my turn to have a pee, we were in.

The auditorium was completely dark, the lights out and the film's opening credits were rolling up on a black background. Feeling for the seat, relief! Kristaps' friend was not there and I assumed he could not make it.

The film was most enjoyable and I would recommend anyone to see it.

Someone sat in the seat to my left, an end seat, who was fortunately quiet throughout the movie - no popcorn, bags of crisps or ice lollies. Kristaps and I, though, had a bottle of beer each.

After the film, whilst waiting for the loo queue to disappear, I went into the courtyard for a cigarette and waited for Kristaps who had probably hurried off to the toilet himself. People were standing around, waiting, as they do. A young man came up to me and says,

"Hello, my name is Peter."

"Oh, nice to meet you!" and then, where do you come from, what do you do for work etc, as one does. He tells me he is an artisan of some kind. Now Kristaps is bouncing down the steps into the courtyard. So, you have met Peter? Really, I say, I thought he was just a random nice man talking to me. Peter looks at me and says,

"No, I am the person you were meeting! I did not speak for arriving a little late."

So funny. With that, we all walk off towards an LGTB+ friendly bar.

I had been there before, last year, for the Pride Week. I had come early during the day when it was quiet, just two others on one table playing chess and another on a table alone, near the pride tent in the corner. I had sat at a table on the far side just watching the occasional people come and go and the two police vans clearly there for the duration of the event. A single pint only because it was one of my first jaunts out on my new electric chair and I certainly did not want to risk being breathalysed so soon. Before leaving, I had asked one of the nice young girls sat under the canopy, selling badges and flags, if there were any groups of older gay men in Riga. 'No!' was the reply, after people get to thirty-five years old, they don't take much interest. But she took my email address and said she would ask around and email me. She never did.

Anyway, back to Saturday evening. I dashed around the back of the courtyard as I knew, or thought I knew, where the loo was, except I didn't - and it wasn't. When I asked the barman, he said this was because of the refurbishments. One now had to go to a bar on the adjacent corner to use their loos.

"Can I not just stand here and have a pee against this bar?"

"Well, you can," he said. "It would be interesting to see what attention it gets."

So, it was over to the other bar. Afterwards, Kristaps said that some of his friends would be at yet another bar, just a short walk to the next corner. Off we went, but not before apologising to the first bar staff for deserting them. Shame, because the bar staff were friendly, but I will get there again in the future, I am sure. The garden area would be quite a draw on a warm summer evening.

A short walk and we are there, approaching it by walking through a large car park. Kristaps and Peter introduce me to a few people, all friendly and interactive. Not so large inside, definitely a homely place for the more relaxed crowd, much more my sort of venue. People arrived more than they left so it gradually became almost like a house party. I was introduced to more and more, sharing stories and humour. It was such fun and the hours flew by, although I admit, I feel disadvantaged being amongst such talented and educated people. My only defence is humour. I shudder to think what their view of me was.

After hours of standing and mingling, I announced that I should go home as my feet, ankles, legs and back were aching. I searched for Kristaps, not realising that he had been around the whole time ensuring that I remained safe. I felt guilty keeping him up so late. I'd told him earlier that he could abandon me at any time as I knew how to get home by taxi. That was kind of him. So sad to say goodbye to so many wonderful people, just hoping that soon I will be there again. Safety has never been a worry for me. I can look after myself in most situations. I listen carefully to what people say and do and how they react through my mask of humour. I think I can identify potential problem people. I met none there, only truly entertaining ones. I felt privileged to be invited for a short time into their world.

Sunday evening two of my best friends here in Riga had invited me to a Barbeque Garden Party, except it had to be held in their home on account of the rain all day. It was a party for a specific LGBTQ+ group which, for their security, I won't name. Suffice it to say, it was a group that I would not normally be invited to as I was an interloper of sorts from another planet.

A dozen or so people from varied backgrounds gathered, mostly for the first time, meeting for real instead of virtually. Wonderful to see them arrive, wary and uncertain, watching them as they gradually mellowed and relaxed, sharing their stories, often to do with cooking, knitting and dramas. Very funny at times. All had brought drinks and food even though much had been cooked by the hostess. Seats were at a premium, so they climbed over each other to reach it on tables covered with all this bounty. I was sort of an outcast as I did not share their particular interest, but I was impressed with how strong and brave they were. I knew too well the pain and angst that they were suffering. A few hours passed until it felt right for me to leave, and for them to feel more comfortable within their own exclusivity, but it had been a pleasure to be there, even if it was to cause my usual chaos.

EXPLORING RIGA

Good day to everyone! The sun is out and it's getting warmer.

My first real chance to explore Riga and indeed Latvia. Now I am out every-day, morning to night and then too tired to talk. Because of my inherent laziness and complete abandon, I have decided to desist from all my Facebook interactions, never appear available and become completely anti-social, just for the fun of it. It does mean that I am going to miss completely World Museum Day or Week, more accurately, where to get the best international foods from or create new menus.

It would seem to be a tad rude to delete all my friends here, but I am sure that it would make no difference. I will let you all naturally drift away. Obviously, I am so self-absorbed and obtuse, it should be a relief to just about everyone. For that reason, once again I leave the expat groups. Such a shame that they could not have grown further. I guess covid had a part to play, too. I have achieved more than I ever hoped to here, albeit because of covid, largely on my own. I do intend to stay here, if that is what life dictates I should do. I will just have to wait and see. For now I am enjoying my mobile and Facebook silence.

BAN THE BOMB

Since writing that and having the time out for quiet reflection, I mused on a memorable meeting once at a 'Ban the Bomb' demonstration at Trafalgar Square in the late fifties or early sixties. From his wheelchair, this elderly man pulled on my sleeve to encourage me to sit down with him whilst the police, who had completely encircled the square, prevented anyone else from entering. I did so for a short while, watching the pushing and shoving all around us, the police getting ever closer as they made more arrests. However, an opportunity arose for me to wriggle my way out of the encirclement and escape, waving goodbye to my new friend. I had not met him before and was unlikely to again. Every year I went to these CND marches in Trafalgar Square but I never did see him again. It wasn't until many years later that I realised who I had been talking to, none other than the philosopher Bertrand Russell. He had a profound effect on my thinking. There are videos of the great man discussing life much more eloquently than I ever could and explaining the reasoning for my beliefs. So my absence has turned out to be rather brief after all.

THE COST OF CULTURE

The past week or so has been eventful. My first trip to the cinema, a social evening with many new friendships, turning upside down on my scooter, an al fresco jaunt in the evening across rivers and fields with a surprise visit from a friend on his bicycle.

News from my legal team in the UK that everything is in order and Her Majesty's government is now happy with my situation and have called off the dogs. As with all creditors from utility companies from my former business who had, to date, not recognised that I haven't owned it for nearly two years. However, the reason for the absence of debts was that the utility companies had drained my two business accounts. They had continued monthly direct debits despite there being no services used. The business bank accounts are finally closed, devoid of funds. This is a great relief to me because never in my life have I been in debt. I understand now how it feels for so many people, in debt and with no way out, having to feed a family and keep warm whilst facing mounting utility bills, regular avalanches of red demand letters and threats of bailiffs descending on them.

At last, I feel free to travel should I want to and not be so desperately frugal in what I spend. I was freed from obligations regarding my sadly deceased partner and used some of the unexpected money to buy my mobility scooter, on which it is an absolute joy to discover Riga.

Now I am planning to test the ease of travel to and from my home in Riga with exploratory trips to Tallinn in Estonia. I will go by train for a couple of days, staying in a hostel, shortly to be followed by a flight to Lithuania, staying in a hotel. It is exciting to be free to travel once more and I hope that next year I will be able to do much more. I now regard Riga as my home. Strange, as it lacks the vibrancy of many places around the world, but I guess my age leans more to peace and tranquillity. Anyway, I have reduced my smoking by sixty percent and feel so much better, but rest assured, I will not reduce it further. Without a cigarette whilst drinking, the moments of bliss are lost. Hopefully by the end of the year, I will reverse the balance of gin against beer.

So that is what I have been up to.

WARMER WEATHER AND TRAVEL

I have moved from my winter quarters, the kitchen, to my summer quarters, the lounge. I have painted the former, spray bleaching the wall and floor tiles but inhaling too much bleach, so I now have a pain in my chest. For a while, I had difficulty breathing, gasping for air, and coughing and spluttering for a couple of weeks. Time to further reduce my smoking, the benefits now being able to climb castle stairs and up-hill walks without too much wheezing. Goodness knows what I would be like in an orgy!

The sun is out, the weather warm and the garden, abundant with wildlife, left to become a meadow of different grasses, weeds and flowers, crossed by a minimalist path.

News came that I could now spend the second half of the money I'd kept in reserve for a divorce. Time to experiment with travel. Could I easily do so again? Covid rules are now mostly gone. Time to test if my Latvian residency ID really worked for me.

First was the trip to Estonia, a mix of bus, coach, train and police car. Brilliant! So easy and no problems, even though I often forget, in the heat of the moment, where I am or where I'm going. Fortunately, only momentarily. Even the policeman looked surprised that I wasn't aware I had just walked across the border from Latvia to Estonia!

Earlier this week, the second part of my adventure. Flying this time, to Vilnius, Lithuania. The full works, an Air Baltic trip combined with a hotel for three days. My British passport, my entitlement to the Latvian or any other EU emergency health service, folded carefully together and secreted out of sight, hoping not to be needed.

I breezed through airport security, holding my boarding pass, only being asked for ID on boarding where I showed my Latvian card. Hardly a glance. The same returning. Wow, it has never been so easy. No visas, no luggage, not even a frisk, which I always used to enjoy, especially asking them if they had done it properly and suggesting they might like to do it again. You can see more on all my Facebook posts, journeys and walks with the locals, as well as a chance meeting with a possible new friend. A barista. I wanted a hot cup of coffee with milk and no sugar, but times have moved on. A million questions, how strong, how big, what part of the world would I like the beans to have come from, milk hot or cold, in the cup or served on the side in a cute little jug, dizzy now with so many questions. Just give me a coffee please!

I did not really mind as the young man, Christianson, had a great smile, affable personality and the ability to not be phased by this old geriatric fumbling through his change. The longer I was at the counter going through the ordering coffee examination, the longer I could engage him, as I do everyone with my inane chatter and outrageous comments. I said,

"It's interesting talking with you. I would be delighted to take you for a beer locally when you finish work tomorrow."

"Yes," he replied, "but not for too long as I have an appointment later," which was sensible, I thought, a get out clause.

Always with safety in mind, I mentioned these plans to his colleague, a young woman with an equally pleasant personality, quite apart from telling you, my readers, on Facebook.

Off we went the next evening at half past six. He led us to a local bar in the historic quarter situated in a narrow, cobbled street filled with tables, chairs and umbrellas. It was neither pristine nor fussy but vibrant with many people chatting and socialising. The bar was reminiscent of the Spanish style but a bit rickety in places. Food was served too, although just one menu choice, scrawled in chalk on the wall outside: Beef Stew. No fuss, no table service, pay now! What a great place! The staff behind the bar were efficient and friendly. So, it was a beer for Christianson, a gin and tonic for me and a bowl of stew each.

Finding a table outside amongst the throng of others, chairs balanced across the cobbles, we ate, drank and talked until around 1 a.m. It is so unusual for me to have the chance to talk to others, I can't stop talking, I overdose on happiness. I remind others to tell me to stop as I want to hear their stories. "No," they say. "Yours are more interesting."

At the table closest to us, almost touching, was a big brute of a man and his woman. He leaned across, wanting to borrow a lighter. Christianson handed one to him. I said, "One euro, please!" That broke the ice. Later, he asked for the lighter again. "This is getting to be a habit," I said. Then yet again later. I'd run out of cigarettes and he needed the lighter so, "The cost," I said, "is one cigarette," and he promptly gave me two. How great.

Suffice to say, Christianson did not need to use his get out option. We stayed until I felt tired after several large gins, happy to note that Christianson did not drink much either. No more buses home. It was dark and the walk back to my hotel was through streets that I didn't recognise. I never normally go out after dark for fear of scaring anyone I might pass, but he walked with me to a point not far from my road and we bade farewell with an uninvited hug to make my evening even more special.

The next morning, with a few hours left on my three-day bus pass, it was breakfast, leave the room maid a euro note under a giant bag of crisps and check out. The bus to the airport arrived at the exact time my pass ran out. Perfect timing.

The flight back was delayed an hour with us all sitting on the tarmac whilst they replaced part of the engine! Most of us had the whole width of the plane to ourselves. During our wait, a big, gruff, bearded man bellowed out to a passing stewardess, "Drink, want drink!" She ignored him. The same when she came back. She told him that there was no service until the plane was airborne. He put his seat back, fumbled in his carrier bag and all was quiet until we are in the air, the stewardess first having to tell him several times to put the seat upright again in between his repeated requests for drink. I labour this a bit because the flight is brief, with just fifteen minutes for the stewardess to drag the trolley the full length of the plane to sell snacks. I did not see anyone request anything… except the man in front. He waves the in-flight magazine at her, wanting a cooked meal. No, she says, there is no time for any food on this flight. Okay, I want sandwiches. No, again. He grumpily settles for a can of beer and crisps. She tells him the price, he waves euros at her. No cash, card only. As she leans over with machine in hand, there ensues a short argument. The beer and crisps went back into the trolley. The hostess glances at me, not expecting that I would want anything, but I replied, "Could I have the roast beef dinner?" That was fun.

Minutes later we are landing and soon back in my own happy little house. The travel experiment worked so well that I am hoping to take more holidays in the new year, but to warmer climes.

A TOURIST IN RIGA

I had planned to venture into Riga as a tourist, much like last week's adventure in Vilnius, however the heat is just too much for me to be wandering about. Currently thirty-four degrees outside and twenty-seven inside. Keeping my doors, windows and curtains closed. Maybe risking a visit later today to visit my friends A... and Z..., but not to sit outside and risk being barbecued.

As I wrote a few days ago, it was wonderful last week meeting my barista friend, enjoying every moment in great company. Maybe I was not clear enough, or perhaps he did not fully appreciate what I had said, that I am not looking for anything other than a great evening sharing a drink and a meal together. That is exactly what we did. He looked thin and had said how little he earned so I was happy to at least give him a good evening without worrying about who would pay. I was more than delighted to do that. Besides, he only drank beer, and it was hardly fine dining.

He was interested in my having a Facebook presence, wanting me to accept an invitation from him as a friend. Having had three gin and tonics already, I agreed, of course,, reminding him however, that my friends are all special and, like an exclusive club, he should feel privileged!

As mentioned in my previous post, at around one in the morning, tired and having missed the last bus home, I said that I should start the walk back to my hotel. He kindly agreed to walk with me to ensure I did not get lost. That was great. He did so, until I said that I recognised the last few streets, that I could easily find my own way now and that he should make his way home from this point. I did not know where he lived other than earlier in the evening he had mentioned, 'the other side of the river' which was in a totally different direction.

Having bade farewell with a hug from him, we parted ways. He was not working Saturday or Sunday so no worries about him being late for work. He hadn't told me what he did on his days off other than perhaps meeting friends, of which he had few. He did have a duffle bag full of stuff, from which earlier he had rescued a pullover as the evening turned cooler. I wondered why as a barista he would carry so much to go to and from work. Later, I thought, perhaps he did not have a home to go to? He did say that he had only been working there since May. The weather now is clement and it's quite possible to sleep in the open. As one would do, I had asked him about his relationships, family, friends, plans and aspirations, to which all he gave indistinct or, I felt, evasive replies, naturally spread amongst other inane chatter. Interrogation is one of my strengths.

I know well what it is like to be homeless, wearing the same baggy joggers and top all the time, rolling cigarettes and looking down at heel. Had he been more forthcoming with his answers, I could possibly have guided him. After all, he was highly intelligent an extremely likeable. Anyway, knowing he did not have access to the internet other than at work, I gave him sixty hours as a friend, time for him to make contact if that was what he wanted. I messaged him the following day.

Having recovered from my jaunt to Vilnius and our meeting, I must say that I was besotted by your friendliness and smile, your empathy for the suffering of those around you and your even deeper feelings for human rights. You are funny and entertaining, young and intelligent. You will have noticed that I have just nine other friends on my Facebook. I do not have any other media or social platforms. My friends are all special although of much greater learning and intellect. As for your own Facebook page, there are few posts, little details of friends or your own adventures, dreams and aspirations. I am not sure you even have a place to live or enough to eat. Perhaps, when you are able, help me fill in some of the blanks. Have a wonderful and happy Sunday.

Monday arrived. He should be working and have access to wifi, but no response. My sixty-hour limit for him to respond on my Facebook passed, so I deleted him with the parting message.

It really was great to have met you and you can still contact me on messenger at any time. But, for my own security, I have taken you off my page for now as it looks like our meeting was pleasant but transient. My best wishes however in deciding your future.

Such a shame, but I am realistic and not so dumb as to lose all awareness. I guess my ebullience and joy can be misconstrued as wanting more than I am prepared to give. Always, when meeting those that might want to know me, I fear their intention is solely to make them rich and give them an easy life.

In Riga recently, I was taken to a bar following a visit to the cinema. So many young, vibrant, friendly people, all wanting to talk to me. One young man said he had no work, no money and had to walk home. I said,

"I have much that I want to do in my home. I have a good friend who does help in emergencies, but he has to work himself and look after his family, so I avoid asking too much of him."

If this penniless young man really wanted to earn something for just one day a week, there would be much for him to do. No problem, he replies, he can do all manner of work, even act as a ghost-writer for me as his major was in English. He could even type as fast as I talk. Sadly, he said that he could perform many other types of service, for a price! My offer of help was thus misconstrued. How sad. He regretted saying it and we did talk again during the evening which was otherwise quite enjoyable. In the end, I don't worry opportunists, even if I don't recognise them as being so at the time. I want to engage in conversations. I love it and enjoy listening and analysing people.

THE QUEEN'S DEATH

I received this invitation:

The British Ambassador Mr Paul Brummell
and Mrs Adriana Ivama Brummell invite

Mr Brian C..... and spouse

to watch television coverage of
the State Funeral of HM The Queen Elizabeth II

on Monday 19 September at 12:15

Venue: R.S.V.P. by 16 September
British Embassy Riga
Residence:Telephone: 67774702
E-mail: RSVP.Riga@fcdo.gov.uk

5 J.Alunāna Street, Riga

Please present a photographic ID on arrival
Buffet lunch will be provided
Dress code: Please dress respectfully

I replied:

I was honoured to receive your invitation. Sadly, I have to decline, however much I would have liked to attend. Waving to the Queen as she was driven past me and the assembled crowds seventy years ago, when I was six years of age, and now having signed the commemoration book at the Embassy, I feel my duty is done. I have spent a lifetime as a loyal subject, albeit serving in the most minor capacities. It would not be appropriate for me to be seen amongst such auspicious company, nor do I have the attire to attend respectfully. Thank you once again for the honour of the invitation.
Long Live the King!
Brian C.....

LAWYERS AND ACCOUNTANTS

The last time I wrote to everyone was from Warsaw, which was tricky, having to do so on my phone. Since then, I have been taking advantage of some glorious summer weather. Bear in mind, I do all this on the UK state pension alone. I've made full use of my free transport pass in Latvia and the incredibly cheap coach and train fares to far flung places, even to the Russian border. I travelled by coach to Poland, Estonia, and Lithuania, the fares averaging just twenty or thirty euros. I carry a tiny backpack containing only my toothbrush, toothpaste, one change of underwear, some sandwiches and water. I plan my trips carefully, travelling overnight to save accommodation costs and staying in hostels briefly before returning home. This has been great fun, especially in Warsaw where transport is completely free for anyone over seventy years of age. There are fabulous bus, train, tram and metro systems in place here and I used them all, every journey being recorded for posterity. Having taken so many trips, one of my Latvian friends suggested that I must be a spy.

Travelling has given me a chance to meet many people from all walks of life and to share precious moments. Here in Riga, I was invited to give a speech on stage to an LGBTQ+ group which I am told was up-loaded to Twitter. Since then I have been stopped at various places where people have recognised and congratulated me, which is really nice.

I follow events in the Ukraine avidly and write regularly in comments to various newspapers. Sometimes, I write to Russian sites, although they are, unsurprisingly, not so well received. The closer to Russian border towns in Latvia I get, the more distinct feelings of special unwelcomeness I feel, perhaps due to the Ukrainian badge pinned to my jacket.

Last month I was honoured to have a personal invitation from the UK ambassador to attend a viewing of the Queen's funeral in his private residence at the British Embassy followed by a buffet. Sadly, in dire need of a haircut and suitable clothing, I declined, watching the event from the comfort of my home almost non-stop for twenty-four hours.

My friends were disappointed that I did not go, but I had met some of the diplomatic staff in the previous two weeks, one as a guest of a prominent business leader at a Chamber of Commerce event, and again on attending the embassy to sign the book of condolences. As I said earlier, I did not have good enough clothes, nor had I found a decent barber, except one a few hundred miles away in Lithuania. I would have felt uncomfortable at the British Embassy.

It is gradually getting colder, and with the energy crisis, living costs are rising fast. My worry is surviving the next few months on a pension that is losing value daily. Any remaining money is spent on filling cupboards with dry foods to last as far into winter as possible. Also, I had to buy a ton of briquettes for my log burner. This was my last acquisition. They have risen in price from 120 to 420 euros, excluding delivery. Electricity and water prices have also soared. In addition to switching on my immersion heater once a week for an hour, I also use water from the butt to flush the loo. I never use hot water to wash up and I only use the washing machine once a month, on a cold wash with no spin. However, I still smell beautiful.

Other than that, it is still wonderful in my rented cottage and garden which would be considered a park in the UK. A tad lonely at times, which is why I love travelling.

That's it for now, except to add a thankyou to Tim Clow for trying to sort out my finances. Hopefully, HMRC will be as patient as I have to be in waiting for the Blackpool guest house sale to be finalised.

My kindest regards to you all.

Brian

EARLY LIFE

Here is a little about my early life.

My father was born in 1895, registered at St Olave's Church, London, although his death certificate states1891. This was apparently a guess by his doctor.

He served in the Kings Royal Rifle Corps from 1914-1920, a private with various kings and victory medals.

He married his first wife, McGill, in March 1922. They had six children:

Elizabeth M	1922
Arthur J	1925
George A	1927
Lilian g	1930
Ronald G	1933
John	1938
Brian	1946 (me)

He had no children by his second wife, surname Wade. This was the one he threw out physically along with a suitcase after finding she had held one of the children's hands over a lighted gas stove as a punishment. She was a lively sort who played the banjo in pubs, known to be able to look after herself in a scrap.

He was unable to marry my mother until one day in 1963 when a member of the Salvation Army came to inform him that his wife had died in a nursing home, alone, blind and disabled, with no family or friends. Now he was free to marry my mother, for no other reason than for her to receive a widow's pension on his demise. I was born in 1946 but not registered until 1951. They did not get married until 1964 when I was 18 years old and the best man at their wedding! My father died in 1969 and my mother around 1999. I was the only one of all my father's children to look after both my parents until the end, bearing all the funeral costs.

As described above, I worked for a while with my two half-brothers as a roof glazier. After the death one of them, falling from a scaffold in 1971, I never saw any of my siblings again. There was a nephew who I had seen being cradled by his mother at the funeral; I believe he has achieved well in life. With such a huge age gap between us, not to mention me being a homosexual, meant that I was persona non grata.

LATVIAN BANK ACCOUNT SAGA: I

Some may remember my last attempt to open a bank account here in Latvia with Swebank and assisted with my lawyer, but that was refused because I did not have a job, even though my lawyer threatened to take them to the European Court. Almost two years on, I thought that I should try once again and not bear a grudge. Today, in I breezed, asked the lady at the front desk if I could speak to someone regarding opening a current and a deposit bank account.

"Did I have an appointment?" she asked.

"I do not," I replied.

She telephoned someone from the back office.

"Please wait," she said, "someone is coming to see you."

A good start, I thought to myself as another lady approached. Pleasant enough, asking me what I wanted and me repeating myself.

"Do you have any documents with you?" she asked.

"I do. I have my lease to the property that I have been renting for the past two years, I have my Latvian five year temporary ID card, my statement from the UK pensions service of the amount that is paid to me every month, my statement of enrolment in the Latvian Health Service, my bus pass and even utility contract for waste removal."

She looked at what I had presented to her and asked,

"Are you working in Latvia? Do you own property in Latvia? Do you have a wife in Latvia? Do you have children or relatives living in Latvia?"

Sadly, I had to answer in the negative to all those questions, pointing out that my age factored against some of those questions. Approaching 77 years of age, I did not think it of great financial planning to buy property now, similarly, getting married and having children might be a bit of a struggle. I know there are dating sites for most everyone, I guess in Latvia too, but how long could I safely manage a courtship? Time is not really on my side. She explained that those were the bank's criteria and so she could not help. With that, I thanked her for her time and once again left with nothing.

I am surprised that a person with a five-year temporary residence ID who is clearly of an age not to work and of independent means cannot open a bank account in Latvia. Not terribly welcoming. I'd told her that I needed a deposit account as my former property had been sold and I would need a way to deposit the money. She was not swayed at all.

I related all this to my lovely I... who exclaimed,

"I know a lot of people who would marry you! Just ask, maybe my mother or daughter, certainly some of my friends."

Now there was a thought. Her mother and I get along great, we sort of communicate with hand gestures and facial expressions, interspersed with lots of laughter, she not speaking a word of English and my only knowing the one word in Latvian, 'paldies', which means 'thank you'. We would never be able to argue and our respective bedrooms would be a hundred metres or more away at the other end of the garden. That was so thoughtful, but I had to say, really, I could not face the prospect of marriage again, however convenient, not solely because of the age difference but because she doesn't drink or smoke and is a vegetarian. It would be tough going, as much as I loved her.

Anyway, on a positive note, following my beautiful haircut two days ago, I rushed to the photographers in Arganskarns to pose for a digital photo which would enable me to renew my passport. Determined to stay where I am for as long as I am allowed, I intend to make lots of trips abroad into the sunshine, returning between frequent explorations to my beautiful cottage, now my home.

In addition, this week, I also collected a tin bath full of hundreds of apples. Nothing much else. Have a great weekend!

BANK ACCOUNT SAGA: II

If you've got to this point, you will have read my recent post about obtaining a Latvian bank account. It doesn't help not being married, not having children, family, property, studies or gainful employment. All this is held against me despite being a few months short of 77 years of age.

Following that post, I remembered that in fact I was a sort of consultant for Regas Porcelans from its inception. Indeed, I was an integral part of the team. I never considered it as actual work, more a hobby bringing to bear my many years' experience in marketing and a pragmatic approach to a business model. The company noted the bank post and was quick to send me copies of my contract and duties, assuring me that I am an important part of a growing and developing business, albeit without the fanfare, not even an executive parking spot. The important thing was that, for bank account purposes, I did have proof of work. So now I can confidently re-apply for a bank account. I will, naturally, continue my input to the company, sometimes controversial, but without fear or favour. I keep further details about the company limited for normal commercial reasons at this stage. However, the re-posting of pictures taken last year earlier is acceptable. The contract and accompanying letter are included on pages:

UKRAINE: MORE THOUGHTS

https://www.youtube.com/watch?v=mN4jOZGdLmE

7.50 a.m. I have been watching events in Ukraine and am appalled at the horror. How can the rest of us sleep, eat, work and continue as normal, knowing this is happening? It doesn't matter that I cannot understand one word of the dialogue. As always, whatever side one is on, it's the ordinary people whose lives are ruined almost overnight. Who knows if or when they might regain something of what they have lost.

Do I wish to rain destruction upon the Russian armies for those they have murdered, raped, tortured and plundered? Many are no doubt vicious, violent animals, but the vast majority are ordinary human beings forced blindly to follow orders. Do they still have heart and soul? I do not know. If they die, Putin will talk of pride in their achievements and reward their families. Refuse and they will face fifteen years in prison or be shot as traitors. Children - dirty, hungry and scared miraculously adjust to the new reality, oblivious to the reasons. It's heart-breaking, as it is for the elderly, seeing their lives wrecked, piled into heaps of broken debris. And here we sit, tutting at the horror, wearing badges of support, trying to offer hope and support and not let it all pass by like some TV soap opera. We must maintain that support, though, share the news and understand rather than complain about fuel and food prices. Would a Russia Today programme express these opinions? Of course not. Otherwise, the whole of Russia would be demonstrating against this useless, mindless devastation.

WINTER DRAWS ON

What a torrid couple of weeks, I won't even bother to tell you. Or will I? I'm mindful of what I have just said about war and our priorities, but nevertheless… two things.

First, British Gas is still harassing me for money as well as HMRC wanting two thousand five hundred pounds immediately.

Second, and this is not a complaint, the hike in the cost of living means I must prepare even harder to survive the Latvian winter. Already my improvements to the heating system are helping, as is using less water, sometimes showering only once every three days. Switching on my immersion heater for half an hour twice a week is working well, too. I alternate between a warm shower, a tepid shower and a brass monkey shower. Fortunately, we have enough rain that keeps my two buckets and baby's bath topped up enough to flush the loo. All I have to do is remember, before I use it, is to bring a bucket of water inside as the mornings can be somewhat bracing. I have bought a saucepan with a glass lid which I fill with water and keep topped up on my wood burner. Now I have hot water to do my washing up and ensure the sink and drain are clear and fresh.

Given the perilous state of my finances, any pension money left over at the end of the month is used solely for food. Well, perhaps a few beers, cigarettes and other essentials. All this, along with a stock of briquettes for the log burner. So, for the next six months at least, I do not have to worry about inflation. I can stay locked in my cottage without venturing out, other than for vegetables maybe once every three weeks.

I am determined not to have to be dug out of the snow this year. Three times last year, members of the public had to help me whilst riding my electric chair. Shopping was a challenge, as was visiting friends. I put on thermals, gloves, scarf, hat, warm jumper and a thick coat, but it was freezing cold and I always worried that I might get stuck in the snow. There was also the chance that the electric might run out mid-journey as the battery lasts half as long in winter. Taking a taxi is far too expensive and a bus an adventure of its own.

Already this week the temperature is dropping and soon my chair will be locked up for winter. The new routine will be not to go anywhere that isn't vital. The happy season is around the corner with birthdays, halloween, firework night, carol singing, Christmas parties, Hogmanay and a whole host of other special events for the excuse to party. Sadly, my budget cannot support such glee, nor my stamina. I am always hopeful that my fortunes might change. However, having spent so long scrimping and saving, I can't think that it would be easy for me to change too easily. But! I will try. So, unless you are prepared to send the Rolls Royce around to collect me and bring me safely home, then take me off of the visitors list. You can visit me any time you wish and be thoroughly welcome.

This season I am fighting against cold, hunger, stress and boredom.

THE ONGOING BANKING SAGA

Like most people, there are days when I don't always feel my best. Yesterday was great. My lovely landlady returned, thank goodness, from her regular trips away. For the past week I have been getting up at dawn to uncover straw and dead vegetation along with a crop of pumpkins in random places in the garden. I venture out again at dusk to cover them as protection from frost. Although my landlady tells me I needn't have bothered as it has not been frosty, I didn't dare take the chance of missing the one night Jack Frost descended, killing her prize crop. But nice to see a live person around again, for a while at least.

Later in the evening my friend and neighbour Kristaps called in for a quick beer and a smoke. Last week, on a rainy day, he took me shopping in his car. Saved me getting wet and I was able to fill what was a completely empty freezer. What a star. He said he wanted to build up some Karma points and easily achieved that. Earlier he had sent me some pictures of a salubrious leather reclining armchair that was surplus to his parents' needs on their veranda. Great to replace mine, propped up against bookshelves to keep it upright, not to mention struggling to get in and out of it. What a fabulous thought on his part. Reluctantly, though, I had to decline. First, in low armchairs, such as mine, I have pillows for the back and the seat to prop me up and ease getting in and out. Second, initially he had suggested that I could simply borrow the chair for the winter, but I would be living in dread of spilling food on it, or worse, dropping a cigarette and burning a hole in the arms. I could buy it from his father and not have to worry about such things although he did say it was thick cowhide so the house would have to burn down first to damage the leather. I did consider it, and what to do with my old chair. I could take it out into the garden and saw it up, put the metal into the wheelie bin and the fabrics into the log burner. However, I decided to err on the side of caution, at least financial caution. But the kind thought was not lost on me.

During the afternoon my new Passport from England arrived, another ten years of travel. All I must do now is make sure I reach 87 years of age to get full value. With that and my Latvian ID the world is my oyster.

You're thinking, what has that got to do with banking? Onb waking up this morning, I decided to contact Citadella Bank and attempt, once again, to open a Latvian Bank Account. Two weeks ago, as I wrote previously, all was fine bar the absence of my passport. When your new passport arrives, I was told, call again. It should be easy to make an appointment; I did it the last time after a slight tussle with the call centre.

I phoned Citadella - a recorded message as usual, but this time only in Latvian. Whilst listening to it, I pressed various numbers on the mobile to connect to someone - anyone. Surely an agent must pick up? But no, it went dead. I tried another number, this time an English recorded message. Great! Press a button and a young man answers. I tell him that I want an appointment and he understands. He will pass me onto another agent who will organise it for me. Guess what? The line went dead.

Tried yet another number and this time a young lady answers. She, on hearing my plight, suggested it wasn't necessary to make an appointment. I could just go to the branch. I may have to wait in line for a while, but they would deal with opening an account there and then. Next, call a taxi to take me to the bank. Probably around 3.30 in the afternoon now. Sauntering into the bank, no one else there other than a bored looking young lady sitting behind her computer screen.

She looks up without a smile and waits for me to explain the purpose of my visit.

"Oh, you have to make an appointment for another time," she says. "We only do it that way."

I said that this was quite different from what I'd been told on the phone by the lady at the call centre. I added that I'd even paid for a taxi.

"I can make an appointment for next Monday, if you wish? What time would you like?"

She turns the computer around for me to see the available slots. 17.40 is the earliest. That will have to do. She writes on a piece of paper Monday's date and the time, '14.40'.

"Wait! Did you not say 17.40?"

"Oh, yes," she chuckles as she makes the correction.

With that another taxi home again.

I do wonder why I persist in trying to do this other than it may then allow me to log into sites where a bank account is needed. My ID is recognised by some institutions in Latvia but not all. Even the supermarket won't allow me to purchase alcohol online. They say they that it is a result of Brexit, even though they have both my Latvian ID and UK banking details. Rules are rules.

COVID AND BUREAUCRACY

Covid injection time again. I haven't had a reminder because I still don't have a doctor. I have a certificate from The Latvian Health Service which I must keep with me. This is part of the reciprocal arrangements with the UK following Brexit. My previous three covid jabs have been done in the emergency facility within the conference centre. I could not access the covid certificate departments online but had to return each time when a doctor would do this and print my certificates. I am now in the system and entitled to treatment. I am told that I am free to use all the medical services available to all Latvians - except I can't. I wonder if it is all worth the bother. Should I leave Latvia for somewhere else? The government here is proposing to cancel anyone's visa if they do not take Latvian language lessons at an approved school and achieve a certain level. No, I like where I live. I will just have to carry on.

WAITING FOR SALE FUNDS

A few weeks ago, a lovely young lady telephoned me to say everything had now been concluded and insurance was being arranged. The next call would soon be to ask for my bank details to effect the transfer of funds.

I am still being cautious with what I spend. For example, would it be safe to light my wood burner earlier than 6 p.m as it is now getting decidedly colder?

Have a great weekend.

Regards

Brian

HOW I PLAN MY DAYS

I was asked how I plan my day, here is my response.

From childhood, my routine is never to get out of bed until I have planned my schedule for the day. And I stay with it. Hour by hour, I have tasks that cannot be avoided, people to speak to, social interactions and each allotted an unmovable time slot. A review before sleeping of progress and adjustment of the morrow to compensate or deal with failures or build on successes.

Personal discipline has always been most important, appearing casual, friendly and loving all embraced within that schedule. Success or failure, judgement by my peers is nothing compared to my own judgement as to whether I have contributed positively to mankind.

My routine is simple. I am aware prior to sleeping of what I hope to do the next day. I am also one of those lucky people who can decide at what time I wish to wake, perhaps allowing extra time in my day if I'm busy or to be somewhere early. However, I am not so self-assured that I don't have an alarm clock! Usually, however, it never quite manages to go off as I wake and switch it off a minute or so earlier. I don't immediately jump out of bed and rush around but give myself five minutes to consider the order of my day.

Apart from the obvious opening of my business on time and the usual cooking or cleaning chores, I pay attention to those activities I know will be challenging and allow myself plenty of time to complete them. Perhaps I have a difficult or potentially fractious meeting or an accounting problem to solve. What I never do is hope that they will go away. I do not procrastinate. One of my goals, in spite of any anxieties, is to do the repetitive, tedious tasks first. These are usually the ones that ought to be done every day.

Some people are morning people, of which I am one; some are afternoon people. They drive me mad as they tend to be less focused and less awake. I do not take a break until I have completed most of my tasks, certainly the most important. Planning my time, however insignificant my duties may be, is important to me. When all is done and I can't think of anything else, then I am able to relax, and often to come up with a new idea. Afternoon people are never able to manage that because they are always playing catch up, spending their time running around like headless chickens and getting stressed.

Years ago, when I employed people, I always arrived at work at least half an hour before anyone else. I could open my post, look at my diary, write a few memos and by the time everyone else arrived I was organised, relaxed and ready to deal with the day. I would be rather pedantic in that I would not tolerate a second's lateness from any of my staff.

I am not sure the foregoing makes any sense but there it is, that was me. However, it's all rather different now, being retired and loving it.

THOUGHTS ON THE WAR

I follow much of the news coming out of Ukraine from many international sources. I often share the dreadful statistics online, but I don't comment on them. My thoughts are always with the loss of so many innocent lives, thrown into battle to be mercilessly slaughtered. Putin and the Politburo can have little or no regard for the human lives they sacrifice daily. Has he been relieved of his power? Assassinated, even? It is hard to know, especially with Russian newsfeeds being so restricted. It's possible that there is an exchange of power going on now, as I write.

I believe that the Kremlin's priority is to withdraw and save as much face as possible. After this, there must be a massive witch hunt asking who to blame, who to arrest and how to stop other territories fighting for independence. How also to tell the Russian people, we got it wrong. How, when the time comes, to pay reparations for the massive destruction, including to all the countries that have supported Ukraine with financial aid and military equipment.

Who do we blame for Russia losing all its youngest and brightest talents? How do we ever recapture our mineral, gas, coal and oil markets? How can we get back the management and ownership of pipelines for oil and gas? It may be that Russia is on the edge of an internal uprising of such magnitude that other countries will have to micro-manage its entire political future.

BRIAN'S CONTINUING ADVENTURES

The past week, a mix of successes and odd disappointments, has nevertheless reinvigorated me. Despite snowfall during the night, I am ready for action, although I think the landlady has hidden the snow plough from me.

Monday, I could not wait to try out my new bank card, so off I went to the cash machine and withdrew twenty euros. Great! It dispensed the notes, no problems. Then into Rimi to buy a few groceries and pay by waving my card at the card machine. Wonderful! It all works. I had also changed the pin number from what was issued; a bit reckless as I did not know what I was doing, but it worked.

Tuesday, my old passport was returned, the new one having been delivered last week. It lasts for ten years and has the maximum number of pages, so I must ensure I am around long enough to get good value from it! I love that it is all black, so distinctive from the EU version. Now with my EU ID card, I will be free to travel, and if I wish to travel outside of the EU, I still have a UK passport.

I am, for the next three years at least, a resident of Latvia, happily retired and loving my home. This might be for the rest of my life, provided I don't get chucked out. You see, the government here is proposing to deport anyone who does not speak Latvian. I really don't want to waste my retirement learning another language. In a couple of months I will be 77 and have coped well not doing so until now. I don't want to be forced to do this because of a political edict. If I were younger, had a business or a full time job, then I would agree it is necessary, but not speaking the native language makes my travels here much more of an adventure.

News from Blackpool, too. My lawyers there emailed me to say that everything I had given away to my partner three years ago was coming back to me. This is due to his sudden and sad demise and me being the only heir. Everything had been auctioned and, after everyone had taken their cut, including the government, they were ready to send me the balance. Where would I like it sent to?

Looking at the documentation from my new Latvian bank account, some in Latvian (okay, chuckle if you must, after what I wrote earlier) it was not clear to me what was what. Another trip to the bank to ask them if they could assist in ensuring that I filled out the details correctly. Sadly, it is still appointments only, but throwing caution to the wind, I dialled for a bolt cab, pressing 'Citadele' for the destination. Within minutes, I was on my way - the wrong way! I realised this as we were going over the bridge into the centre. Looking at my choices on the app, I could now see there were lots of Citadeles. Never mind, I duly arrived at the headquarters. Shouldn't be a problem, after all, I only wanted them to fill in the correct details on my form.

The lady receptionist enquired what I wanted and whether I had an appointment? Actually, no, I just needed to confirm some details, so would she be so kind as to check them. Oh no, you have to have an appointment. Well, perhaps just the swift code then? She wrote it on a business card, also telling me that the IBAN is part of the account number.

Great, now I could carefully complete the form with all the details. I was advised to post all this information along with various signed documents back to the lawyers. Not looking forward to another trip to the post office! However, my friend A... had volunteered to come with me. They don't willingly speak English at the post office - yes, I know, but I am not changing my mind.

Before doing so, I emailed the lawyers to let them know my plan, that the documents would be winging their way to them that afternoon.

"No need," she said. "We already have power of attorney from you." Apparently, I had signed the necessary e-document - well I can't remember everything. "Just scan the forms and email them back to us; the accounts department will then deal with it."

Great, no more taxis to and from the post office. I feel that I might just as well have bought one with so many journeys.

Everyone knows that computers, printers and technology in general, in times of urgency, will not play along. My printer, albeit old, decided it would not co-operate, just refused out of hand. Not connected, it said, bla bla bla. No problem, I will take a photograph of the documents and send them in an email.

Snap, snap, snap, snap, all done. Now, how to get them onto an email? The email is on my computer, the app on my phone and they don't talk to each other. Maybe I can send the pictures to Facebook, and then on to my computer, copy from there to my email…?

It worked!

An hour later, the lawyer says they need the bank's address and that the IBAN or swift code is not correct. More emails but nope, still not working. Later that night I told A... what a problem I was having. Yes, she agreed, what a performance it all is. She had had the same problem setting up her account. It seems that the IBAN and SWIFT are encompassed in the twenty-one digit account code. Wait! I counted all the digits and letters on my account number. Damn! I have written down only twenty. All these letters and numbers without a break and a multiplicity of zeros that move about as you try to count them. So, one o'clock in the morning, another email with the correct number.

No reply from the lawyer on Friday. If it had been wrong, she would have emailed me back. So now I wait with hope it will all be completed soon. Depleting my emergency fund ever more in the expectation of riches to come, I threw some more briquettes into the log burner and opened a beer. What a day!

I had said some weeks ago that now winter is here, I would not be using my electric chair and, because of financial constraints, not visiting anyone either this side of Christmas. But with new hope, I have started using taxis, although not too often. Ha! A visit to A... and Z... yesterday by taxi and then in their car to my favourite supermarket, G.... He offered to drive me straight home and that was a joy, no standing about for a taxi dragging my trolley around. He is such a star.

I can't sleep thinking of all the things to do at home. Four a.m. up again, this time looking at possible purchases book-marked over the past few months. A bit precipitously, I start to order insulated floor tiles, hanging low energy infrared wall heaters, blackout curtains, an armchair and footstool, wallpaper and, last but not least, a log burner exhaust fan. Also planning to have the outside painted, maybe make a sort of conservatory at the side that is already half there - it just needs a roof and windows, perhaps with triple wall perspex. I must repair my log store and support the beams that I am careful not to bump into as they are not fixed to the roof; cover over the single glazed and rotting window frame on my roof with stained marine ply - that should certainly help reduce the heat loss through the gaps; cement the jaunty angled bricks on the chimney too.

My friend A... suggested I could keep her company on a holiday in January somewhere warm. Okay, I agree, but knowing how difficult I am to live with (I must have my own accommodation, a balcony and en-suite) she plans everything - hotels, flights etc. and then I will mirror the arrangements for myself. Something to look forward to.

Just to end with, you may remember that I was pleased with the trunking to distribute heat from the kitchen to my lounge which was a great success - until the temperature outside dropped to below zero.

My log burner is not able to produce the heat needed, hence the ordering of hanging infrared heaters, no elements just infrared rays keeping the ambient temperature no higher than 65 degrees. I love not having to live in the kitchen all winter, so these will help when the log burner can't keep up.

My attempt to save water by using buckets and a baby bath catching the rain from the down-pipe works well, except last night, I dragged a bucket into the loo but, when tipping it into the basin, out comes a great two inch thick dinner plate piece of ice. Ten hours later it is still not quite thawed out. Maybe I should rethink that. My place is not big enough for buckets or water standing in my hall to stop them freezing, nor would I want them.

That was my week. I hope yours was as eventful. A happy and successful week ahead for you.

END OF CHAUCER HOUSE

Good Morning, Mr. C……

You should now have received payment and we have now closed our file on the above estate following the completion of the case. We would like to take the opportunity to thank you for choosing B…….. Inheritance to represent you in the estate of M…..

Following the completion of the Estate of M….. we would appreciate your feedback. I sincerely hope that your experience with us was satisfactory, as we are constantly striving to improve our customer service.

Whilst a review is not obligatory, I am writing to ask if you would be willing to leave us a review on our google business page:

(link removed)

'Leave a review' will also bring you to the same page.

We ask this because the calls for these cases often come out of the blue and cause distress and concern that they are being scammed. As a result, hundreds of beneficiaries miss out on receiving their inheritance.

Often the first thing potential beneficiaries do is to search the company online. We would like to ensure that future beneficiaries feel reassured and know they are in safe hands with us. Having reviews from beneficiaries from previous cases will help us accomplish this.

We hope this matter has been concluded to your satisfaction, you are welcome to contact myself, as the client care officer, if you require any further assistance on this or any other matter.

Thank you so much, I have left a review, a bit confusing as the link above took me to an American coffee shop. Searching again, I found you, but had to translate the site from Latvian. In any event, you should have it on Google reviews now. Just in case, here is what I have written. You are welcome to use it how you wish to promote your service.

The whole service, tracking me down in a different country, guiding me through all the legal formalities, the care and patience shown, the professionalism in taking care of all liabilities, liaising with my own accountants, solicitors in what was a stressful period in my life.

The prompt responses from a dedicated named person to oversee everything. Because of Covid, delays were inevitable obtaining probate etc and it took around 18 from the start and payment. I am in awe of how efficient the service has been.

Now, without being creepy, I can say what an absolute star you have been in gently guiding me through this stressful experience, patience and care at every stage. All my lights are on now, physically and mentally, heating, too!

Thank you once more.

Very kind regards Brian

All completed now, including having my Revolut stopped of any activity for an hour or so whilst I sent them details of where the money is coming from.

CONVERSATION WITH LANDLADY

Brian:
Tomorrow is Rent and electricity day and I will send you the readings as soon as I get up. Hope you and your mother are well and warm. Give her my love and a chocolate cake will be accompanying the rent for you both to share.

LL:
Oh, Brian... You want us to become fat! We are fine but not very warm - only 13. When we arrived, was +6 .

Brian:
Turn the heating up and charge me for the extra gas bill. You must

both stay warm! If I added 50 euros to the rent, just for help with the gas bill and you can turn it up a bit more! Every month.

LL:
Darling, it's turned up more then usually, but the hause is like made from paper. If there is Sun shining - immediately is 18 and more! But we feel good, don't worry, please!

Brian:
Well, I think that now I have a beautiful new floor, I should pay more rent... So I am having to increase the rent to 250. The reason you can't see my lights is because of the new blackout curtains that stop the sun and daylight waking me early and also they help with insulation.

LL:
No, no, no!!! No more rent! You can donate to Ukraine, if You want! About lights - maybe let a small thin line from one side, very small, that I can see You are at home.

Brian:
OK, curtain opened just a little for you! Donating to Ukraine will not help at all, it's you both I want to help stay warm. So, I am afraid I am having to increase the rent, no arguments. I am sure that this is not the way rent increases work but I am happy and you will make me feel happy anyway, see it as my contribution also to snow clearing.

CHAUCER HOUSE POST SCRIPT

Right at this moment, calm and quiet in Riga, I cannot believe how I managed to run Chaucer Guest House for twenty years. In addition to sleeping on the floor in my office/lounge 24/7, I cleaned all the rooms, did the never-ending laundry, cooked breakfasts, did the accounts, attended to all the health and safety measures and entertained guests, even physically throwing the occasional misbehaving ones out.

My partner did at least deal with maintenance, which he was good at. When the end of the season came around, in November, I would go on holiday, we officially would be closed and he would do the work that had accumulated over the year. Normally, this was done prior to my return. Except on two occasions. Once, on stepping in through the front door, I fell into the cellar because he'd removed the floor. Another, I fell from the first floor to the ground floor, again because he had removed the floorboards.

I always took away enough sterling when going on holiday to ensure that on my return, I had enough money to buy essential supplies to prepare for guests' breakfasts the following morning. These were guests who had booked whilst I was away. I used to check the bookings everyday wherever I was in the world as my partner did not read emails or answer the telephone when I was away. He was never a natural host but he allowed me to take holidays and I knew that Chaucer House would be safe from fire, floods and morons whist I was not there.

After gifting my premises, business and everything I owned to my partner some months before my move to Latvia, I instructed him one last time how to do the annual Fire Risk Assessment. This is a legal requirement that had to be readily available for the attending officers at any fire incident. It also had to meet periodic compliance visit checks from the fire brigade. It seems strange now, changing my name to his after all these years, and crossing my fingers that he would manage it, including any future changes to the FRA. All he had to do was carry out and record external examinations of alarms and extinguishers on the due dates. Fortunately, in all the years we had an A1 compliance notice. Here it is:

Fire Risk Assessment

Chaucer Guest House
59 High Street, Blackpool
FY1 2BN

Audit carried out by M…..
Responsible Person

Sunday 16th of August 2020
Next Review date 17th of August 2021

Introduction

The premises are a traditionally built corner house, circa 1870, being changed to a guest house probably between the wars complying with all the planning requirements in place at the time. The premises have continued to operate as such continuously up to the present time. Chaucer House is subject to a continuously rolling programme of updating to reflect the changing needs and expectations of guests and incorporating the best practices in Health and Safety, including Fire Prevention and awareness.

The premises are arranged over three floors.

Ground floor, with the entrance from High Street and a short hallway direct to stairs to the floors above. Also from the hallway is a door into the guest and owners dining room/kitchen, the owners workroom, a utility room and the owners private lounge. From the owner's work area is access to the owner's private sleeping quarters in the basement area, consisting of one room.

The first floor has 3x en-suite rooms and one standard room, for which a separate shower room and toilet are situated off the stair landing.

The second floor has two small single standard rooms, Rooms 5 & 7, (these are no longer in use for letting). plus one owner's dry store room. Room 6.

(The Fire Precautions Act 1971) did apply to the premises and an original certificate was issued on the 1st of May 1977, subsequent changes of ownership being notified to relevant authorities up-to and including the present owners).

The present responsible person Brian C..... has a certificate from the British Safety Council, "level 2" qualification in Risk Assessment dated 23rd of May 2007.

This risk assessment will be reviewed in 12 months or earlier if any structural alteration takes place or should the operation of the business change in any significant way.

Occupancy

Chaucer house caters now for a maximum of 8 guests, all on the first floor between four rooms. Along wiith the owner, The maximum number of people on the premises at any time is 9 persons. The guests are mainly able bodied couples and single people on short breaks. Families, stag and hens or any groups are not accepted. Because of the style and build we do not cater for the disabled or those with special needs, however elderly or those generally slow on their feet are only accommodated on the 1st floor level.

(Note. During the Covid-19 Pandemic until further notice the number of guests allowed throughout the premises is restricted to just 4, at any one time, to ensure social distancing. Additional signage and protection screen). The Dining room and kitchen are permanently closed. There is no lounge area.

Identified Hazards

Guests own equipment, hair dryers, irons, curling tongs etc.
Electricity supply throughout the premises
Electrical appliances as standard equipment
Guests Smoking in rooms
Combustible materials
Water supply

Gas Supply

The gas supply enters the building from the High Street into the cellar, the consumer unit and cut-off valve being situated to the left of the far wall in a cupboard at chest height.

The single supply then goes directly to the kitchen domestic cooker, this being the only gas appliance in the premises. The gas installation and cooker are checked and certificate issued annually byJB Gas & Electrical, 35 Hesketh Ave, Bispham. Tel 07973 816359. Installation of 2 Carbon Monoxide detectors August 2015

Electricity Supply

The supply enters the premises to the basement from Banks Street into a cupboard on the far wall at chest height behind removable doors to access the consumer unit and distribution boards.

The 5 yearly "Electrical Installation", test and report having been renewed 24/05/2020 by Total Protection Electrical Fire & Security Ltd, 14 Blackberry Way,Penwortham, Preston. PR1 9LQ Tel 01772 466222. Replacing consumer units,testing, certification and Building Control Notification issued.

Electrical Appliances

Electrical appliances in all guest areas and bedrooms are PAT tested annually and certificated together with an itemised log of condition and tolerances, the responsible person being certificated to carry out the tests.

Guests Own Equipment

Rooms are checked daily and advice given to guests using their own equipment and also the in-house equipment. Particularly curling tongs, irons and hair-dryers etc.

Guests Smoking

No smoking is permitted in any of the public areas, however it is permitted in allocated guest bedrooms. These are supplied with heavy glass ashtrays and metal waste bins, which are serviced and cleaned daily, special attention being paid to those guests that do smoke.

Combustible Materials

All means of escape are kept clear of any combustible material and are checked frequently during the day as we perambulate around the building. Rooms are cleared each morning of waste bins and guests clothing and other detritus deemed to be a risk in and around electrical points and equipment. All rubbish is bagged daily and removed from the premises and stored in the ginnel for collection by the council. A Duty of Care Waste Transfer Note is renewed annually by Blackpool Council.

Water Supply

The external Stop Cock for the building's supply is situated in the ginnel that exits onto Banks Street, the internal stop cock is situated in the owners work room beneath and behind a panel, (access aperture), below the work-bench on the left.

Fire Protection Equipment and Emergency Lighting.

The L2 fire detection system was installed in April 2006 to comply with current standards and requirements for the premises. This is serviced twice yearly by HS Security Services,(formerly Ace Security Blackpool). In addition weekly call point tests are made and logged along with checks of the emergency lighting system to include a monthly battery drain test. This is also maintained by Ace Security twice yearly. Emergency Break Glass points are situated at the entrance/final exit door to the road, on each landing, in the workroom, the utility room and the kitchen/diner.

Note, the normal six month service being 29/10/19 The following service has been delayed until February 2021 because of closure, ref Covid-19. However the partner owner Brian C....., competent person, continues to run normal routine tests and checks of the fire and emergency lighting systems and recorded them in the logs.

The Fire Control Panel is situated in the hall area entry point to the dining/kitchen from the main hall-way. This is sectioned into two zones, each being identified and areas covered by each zone on the panel, along with access code and instructions for procedures. All guest rooms, public and private areas are equipped with L2 fire, heat and smoke detectors including sounders, maintained as above by Ace Security twice annually.

There are 14 detectors and 5 call points in total.

Top floor landing, plus one each in the two single guest rooms and another in the dry-store room. A call point situated on the top landing. On the first floor are detectors in each of the four guest rooms and the landing, on the landing is another call point. On the ground floor there are detectors in the hall, owners private lounge, dining room/kitchen, utility room and the workshop.

Call points located inside entrance/exit doors, owners kitchen/dining room, and workshop area.

Fire Extinguishers (water) are located in the ground floor hall and on the landing areas of the two floors above. A dry powder extinguisher and fire blanket is located in the owner's kitchen/diner and a dry powder extinguisher situated in the work-room. Serviced annually by Embetter Fire Protection.

Escape Route Signage

Escape route signage is located throughout the hallways, stairs and landings in addition to the Evacuation Procedure and Assembly Point notices located in each guest bedroom which are checked daily to be in place and in good condition as part of the cleaning schedule duties.

Means of Escape

The primary means of escape is the entrance/exit doors leading onto the High Street. These doors require no keys to exit from. The furthest point in the premises takes a direct route to the exit doors and takes no longer than 90 seconds at a normal casual walking pace to exit to the road. The assembly point being on the pavement opposite.

Maintenance and Testing

In addition to the statutory checks and obligations, all guest rooms are checked daily to ensure signs and notices are in place, doors & automatic closures are functioning correctly, to ensure closure into their rebates, intumescent strips and Euro locks are in good condition and doors are kept closed at all times, occupied or not. Luggage, equipment, free-standing are not allowed at any time to be left anywhere other than in guest rooms or service rooms. All guests are made aware of the emergency procedures in the event of an alarm activation.

Owners Procedures / Emergency Action Plan.

The policy of Chaucer House is to ensure that all visitors and guests can quickly and safely evacuate the premises at any time of the day or night. The premises are staffed continuously whilst guests are on the premises. There is 24 hour CCTV monitoring the safe arrival and departure of guests to ensure the security of the premises.

Should there be a fire alarm activation M....., (the responsible person), will inspect the fire panel and investigate the location indicated. M....., (proprietor), will remain in the hall to give instructions and to reassure and assist any guests.

Should nothing be found, the system will be reset and the details recorded in the log.

If there is any doubt as to why the system activated then the fire service will be called and an immediate evacuation instigated by M....., will ensure that all guests are compliant in following the procedures from their rooms and be ready to assist any that may need it. Including any visitors or traders working during the day within the premises. To ensure that all guests are accounted for with reference to the guest register by M..... who will check them off as they exit the premises to the assembly point.

Ensuring that the premises are clear of all persons the alarm will then be silenced but not reset until the arrival of the fire service.

Guests will not be allowed to return into the premises until agreed, on the instructions of the attending fire officer.

Signed: M..... responsible person.
Proprietor: Brian

Years before, when this report became mandatory, I immediately took a course in Fire Risk Assessment in conjunction with and monitored by The British Safety Council. The course was for assessments for all industrial premises and ranged from basic walk around to buildings compliance with fire control systems and the design of installation of alarm systems, taking in escape routes, distances of fire detection equipment and, importantly, the time it would take for anyone to escape safely from anywhere in the premises, be it a factory, office block or humble guest house. A detailed plan of a random premises was given to test your observations and to design the correct placement of all detection and exit points including alarm buttons and signage.

At the time, it served me well, as I was able to recoup the cost of my equipment and the courses which, by the way, I passed with full certification. My tutor even asked me to teach him the finer points of fire safety as he did not have a full certificate! I also took exams in Manchester and additionally online gaining yet more certificates from the British Safety Council on Portable Appliance Testing (PAT). I was therefore able to recover the costs of equipment and course fees by selling my services to other commercial businesses, being authorised to write and certify their electrical, fire and other compliance.

A POTENTIAL JOB APPLICATION

To Nasa Aeronautical Astronaut Employment Programme.

Dear Sir or Madam.

My deep interest in travel and exploration leads me to apply for the position of Astronaut on your next mission into deep space! Below is my work history. Full documentation, i.e. contracts are available if needed:

1951-1961

Wightman's off licence, Vassall Road, Brixton, London. SW9. Hours 17.30 to 10.30 Monday to Saturday, 19.00 to 22.00 Sundays (part time), salary ten shillings per week.

Duties: everything, cellar stocking, shelf filling, serving and being left to open and close one day per week after the first two years whilst the owner took a day off. In 1961 my Monday to Friday hours changed to 19.00 to allow for my first full time job on leaving school.

The junk and television disposal shop, Cowley road, Brixton. SW9. Hours 22.30 to 01.00 Seven days a week, salary zero, but any television that I could get going again.

Around 1960 the owner ran away and the building was almost derelict. He was a Canadian Soldier, staying illegally after the Second World War.

Duties: dismantling televisions, bought hundreds at a time from television hire companies. Burning the wooden and bakelite in an open fire, dismantling every component from the aluminium chassis, saving the valves, brass screws and anything else salvageable to be sold to scrap metal merchants or on the open street markets on Sundays.

1961-1964

The Post Office Engineering Department, 2-12 Gresham Street, London EC4.

Hours 09.00 to 17.00 Monday to Friday, Once every three weeks it was required to be on duty Saturdays 09.00 to midday, alone, just to listen for the telephone. Should it ring with the caller saying, 'War has been declared', without further conversation I was immediately to relay it to another number with the same message. Fortunately, it never did rang. Duties Internal Messenger, salary £4.19s.6d per week. Aged 18, transferred to HMTS Monarch, a deep sea cable layer, duties, officers steward, UK to the far east.

1964-1965
Faulkner Green, Marshalsea Street, London SE1

Duties: roof glazier's mate, salary £20 per week. Hours 08.00 to finish the build, usually 18.00. Start time for travel anywhere in the country could be 04.00.

1965-1966
Securicor, Old Swan House, Chelsea Embankment SW3. Security Guard for any of 300 premises around greater London. Hours minimum contract of 60 or 72 per week depending on clients' needs spread over seven nights and or weekend days and nights. The latter 24 hour shifts. Salary £18 per week.

London Underground just one month to learn how the system worked, salary £8 per week.

1966-1967
Milkman, United Dairies, Croxteth Road, Dulwich. Hours 04.00 until end of round of deliveries, the choice of start time my own.

Duties: unlock the depot and be first out after loading the milk float. Finish time around 13.00 hours except for money collection days Fridays and Saturdays when I would finish around 18.00 hours or whenever every customer had paid. Salary £20 including tips/gratuities.

1967-1968
Popular Book Centre, 118 Camberwell Church Street, Manager, Fulham Palace Road shop. Salary £15 per week. Hours 09.00 to 18.00 Mondays to Saturdays.

1968-1972
P&B COW, Streatham Common, a factory one hundred years old, now producing windscreen rubbers and lilos but best known for Durex produced elsewhere.

Duties: labourer, leading hand. Hours 18.00 to 06.00 six nights per week. Salary £22 per week. Just three months here, but fascinating ones.

Securicor: rejoined for four years. Guard, Sergeant, Inspector, Chief Inspector, Superintendent, Vault Controller. A job I loved but I was asked to resign when it was discovered that I was a homosexual, illegal at that time in the UK. Salary £20 per week. Hours normally around 60 to 84 per week.

1972-1973
Superdrug, Central Avenue, West Molesey, Trainee Manager at Putney High Street and stand in manager or other branches. Salary £22 per week. Hours 08.00 to 18.00 Mondays to Saturday.

1973-1974
Indesit, 292 Streatham High Road, London SW16. Field Service Engineer, washing machines, dishwashers and refrigerators mainly for machines on customer premises still under warranty. Salary £25 a week and a free pass to use vehicles personally. Hours 08.00 for twelve customer visits per day; mostly I was finished by 13.00 Mondays to Fridays.

1975-1978
Association of County Councils, 66a Eaton Square, London SW3, Print Room Operator, Salary £25 per week. Duties: operating solo, three Gestetner machines, two scanners, copiers etc printing, collating and occasionally going to other government departments, The Lords, The House of Commons with important missives that I had just printed. A fabulous job with free access to most government establishments and a chance to see what others might never be able to see. Here I met and was introduced to another world. People, one in particular, would wine and dine me. Hours 09.00-17.00 Mondays to Fridays. My first normal job was only five short days per week, with two weeks holiday, bank holidays off, and being able to read The Times each day on the bus from Wimbledon to Sloane Square.

1978-1982
International Computers Ltd, Beaumont, Old Windsor, Berkshire. I, and my partner to be for twenty-six years, had the offer of a large apartment in Maidenhead, so it was with great sadness that I had to leave my previous job, but not my friends. Duties: porter at Hedsor House, Taplow, a magnificent country manor, next door to Cliveden which everyone would have known at the time. This is where ICL feted, fine-dined and accommodated leaders of industry for the opportunity to sell computer systems. My only duty was to care for their comfort and answer their requests. After a few months I was promoted to Beaumont Windsor to manage their student facilities, then to absorb the conference facilities, graphic department, audio visual operations and the film studio where advertisements for ICL training were produced, along with the catering department and coffee shop, bar, hotel accommodation and coach fleets, catering for five hundred students per week. Also, to negotiate and produce contracts directly with suppliers which involved visiting many around the country. Took them from an initial budget loss of minus £90,000 to a profit of £1.5 million. With my own key to the executive loo, I was standing next to

a director having a pee. He said, 'Christ Brian, if you had your own business, you would make a fortune!' Forthwith, I handed in my notice, to do just that. Salary £8,500 per year. I had asked for more. The reply was, 'You don't have a degree.'

1982-1983

My first business, The Mace Foodstore, 26 Ash Road, Woking. The name was the buying group it was trading with. Having had to get a loan of £9,000 after paying £12,000 for the lease, I built the turnover enough within nine months to be able to pay the loan back and sell the business with enough to purchase the next business outright.

1983-1986

The Mace Foodstore and Off Licence, 9 Chart Downs, Dorking, Surrey. This time it took longer to build what was a store verging on bankruptcy to one that was profitable, selling it three years later with an extended new lease from the local council.

1986-1987

The Swaffham Lighting Centre, 14 Plowright Place, Swaffam, Norfolk. Purchasing the lease from the owner of a bankrupt mobile phone store for zero pounds but paying him for the shelving of a couple or a few hundred pounds, I can't remember now. I had decided from three choices of needs for the area: a toyshop, a cycle shop or a lighting shop. I chose the latter and decided to specialise in crystal only, lamps, ceiling chandeliers, wall lights, standard lamps etc. My partner, after the first few weeks, decided it was too boring to travel to the shop each day and stayed at home to look after the dog and the house. He was actually a good housekeeper and cook. My dinner and a glass of sherry were always waiting for me when I return in the evenings. Sadly, he refused to leave the house unless with me. He would order all our groceries by phone from the butcher and grocery shop a hundred yards away on the other side of the road. I put the shop on the market and it was sold quickly. Now I had to look after him and earn a living until deciding what we should do next.

Editor's Note: at this point, if not earlier, (well, you try editing this kind of raw material) Brian's astronaut CV lurches into descriptive narrative so the font should revert to normal. However, Brian never does, so let's stick with it...

1987-1988

A brief stab at trying to see what I could do from home, set up a removal company, using our garage for storage and driving an eight-ton pantechnicon was challenging, to say the least. That had just the one customer, who was extremely happy as it happens, moving him and his partner from Brighton to Manchester and storing all their possessions in our garage for a few weeks.

A new company, GLS services, loft boarding, building maintenance with labour from a man down the road. Sadly, it could have been successful but again my partner would leave halfway through a job and never return.

1988-unspecified

Mason Seely, Downham Market. I was approached by this company to work for them as an estimator. They had many government contracts but were losing them simply because they could not create the estimates in a timely manner. Most consisted of hospital, road signage etc as well as the normal businesses wanting signs to be made. They had computers scattered around the offices but not connected or ever used. I devised and wrote my own programme to encompass all the variants of signage, size, material, wood, metal, plastics, amount of spray painting and time, vinyl, brass etc. From there, putting in all the costs of each material by volume.

Now what took their own estimator weeks to do, one person was able to do in an instant. Input the details of size and materials and time and up would come the price for the estimate. Also programmed in was an element for wastage and a healthy profit margin. Taking this with me, I presented it to them for free, and showed them how to use it. At the same time, they had their own estimator and other directors do it first by long hand then compare the results. They were delighted. However, they were now financially struggling because they were getting all the contracts they quoted for and had problems raising the money to buy the materials, so the potential contracts were being lost. I left them to work that one out for themselves as my mother who was living in sheltered accommodation was not well. My frequent visits to Clapham, London, and giving money to carers to look after her was literally exhausting me. Time for a short break of not earning anything.

Campbell Soups, Kings Lynn, Norfolk

A temporary job on the production floor for a few months, filling huge drums from set menus for the soup of the day, 30k of potatoes, 10k of peas, 2k of onions etc. shovelled up, weighed and then transported to the guys on high platforms with huge boilers tipping all this in. Behind them were huge canning machines shrouded in steam, turning and chucking out the other end at great speed the tins of soup ready for packing. I really enjoyed this too. Tomato soup, beef stew, mushroom soup etc. Well, I guess you all know the range. Different qualities and quantities depending on who they might be produced for, with the supermarket's own branding. A month of this and then promoted to quality control, examining the temperature of the product as it was cooked, taking tins as they whizzed around, using a special lever where you could open a gate and six tins would fly out. Back to a workbench, check the information impressed on the lid, check with a micrometre the thickness of the can itself. Tipping all the contents out and

then separating each different ingredient and weighing them, then counting out meatballs which the machine seemed to find extremely hard to do. Finally, someone on the factory floor would place a can of each product onto a table for me to do a taste test. Open the can, take a spoonful and then add comments to a form. Salt, too much too little, sugar, etc and then the most controversial part in my own opinion - was it good, nice, not so nice? After a few weeks the production manager asked why I always marked every product as not nice?
"I don't like soup, I told him."

The mushroom farm, Stoke Ferry.
One day a local bank, not mine, emailed me to ask if I would be interested in producing a report for them for why a nearby mushroom farm was in financial difficulties. It was a fairly big business, employing a fair amount of local labour such as pickers, packers, drivers and labourers. Why had they contacted me? It was your accountant, they said, he recommended you as being the best to evaluate a company's performance. I judged that the best way to do this was a couple of days picking mushrooms myself. I duly applied and was accepted. Cutting through all the detail, it came down to them producing more than they could sell. Every few days they had to drive the excess to Covent Garden in London and sell them for less than it cost to produce them. They may well be still trading, so I will not give my report here. Suffice it to say, the bank asked me to consider buying them out and would advance me any amount I needed. He had in the meantime done due diligence by checking my own bank record. If I was not interested in this, he had a large supermarket that was in trouble and he felt I could quickly turn it around. Wow!

1988-1992
Bar Aguila, Palma Mallorca. My partner had been scanning property pages for businesses in Majorca, Spain and pleaded with me to go and look at one. I flew over a few days later and bought a tiny, closed-down bar in a village, flew back, sold the UK business and within a few weeks we were off to Majorca. We had to obtain residency and working permits, tax and social security, (this was prior to Spain joining the EU) which involved endless queueing and paper stamping. It was worth it though. When the police eventually came around to check businesses, a horde of people who had not had their papers stamped could be seen closing shop and running off until the coast was clear, even my own staff! It gave me great satisfaction when three burly Spanish police officers brusquely demanded my papers, saw the papers, smiled and shook my hand. I still have the documentation in Latvia, the only documents small enough to keep as souvenirs.

Sadly, the economic crisis at the time the collapse of the ERM caused me to lose my customer base as they all went back to their home countries. My partner decided to leave me and our dog and return to the

UK, the end of 26 years together. Impossible to sell my business in the current climate. I ended the lease on three shops and gave the lease and business to the staff in the fourth. I paid all my taxes, solicitor, accountant rents and gave my bar, now a huge apartment, to a friend and partner in the furniture shops, again for nothing. With my backpack, I returned to the UK, ten pounds to my name and a long walk to the soup kitchen at Charing Cross to sleep under the bridge. It was January and freezing cold. I decided to jump into the river - but that is another story and another adventure.

1992

Redgate Couriers, Redhill.

I was now living in someone's loft in Redhill, on the floor but warm. I had gone to the unemployment office because I only had enough money left for a packet of cigarettes or a cup of tea. I chose the former because they would last longer than the tea! The first time ever in an employment office. Looking at my CV, the clerk said I should not be at this office but upstairs in the executive office. I was shown a desk to use, a computer, newspapers, tea and coffee, plus printer and fax machines. In addition, I was given two weeks unemployment money amounting to £98, the first and only time ever to claim or be unemployed.

Just a couple of days here and I came across a motorcycle courier company looking for self-employed couriers, travelling anywhere in the country with paid mileage. The only problem, I needed a motorcycle.

Looking around several motorcycle shops, I found the perfect bike, just a 400cc shaft driven Honda, an American import. "I'll take that," I said to the dealer, "here is my credit card."

Within a few minutes, I was called on the telephone. It was Nat West Bank wanting to talk to me.

"Are you Brian? Where have you been for four years? We closed your account, but now you are back, it is open for you again. Your purchase is approved."

So, guys and gals, always pay anything and everything you might owe or be liable for, even if you plan to emigrate and never come back. I did, before going to Mallorca, even the tax office, against the advice of my accountant. But now I was so pleased. I had an identity back, a bank account, albeit empty, and a credit card with £2,000 credit.

Registering as self-employed again, for the next couple of years I was not only the oldest courier on their books but also the highest earner. They said I had a death wish.

During my time doing this, I replaced the bikes every six months, simply because of the high mileage and treatment. My last bike was a BMW ex police 900cc with full fairing, top box for parcel and radio contact, panniers etc.

However, the day came when I realised, I was getting too old for it, especially as my feet only just touched the road. To stop, I had to kick down the stand before and allow the bike to lean onto it. Occasionally I would miss the stand and fall over. Passers-by would help me lift it upright again.

1993-ish

Reigate Manor Hotel, Reigate Hill, Surrey

I needed to earn more money quickly to pay off my credit card at the end of the month. I drove into this hotel car park and enquired if they needed any part time staff. Yes, was the answer, as a night porter one night per week to give their permanent man his days off. Friday and Saturday nights. I could finish my courier work Friday nights and earn as a night porter. Plus, free food! At the same time I got another part time job, just for a few weeks, cleaning school toilets two hours a day, for three weeks. In the courier's office, waiting my turn for the next journey, I would wake up to everyone shouting "BRIAN! BRIAN! Wake up, there's a job!" Only once did I manage to fall asleep on my motorcycle nearing my turn off the M25 and missed it. Waking up sharply, I never did that again.

1994-1995

Ratedale Security. This was a small security company covering the local area and Gatwick airport periphery, just thirty static guards or so, a dozen mobile patrolmen and a few cash in transit vans. I started as a guard but within weeks was promoted to mobile patrols, then inspector then controller. I took a Gatwick airside driving test to be able hand sacks of cash direct onto and into the cockpit of planes every day. One of the things I did was to re-plan their system of allocating staff to jobs. I was still looking to earn more, though, so one day I called into a hotel, spoke to the general manager and hey presto, another job!

Editor's note: From this point on, Brian's CV has fully morphed into descriptive memoir mode, so the font will return to normal, something, as I said earlier, that Brian has never done.

1995: Nutfield Priory Hotel, Redhill, Surrey. I started as a night porter in this expensive hotel and fine dining restaurant which also had a sports centre attached. It specialised in wealthy private guests, the international corporate market for conferences and high-end weddings. Although it's now nearly thirty years on, you could google it as I imagine it is still in operation.

Duties: after the restaurant had closed and the receptionists and duty managers had left, I had to hoover and clean the grand hall, look after security and download the business for the day using Fidelio Software. In the morning, when all the guests were checking out, their bills were thus itemised including food and drink. In addition, should any guests require the odd bottle of wine or champagne, sandwiches or snacks, maybe a VIP arriving during the night, it was my duty to deal with it.

The rooms had no numbers but were named after famous poets and writers. I remember a well-known comedian arriving late one night.

"Welcome to Nutfield Priory Hotel, sir." He apologised for being so late as the plane had been delayed. "Allow me to take your bag and I will take you straight to your room. Should you require anything to eat or drink, you can telephone me at reception and I will do what I can."

He insisted on carrying his own bag so off we went, chatting as we climbed the grand staircase. I pointed out the Minstrel's Gallery on the way with the beautiful stained-glass windows adorned with coats of arms. Then I showed him the 18th century organ below, along the first landing.

"Damn!" I thought. "This is not the floor for his room! I'm lost!"

Never mind. As we walked the length of the hotel, I gave him some history and pointed out the secret door down to the kitchen. We ascended to the next floor and the same again. Up we went, me pointing out that from here you could see Gatwick Airport in the distance and the Surrey hills. He laughingly said to me,

"You don't actually know where the room is, do you?"

I admitted it, but fortunately we had arrived. He proffered me a tip. I said,

"Absolutely not! You've been carrying your own bag all this time."

He insisted and said it had been entertaining, just what he wanted after a long flight. Later it became a comedy sketch in his act! I wish I could remember his name. He was Canadian and sang and played the guitar. Something 'Red' maybe?

Two weeks later, the general manager was waiting for me when I arrived for my late shift.

"How are you liking it, Brian?"

He only ever called by my first name, so nice.

"Very much Mr P." I replied.

"I think you are wasted as the night porter," he went on. "I want you to be here in reception, to meet and greet the guests as they arrive. You will do nothing else. You can order a porter to take the guests' luggage to their rooms whilst you escort them yourself and ensure they are comfortable. Sometimes guests will arrive by helicopter. You are to take the large multi coloured umbrella into the field opposite where the pilots will know where to land. You are not to do any other portering duties other than look after the VIP guests' needs and wants. Should they require any shopping, take one of the staff cars. You will be the only person on the staff with insurance to drive guests' cars and park them. What do you think?"

How could I refuse? Additionally, he told me to learn about the computer systems and who has responsibility for each department. It was great. I would get a list everyday of VIP's arriving and, as long as I was around for them, my time was easy. As the months went by, I would be given responsibility for instructing the gardeners when to use mowers so as not to disturb conferences and many aspects of garden maintenance. I would walk every floor looking for anything out of place, especially in the mornings when guest trays had been left outside the rooms and not collected by the porters. I'd also check that the domestic staff had not left dirty linen in corridors, weren't sitting down watching television and that all brass was clean in public areas. Easy!

One day, the restaurant manager asked me to help move some huge round tables from one end of the hotel to another for a wedding event. He was a prestigious person, so 'no' was not an option. As I was doing so, the hotel manager came along.

"What are doing moving those, Brian? It's not your job."

He was angry, immediately sending a letter to every department head stipulating in no uncertain terms, 'Brian is not to be asked to do anything, whatever the circumstances. In addition, if a guest has a complaint, you must not deal with it yourself, but call Brian immediately'. He confided in me later that most of the staff, such as trainee managers and reception staff were young with no common sense. He had instructed them with the same edict – if there's a problem, call Brian!

"You and I," he said, "are the only people at the hotel that work 9 to 5 Mondays to Fridays, avoiding the wedding parties, ordinary guests and being involved with the normal herd."

The job was great, despite occasional dramas playing out as in any hotel. The lift didn't work, there's no water, the lights had gone off, the room was locked and the keys didn't work. When I arrived at any scenario with trainee managers, department managers, porters all wondering what to do, I solved them all, quickly, even if it meant some damage. I kicked the door in one day to the head of the maintenance workshop; he was somewhere else, but I needed keys and tools. He went mad. The general manager castigated him for not having his pager on and said, "This is why Brian's here."

Such fun, getting guests out of an elevator that hasn't reached the floor using a special key to open the doors. Really, the fire brigade's job, but hey, this is a hotel and guests are prime. None of them want to be stuck for an hour or two in an elevator waiting to be rescued. VIP guests would arrive in their Bentleys, Rolls Royces and Bugatti's and just jump out at reception. I would take their keys, see them into their rooms or the restaurant and go back to park their cars, occasionally taking them for a short spin around the grounds. The manager told me I was a lucky so and so, that I was the only one suitably insured and that the staff watched me in envy. Ha ha!

A day came when Mr P, the manager, had to go away on urgent business. By now, I stood in for him regularly. He insisted that I wear a suit so he could take a day off and not just trust the running of the hotel to trainee duty managers. I had the same duties but the guests did not tip me out of uniform. However, I did stay overnight in any room that I chose, which was great! The cheapest room back then was £495 plus breakfast.

One day, he tells us to be on the lookout for an AA hotel inspector who is likely to make a surprise visit at any time, unannounced and with a false name when checking in. The staff were all primed to be alert to any strange cars in the car park, suspicious guests etc. Reception, around lunch time, called me urgently. Someone had just checked in and in the back window of their car was an AA book. It must be them. No problem, the hotel was spotless as usual. I assumed that if this guest was indeed the AA Hotel Inspector, they would shortly be telephoning down to reception to test the services. Sure enough, within half an hour, "Could I order a sandwich please?" My only intervention here was to instruct the kitchen staff not to spend half an hour prepping it, it's wanted now!

Extra attention was paid to ensure no cup and saucer was left in the lounge, no cigarette left in an ashtray, no newspapers left unfolded on chairs and so on. All was well. The next morning, down this guest came to check out. I went through the procedure and bid him farewell. He looked twice at me and then returned to reception to announce that he was the Hotel Inspector and would like to speak with the general manager. I am in my slightly uprated porter's uniform.

"I am sorry sir, the general manager has not arrived yet, but he has instructed me to act on his behalf."

With that I take him to a small cosy conference room, order tea and biscuits and we begin. Now he is suspicious! It was so funny, he said to me,

"You're really the general manager dressed in a porter's uniform. I recognise you from yesterday."

"No, no. I am afraid it's the other way around. Yesterday I was just standing in for him!"

He took some convincing, asking the waitress who brought in the tea, "Is this your manager?" pointing at me.

"Oh, no, sir that's Brian the hall porter. He looks after everything when Mr P is out."

With that, he congratulated the hotel on its high standards, staff attitudes and helpfulness, the evening meal and breakfast. He had only one point to make - he thought there was a little too much starch in the sheets (I will have a word with the laundry, sir).

"Okay," he said, "I am pleased to report you have your four stars."

Thanking me, off he went.

Lunchtime, Mr P returns. The receptionist has already told him the Hotel Inspector has been and left. He hurriedly chases me down.

"What happened, Brian? Did you sit down with him, did you… did he… did…?"

"Don't panic, Mr P! All is fine. You have your four stars still."

The hotel was part of a group, The Nutfield Priory being the flagship on the Island of Jersey in the English Channel.

"Brian," he said, "I need eighty banqueting chairs which they have and I don't. You've got a full driving licence. Would you like to take a trip there and collect them? Drive to the hotel, stay two nights. They will load everything onto the lorry for you to bring back. I will hire the lorry to be delivered here and book the ferry. They will not know who you are, other than the lorry driver, and they will be instructed to give you one of their best rooms following your long journey, including mini-bar and meals, eaten in their dining room. You will check their services, their cleanliness, the staff and all the areas including the standard of meals and room service, so order whatever you want to be brought up to the room, but do not let them see you taking notes. When you return, you are to report your findings."

Fantastic! The day arrived. He ordered a seven-ton, tail-lift lorry for me and off I went. Joining the line of vehicles to board the ferry, a man comes along with a long measuring pole, holds it against the vehicle and says, "You're too high." "Never checked that, did you Mr P." I thought to myself. I gave the man a long story that it wasn't my fault and that I could be in trouble if I didn 't get on board, all whilst smiling nicely. He relents and pulls me out of line to be the last one. I would have to park on the stern without going into the ferry. Done.

They strapped it down and there followed a few hours of cruising.

On arrival, the island was dead. No traffic, no people, but masses of flowers everywhere. It was the day of Princess Diana's funeral. The hotel was great, luxury living for me, noting every aspect as instructed. I took the lorry next day for a tour of the island. Parking at some of the tourist spots was at times a little tricky but a fabulous day. Next morning, my lorry had been filled and I began the return journey to Redhill where I typed out my report - in my own style, of course. They were so pleased with it, they published it in their own in-house magazine for all the other hotels in the group to be aware of the secret inspector and what he might find.

Sometime later, the receptionist called me to report a guest had not checked out and was refusing to leave the room or talk to anyone. I go to the room, announced myself gently and asked if there was anything I could get for her.

"Don't worry, I will not come in, unless you want me to. I will wait here as long as needed to ensure your safety…"

Bla bla bla and more bla. She is apparently having some kind of breakdown. I have friends who work in the local hospital, I tell her. Maybe if she was to speak to them privately, they could help. Thank goodness, she agrees. I ask the receptionist to call the local hospital, outline the problem and within half an hour or so a couple of really nice people arrive to chat with her. An hour or so later, they take her to the psychiatric unit at Redhill Hospital for assessment.

I never heard any more, but that same weekend there was an advertisement in the local newspaper for an open day at the same unit when one could look around, get a feel for this kind of specialist nursing and apply for a job. I went and applied with no hope in the world of being accepted. I told them I was gay, had had a partner for twenty-six years, had gone broke, slept rough and had many businesses and employments, little education etc. Well blow me down if they didn't say I was exactly what they were looking for! Someone to interact with the patients, gently teasing their stories out of them. I would be allowed to wear my ordinary clothes and even smoke in the small garden. It was all just about gaining the patients' trust and calming them. I resigned from my job at the hotel. They had a collection for me and presented me with a large, expensive crystal cut fruit bowl which, many years later, was left behind at Chaucer House and, I guess, auctioned off.

Whilst still living in Redhill, I was invited to the hotel's Christmas parties, although I never went to any of them. However, the hotel closed between Christmas night and New Years Day, when Mr P asked me to sleep there alone, ensuring its security. I was given the keys to the bar and the kitchens and a grand room to sleep in, also a large screen television in the library. This went on even when I was working at the hospital, until I changed job again and moved to Hastings on the south coast.

END OF YEAR 2022

Now that I have a Latvian bank account, and a five-year temporary residencia, I must pay ten euros a month for the privilege. That is a requirement by the government. Plus of course, the hundred euros to open the account. I could have chosen a card with extra benefits for an additional three euros each month, but I am informed that none of those benefits will be relevant to me because I am too old! It pays no interest either unless I was to open a fixed term deposit account and give many months' notice for withdrawals. However, it works, and so I am relieved to be able to finally download things like Covid records. With my letters of confirmation that I am enrolled in the Latvian National Health Service, I am free to find a doctor, either private or as a resident. I carry with me a letter showing all my details in case I need to be swept up from under a lorry and require medical attention.

My lovely landlady has spent the last month telephoning every doctor on the list from the health department to enquire about taking me on as a patient. She has told them that I do not suffer and have not suffered from any ailments, diseases or anything else. My only wish is to just have a doctor in case of emergencies.

Sadly, each time she has been told that (a) they are not taking on new patients, (b) they don't speak English, so would not be able to communicate anyway, (c) they are swamped with coping with the refugees from the Ukrainian war. To date that is a failure. Fortunately, being fit and healthy makes it not so important, at least for the time being.

Lastly, I wanted to find a notary to write my Last Will and Testament, preferably one who would not see it as an opportunity to write themselves into it or make a mountain out of a molehill and inflate the costs. Having no faith in the integrity of local lawyers due to previous experiences in Latvia, I asked around for references. Those I contacted did not reply. Ha! I love where I live and my new friends, and it might be the right place for you, my readers, provided you don't want banking, medical or legal assistance.

Anyway, this is what I wrote to a notary, part of a group practice:

Good day to you!

I asked my friends here to recommend someone to draft and notarize my last wishes and you were recommended. Do you think that you could help? I own no property, here or anywhere else, just a small amount of personal possessions and what would be left in my two bank accounts. No investments, only what is in those accounts. My beneficiaries list will be few and local. I have pasted the details below to save me writing it all out again.

As Wills go, it will be incredibly simple both for me and an executor. My aim will be to keep the process as simple as possible for heirs not to be encumbered by unreasonable costs or convoluted legal interventions. I shall nominate an executor who would not be a beneficiary. Are you able to help?

To date a stony silence. Haha!

ON HOLIDAY

Shortly after this, I go on holiday. A fabulous friend and neighbour is going to help by decorating my home whilst I am away.

Money issues. For three years, HMRC in the UK have been sending me fines and penalties each month. Last week they sent another for £1,200 to be followed yesterday by another letter, this time to say ***they owe me*** £1,100 and where would I like it paid to?

It's rather nice that they keep in touch. And to pay me! That's a first, so I am delighted to be able to add it to my holiday fund. An exciting and at times dramatic year, but still able to keep my sense of humour and fun. Happy Christmas everyone and an especially successful year ahead.
Brian

WINTER HOLIDAY

Tomorrow I shall be getting the bus into Riga around lunchtime, doing some food and snack shopping at Rimi in the train station shopping centre and then catching a bus to the airport where I have a twin room booked should my friends A... and Z... decide to join me later in the day. The reason being that, as of yesterday, A... had not managed to sort out transport. She was sure that it would not be a problem getting a taxi to the airport at four in the morning on New Year's Day. "Leave it to me, no need to worry," she said. I was not so sure. I suggested that she try to pre-book a taxi. She reported that of five different companies only one was marginally interested. She had been quoted eighty euros with no guarantee that they would turn up. Given the precarious nature of that kind of arrangement, I decided to ensure we would be there on time by booking a twin room at the airport hotel. They could then relax, be early, use the room and we could dine at the hotel, celebrating with our own private party. A... said I should not have worried, that perhaps it was my way of avoiding going to their own party. That was partly true. Too much drink, too many snacks and foods from around the globe, conversations in Latvian, non-smokers, vegetarians and fitness fanatics with me trying to stay awake, worrying if transport would turn up.

A... said that one of the members of a transgender group had volunteered to drive her to the airport early. I was not happy with that myself. I'd met some of them - all young, a disparate mix of unemployed heavy drinkers with a high number of scatter-brained drug users. They did not fill me with confidence.

Today A... informs me that it is sorted. A friend has organised a taxi. That would be great, just too last minute for me with no plan if it doesn't show up, breaks down or the driver gets breathalysed on the way. Some of the conversation shown right now:

Brian

I plan to meet you at the terminal if you wish to take a chance with taxis. You sent Stay at Sky High Hotel Airport 200 meters from the terminal Saturday 31 Dec 2022 – Sunday 1 Jan 2023 Location Lidosta Rīga, Rīga, LV-1053, Latvia View map

A.P.

Ok.... will mosey over to the Sky High... we can sort the timing later on.

Brian

The restaurant closes at 19.00 hrs on Saturday and not open at all on Sunday. Just for information. You will have to let me know if A... will be joining us, if so allow you both being their if we wish to have an early evening meal together at the hotel.

A.P.

That's early!

Brian
It is, I guess it's something to do with New Years Eve... haha

A.P.
True...

Brian
Will leave you to think about it and catch you later. Just need to see if I can check in with Air Baltic now and print out a boarding pass, even if I do have to book a seat. You are cordially invited along with your partner to the New Years Day soiree at the Airport Hotel commencing 02.30 hrs. A room has been booked for you both, should you require to sleep after the round of drinks and snacks. You both can sleep until I return from the airport terminal in time for A...'s and my departure. You will be welcome to wave us off and return to your room until checkout at midday for more sleeping. Taxis then will not be a problem and even the bus number 22 is frequent and free on the day.
Happy New Year!
p.s.
Do not worry about where I sleep as I will have already been occupying the room from midday Saturday and will happily have slept through all the celebrations. Wide be awake and ready to host you both.

A...
Happy New Year to you too. Thank you for the invitation but I can't come. The house needs to be cleaned. I don't have time. I am leaving the same day at 16.00

Brian
Bring your luggage with you. You won't have to do anything as you will already be at the airport. A... can clean the house three weeks later!

Z...
Sorry Brian, I can't leave my house not clean. See you in January when you get back.

Brian
Just ensure A... does not drink too much as it would be nice for her to present herself in an upright position at check in.

So that's my schedule. Evening at the hotel, sleep early and be awake to greet A... at 02.30 on New Years Day, give over the room to her to get some sleep, returning to wake her later for us to walk over to the terminal and check in for our flight. Refreshed, relaxed and sober, almost!

NEW YEAR 2023

Saturday up early for the start of my holidays following almost three years of living like a pauper. Becoming a professional master in the art of scrimping on everything including foods, heating, clothing and even water.

It was the bus to the shopping centre first to add to my luggage with sandwiches, cakes, biscuits and beer. Dragging my suitcase around with a shopping basket perched on top. It was a miserable day and my plan initially was to go to the airport by bus. However, the prospect of waiting in the drizzle changed my mind. Hoping not to be spotted but a friend, G... spotted me. Although it was New Years Eve and he was busy shopping along with his daughter, he still offers to give me a lift. Wow, just so kind, but I couldn't bring myself to accept his offer, telling him I was going to get a taxi to the airport as he watched me packing my suitcase on the bench outside Maxima. What a star he is.

Thirty minutes later, I am checking into the last room available, one for the disabled, next to reception and the entrance door. Fabulous, a wet room, and convenient to pop outside for the occasional cigarette. Few guests in, mainly airline staff. To repeat, my idea was that A... was to join me at 02.00 New Years Day so that we would have somewhere to relax before our early morning flight.

The hotel is almost obscured by major building works for the first railway station to Riga, the road with barriers, trenches and mud, dark, gloomy, constantly drizzling and desolate. So, I send a message to A... which she can share with her taxi driver. Including a video of the location. If she gets dropped at the wrong place, she would still be able to find her way here. Not easy – even the main hotel entrance has been closed, replaced by another at the other end of the building obscured by barriers over the mud.

Video posted, a luxurious shower and to bed, not waking until

01.00 New Year's Day. Yes, I missed everything. Another long hot shower, dress and repack my suitcase. Two in the morning, A... is messaging, she is on her way. Just a chance to set out the sandwiches and snacks, beers and cakes; she would be bringing the wine.

I stand outside and await her arrival and to guide the driver through the dark muddy barriers. Standing there waiting, sheltering from the drizzle, a chance for a cigarette. In the gloom I spot someone slowly making their way towards me. A young Indian man. We exchange hellos. I'm relieved that I'm not about to be mugged as no one would know; even Reception had closed. In almost complete darkness 1 unlock the door.

The young man, I guessed in his thirties, and I engaged in conversation. He was from New Delhi, now living in Germany and working in Norway, to which he had an earlier flight than ours. Sharing and exchanging experiences of India. Twenty minutes later A... appears, her taxi driver struggling with her luggage to reach us. Best not to interfere as we continue talking. Now introducing A... who also joins in the conversation. Half an hour later we separate to go to our respective rooms. I carefully lock the hotel door. I could sense A...'s wonderment to be talking to someone in such a desolate place.

Snacks wine, beers consumed, talking until 4 a.m., an hour's dozing when we leave for the airport terminal a thousand yards across the still muddy path, locking the reception door behind us. No sound of anyone and still in almost total darkness.

People start to arrive for later flights, a queue is forming for our flight, A... tells someone in uniform that she has a wheelchair booked. We are directed to the desk next to the one where everyone is lining up to check in. Just us. The person checks us in immediately and sends someone else to organise the wheelchair. A few minutes later and a personable young man appears, A... is shoe-horned into the wheelchair and I place all her luggage on her lap, leaving just enough room for her to peer over it. The young man strides to security with me struggling to keep pace whilst talking and teasing him. We are taken to a separate security man waiting for us and pass through in a couple of minutes, but now an electric golf buggy awaits. The personable and cheerful young man helps A... onto the back of it whilst I excitedly decide that I would rather sit next to the young man at the front. He laughs, not minding at all as we whizz next to passport control. Parking up, we are shepherded to the front of the queue to pass through. Some do not look happy at us jumping the line and I suggest to one that he should fight A... for the place.

Back on the golf cart once more, this time up in an elevator swooshing through the terminal, flashing lights and bleepers warning more and more people to stand aside or risk being mowed down. We are delivered to the business lounge. Apparently, my bank card is supposed to give me free access, but it does not, so A... pays for me.

The offering, being early morning is surprisingly pathetic. Oranges, bananas past their prime and pears. Usual cereals, juices, tea, coffee, ice cream, porridge and some rather sad pastries. No sandwiches or any meat products.

Two staff come along every few minutes and re-arrange the offerings, stir the porridge and generally just move around. We pay a heavy price for a pear, a spotty banana, a coffee and a gin and tonic.

Our nice young man returns an hour later to take us to the boarding gate. A few minutes later we are boarding.

(Ed. Flight details missing, but I imagine they slept and did not cause a rumpus)

On landing at our destination, we are met by a man who escorts us through all the procedures, customs emigration, baggage claim and in minutes are out and fast-tracked into a taxi to our hotel.

I'm having a blast for the first time in years, and I think and hope A... is too.

LARNACA

A walk around in the morning then coffee at one o'clock in Costa Coffee opposite the hotel where I was able to make the latest video and see A... emerge on to her balcony. Great. Finish my video and coffee and return to check if she was ready to hit the streets. Two o'clock and we are slowly wending our way to the beach front road to find the times of buses to Nicosia. They leave every thirty minutes, cost four euros. From there, A… wanted to see the fort further along the road, but not before finding a shop to purchase feminine items, purchased and put in my shoulder bag - a first for me.

We reach the fort where A... suggests I could look around on my own whilst she would wait in the bar around the back. This offer I declined. It was extremely small and looked like an opportunity to strip money from tourists. A window cleaner's ladder is all that would be needed to scale the walls and invade. So, we both went to the bar where I had a sumptuous pork chop lunch and coffee, plus a beer and wine and water for A.... Two hours later we are ready to return to our hotel's sports bar where I left her and returned to my room. Two hours passed so I called into the bar to check if she was okay. She was happily ensconced on the settee watching football on one of the many giant televisions. Another first for me.

A bottle of beer and twenty minutes later, I could suffer it no more. She came up to my room to collect her feminine purchases before going to the roof terrace bar on her own, messaging me a little later to say there were a few more people about. Poor A... has a problem walking any distance. The walk to the beach earlier should have taken ten minutes but it had taken an hour with frequent stops to sit down and rest. Hence her reluctance to go anywhere involving walking, her preference being to spend the whole time in hotel bars and restaurants until around midnight - or later.

Selfishly, perhaps, I suggested that this was not my pleasure or what I'm on holiday to do. She suggested that there might be more options in the places we are going to tomorrow. I replied that with her problem walking it would probably result in the same outcome – leaving mid-afternoon each day to see no more than the inside of bars until gone midnight wherever we happened to be. This now is a concern for me. She needs a carer, and it is not what I had envisaged or want to be.

My insistence before agreeing to join her on holiday that we each book independent accommodation, travel and food has worked well. At any time, either of us could head off in a different direction, which is what I am thinking that I should do, forgetting the money I have already spent on flights and accommodation. I seriously don't want to spend three whole weeks in bars, wherever they are. But now I have the dilemma of leaving A... to her own arrangements along with her mobility problems. I love meeting new people, but I don't want to be propping up a bar with them. I am writing this at ten p.m., stopping only to go up to the roof bar to check on A... where she is sitting alone. The bar is busy, disco music pumping out, several tables occupied with customers smoking shisha pipes. By twelve midnight, most have left and it's time to return to my room, leaving A... to finish her drink. Hopefully, we will meet for breakfast as we must check out and walk to the bus stop. A... insists she will be okay dragging her luggage.

We get on so well and we do enjoy each other's company, especially when out and about so it is really advice I need. She requires medical attention, especially her legs, but has already paid a lot of money for an inconclusive consultant's report. I fear for her well-being as she is not able to cope on her own, at home or abroad. She requires constant company.

Monday afternoon, on returning from one of my bus journeys, I popped into the travel agency we'd used to book our trips to Tel Aviv. I checked for day tours this week and with a list in my hand, hotfooted it back to show A... sitting in the hotel sports bar. There's a tour Wednesday to Famagusta, we could go together, all we needed to do was walk into the travel agents and book it. Great! She agreed. A bit of reshuffling today's itinerary and, at midday, we visited the agency to pay for the trip.

The plan for next day was - up at 06.30 and a walk down to the beach bus stop at 07.25 leaving lots of time for A... to rest on the way and catch our tour at 07.45. Although I have my bus pass, A... suggested that I could go with her, first to Mr Singh's Variety Emporium to purchase a couple of international travel adapters and later a sex shop, recommended by a chemist for something to help with her recovery and mobility. If I haven't mentioned it before, A… is transgender having had the operation a short time ago. Anyway, after that, another taxi to the mega mall to purchase other lady things, finishing with an early dinner that would leave her clear for Wednesday's day trip. She would pay for the taxis. A good deal that I couldn't refuse.

So, travel adapters bought, it was back to the hotel to drop them off, a chance for quick refreshments in the sports bar, a lively chat with a shabby looking Lebanese man from Canada and it was off to the sex shop. Mostly they all look the same to me, not well lit and the usual array of apparatus and things to fill various cavities.

Whilst A... was deep in conversation with the woman assistant, I enjoyed walking around the store marvelling at the variety. The enormous size of some dildos made me wince. Anyone who has dared to read Darryl's Diary will know that, after owning a gay friendly guest house for twenty years, there is little I haven't seen of people's predilections. Still…

So, wandering around the shop, I spot a selection of Blow-Up Dolls, male as well as female. I was drawn to the pictures on the boxes - fit, strong men with six-packs and boasting lifelike anatomies which could serve anyone's desires. Cheap too. I mused to myself, although I don't like to see anyone naked and would not want to do what one might be expected to do, I could dress one up and then have someone to talk to other than Doris (the microwave) or Rocky (the boulder in the garden). At least, it could be great fun sitting in the garden on sunny days, taking him for a ride on my electric chair or watching a movie together. I made the purchase which was put into a discreet carrier.

I showed A... and suggested she could borrow him, for a price, of course. A..., having obtained what she needed, we left in another taxi for the mega mall. Here she was able to stock up on her needs whilst I occasionally reassured Justin, my new friend, that he would be safe and that I might buy him some new clothes. But then, I realised, I would have to blow him up in the store's changing room to try them on. For the moment, I told him, he would have to stay naked.

A... and I made our way to the mall's main entrance where we sat outside on a bench to have a cigarette before calling a taxi to take us back to the hotel. Now, I could open the sealed box holding my new friend, Justin. Hastily tearing the box open (disposing of it responsibly in a nearby bin) I saw what looked like a folded up paddling pool, allowing him to unfurl to his full height. Wow! He is hideous! No mop of hair, no six-pack, strong muscled arms or footballer's legs. Holding him up at full height he resembles a large pink balloon that someone has just popped. Could I still dress him, maybe? Socks, gloves and a ski mask to cover the hideous head, especially that gaping red mouth? He could sit between us in the taxi back to the hotel. I suggested this to A… but could see that she was not overly enthusiastic. I folded Justin up and shoved him back into the carrier bag.

I told A... that I was planning to blow Justin up in my bedroom and leave him sleeping in bed whilst we went off to Famagusta tomorrow so that the domestic staff would find him when they came to clean the room. Once back in my room, I again got Justin unfurled and laid him on the bed to take a picture for his Latvian visa. But wait, he's a eunuch! He has no cahones! I just had to put a pair of my underwear over his midriff to save him any embarrassment. Now to blow him up. But, after just three puffs the thought struck me, what if it is a non-return valve? I couldn't possibly take him back through customs and immigration with his arms and legs sticking out the ends of my suitcase. He will have to wait until I get home when I can use my electric foot-pump, taking care not to explode him. I later showed the hotel owner the picture and my plan to leave him in bed for the domestic staff to discover. She roared with laughter and gave every encouragement, wondering what their reactions would be, having this very morning voted me the cleanest guest in the hotel ever. Anyway, Justin is now at the bottom of my suitcase looking to make many Latvian friends.

Later that afternoon, A... and I went to a small Greek restaurant a few hundred yards away. We had a great meal, talking to other customers and returning to the hotel where I left A... in the bar to call me when she was ready, which she did a couple of hours later. I joined her for an hour with one small beer which she kindly paid for. The bar was extremely busy with two large groups from different countries, so the owner told me later. She is an Australian herself, having bought and fitted the hotel ten years ago, now a citizen with her own family.

ANOTHER HOLIDAY OF A LIFETIME

Okay, I can now announce my imminent plan to spend five weeks in Thailand, less than two weeks before launching. My suitcase is beautifully packed, this time with lots of shorts and tee shirts for the 80 degree heat. Also, a few shirts and trousers for formal wear. My flight is from Riga to Helsinki and an hour later a connecting flight to Bangkok. One ticket for both flights which means when I wave my luggage goodbye at Riga Airport, I shan't see it again until landing in Thailand.

Checked where to get my bus for the two-hour journey to Pattaya, and the cost. I have a simple currency converter on my tablet and phone. All I need do now is exchange some euros to Baht for initial currency to see me to my destination. My first task will be to get a local sim card. Usually, however, wherever I am staying, they help with this. For me, it's a nightmare.

I am planning where I want to take trips to in Thailand by train and bus. I may even stray into Cambodia and Vietnam. Just so much to see and do! I will download maps onto my mobile and tablet, then highlight all the bus and train stations plus places I want to visit. Really looking forward to my adventure of a lifetime this time, and provided I am not mugged, murdered or fall off a cliff, it should be great.

Over the years, I have travelled to many Asian countries, but this will be the first where I will be eager to explore the vibrancy of the gay areas, too. I will probably look every bit like an old pervert seeking a good time, but worry not, I will be sensible and hopefully safe. Laughter and fun are my only desires, and I am sure I will achieve those easily enough. Looking forward also to an en-suite and a balcony, maybe even meeting other guests and sharing tips of where to go and what to do. More news as I get it.

Have a great weekend everyone.

P.S.

I do have a helper, courtesy of my landlady finding someone to advise me. He is already helping with planning and schedules. My special thanks to M.D.

TEACHING IN VIETNAM

I've been to Asia before so now is the time to tell you about some of my time there before I go again. I could have been a teacher if I actually knew anything. Possessing no formal education or qualifications of any kind, other than sixty years or life experiences in a multitude of employments and businesses, it was only in the latter decade that I was able to take holidays, each one for a period longer than the previous.

My budget being small, it was initially for a week at a time to places like Greece, Tunisia, Spain and Paris, then longer holidays to Egypt

In Hanoi with students

and India. In those countries I managed, over several years, to travel the length and breadth of the land using every class of train, from super first-class sleepers to riding on the roof out of Mumbai.

I always travelled solo, the only interactions being with hotel staff and the people I met whilst walking around. An adventurous spirit and enquiring mind led me to explore those areas where travellers were generally advised not to go for reasons of safety.

A few years ago, I decided to go to Vietnam. An avid follower of the Vietnam War whilst working in London in the sixties, buying the Times newspaper to read on the bus every day to work, I followed events avidly, not only the fighting but also the politics. I was, albeit secretly, an admirer of Ho Chi Minh. Vietnam, therefore, held a special attraction and in particular Hanoi where there were many sites I wanted to visit, not in formal tour groups or packages but by local buses, motorcycles and simply walking.

Leaving the Hotel on the first day, I meandered along to Ho Am Kiem or Sword Lake, in the middle of Hanoi's old quarter. Six in the morning and already hundreds of locals are taking morning jogs around the lake. Others are on exercise machines, frantically working out before going off to work. Impressive!

After exploring the old quarter, street by street, named for the dominance of the trades carried out in each, it was back to the hotel for breakfast, a change of clothes and return to the lake around ten o'clock. The tourists now numbered in their hundreds along with peddlers, traders and scam artists. But also, countless students from the many universities and colleges in Hanoi.

Within a few minutes, I was approached by a couple of students, nervously and respectfully asking if I could spare them a few moments to talk with them and answer some questions. I agreed. I will talk to anyone, short, fat, old, ugly, poor or all of the above. There is only one person I know who can talk for longer than me, living here in Latvia, not a million miles away.

Many of the students had project sheets in their hands. They had been assigned the task of engaging with Westerners, ask some set questions and write down the answers. I listened patiently whilst they struggled with pronunciation, so I would then attempt to teach them how to form and speak the words. Great fun. Soon, they were joined by another group of students wanting to join in, and yet another, until within thirty minutes I had a crowd of fifty students, including some local Vietnamese interested in how I spoke. Apparently, they loved my voice, talking slowly enough for them to understand as we slowly circled the lake.

The questions were similar: where are you from, how old are you, where is your wife, how many children do you have, what is your work, how did you get here from England and so on. It was great fun for them and for me, too. Sometimes, I gave the most ridiculous answers. I would say, ‘China, 29, ran away with another man, 27, paperclip maker, walked here'. Some of the students avidly wrote down those answers whilst others would be filming me on their mobiles or recording for their tutor. I put right those who were simply going through the motions, then I went on to explain that to truly learn English they had to listen and think of an answer or follow up question and not just nod their heads. The better students laughed raucously and explained to the others.

Some of them were accompanied by their tutors and a few of them asked if I would go to their colleges to speak. They would send some students to my hotel on an agreed date to escort me. Fabulous, although I insisted on them using motorcycles. I loved the traffic in Hanoi and for that matter Saigon too and hired my own motorcycle. I remember the hotel manager coming out and crossing himself as I wobbled away into the swirl of traffic. I used to ride around until the petrol sank to emergency reserve levels, then was horrified to have to join the melee in garages, pushing and shoving to fill up. Like Latvia, my language skills were non-existent. Anyway, once refuelled, I would return to my hotel to give the bike back.

SOVIET ATTITUDES IN LATVIA

The talons of the former Russian rulers of the Baltic states state still dig deep into the politics by those who choose to stay after the breakup of the Soviet Union, half the general populace still bearing allegiance, albeit secretly, to the Russian state and way of life. Many are in power through the government and their quangos. Progress in changing the balance in places like Georgia and here in Latvia is notoriously slow. Latvia, which I know best, still lags behind in human rights. The youngest and brightest are leaving, as are the highly skilled, for more enlightened countries with better opportunities and freedoms. It flies loose honouring its EU responsibilities and there is corruption on a large scale.

Something similar is true for individuals. I am a temporary resident so, for five years, by reciprocal agreements, I should be subject to the same rights and benefits as before Brexit, both in Britain and the EU, but that does not seem to be the case. There are many more Latvian citizens living in the UK than UK citizens living in Latvia, but they continue to benefit under the pre-Brexit agreements, entitled to British health care, social benefits, working opportunities, access to legal and banking services as for their own citizens whereas I do not. It took over two years to able to open a bank account and I still cannot find a doctor. It might help if I was to marry a Latvian, buy a house or invest in a business but none of those will happen. I am into my third year here and in spite of Latvian friends here calling every single GP Practice on the Latvian national health service, no luck. They say they don't speak English so they won't be able to help. For the private sector, too, the door is closed. Despite being registered with the Latvian National Health System in principle, I can't access it at all.

I love my house and garden, Latvia's countryside, even the winters and especially the summers. As you see, I also have some special friends who really want to help me. But Latvia makes it so difficult and deservedly is described as the most unfriendly country of the EU. The latest kick is that however long a *foreigner* may have been in Latvia, even those with permanent resident visas, home owners or not, working or retired, no matter how much financially they might be contributing to society, they will now be required to leave the country immediately if they cannot speak Latvian or prove to be able to do so by producing some kind of certification.

Unless they happen to be over 75 years old or more.

THAILAND

Never having been to Thailand before, I think now would be a good time to go. I could explore at least part of the country and maybe take trips along the coastline, even venture into Cambodia. Given Bangkok's vibrant sexual reputation and red-light districts, I have always avoided the country, not wanting to be viewed as another tourist looking for a good time. Nor do I want to risk ending up with an expensive life partner many decades younger than me. The internet is awash with truly desperate stories of those who have succumbed in a fog of promiscuity and lust to find they are led along a well organised and merciless business preying on such tourists. Not to say that I won't also want to explore these areas, but as a voyeur, not a participant.

The real draw is the Asian lifestyle, the frenetic cities, the dramatic countryside and getting to know the people, smiling and friendly. Plus of course the climate and the unexpected adventures of travel. Every day doing what I like best, walking, exploring, savouring the smells, sights and sounds, watching people going to work or at work, sitting amongst them chatting and laughing, to return as dusk falls to the safety of my hotel. There I can relax in the coolness of the air conditioning, watch the news, enjoy some snacks, unwind with the occasional cigarette, musing on where I have been and the people that

I've met before deciding what to do the next day.

Planning

Firstly, the flights - when, how much and the special offers that change in the blink of an eye. If I mask my nationality or where I live, prices for flights and hotels are much cheaper. When I unmask to make the booking, prices jump by ten percent because I'm a westerner and have to pay a premium. Such is the market. Never mind, that's par for the course. Luckily at 77 I don't have to worry about dates too much - 'tomorrow' is always my preference.

Next, how to negotiate booking forms! Not helped that I am a British citizen living in Latvia. That seems to throw their systems into a whirl. Choose your language and up pops English. State your telephone number is generally followed by endless buffering before the system times out because it can't recognise my Latvian country code. Maybe it assumes I'm in the UK and only shows UK country codes. Hey ho, one manages, eventually. What extras do I want? VIP lounge? Choose a seat? Insurance? Car hire? Hotel booking? Taxis? A rub down with an oily rag? So many inherent traps to fleece you of your last penny. No extras.

Finally, it's done. I cross my fingers hoping that all is well before receiving endless confirmation emails including separate details for each leg of the journey and twenty-eight pages of terms and conditions.

Hotel requirements

Priorities, a 3-star hotel, not posh but neither too run-down. I don't smoke as much as I once did so, should I end up with a non-smoking room on the top floor without a balcony, it would not be a problem, as long as the lift works. Ha ha! Air conditioning and an en-suite where I can leisurely primp and preen myself; a view of the city; walking distance to bus stops and train stations; a fridge to store food bought from local shops as well as my own stock of beers, gin and tonics. Plus, of course, a television. Not so important is a bar or restaurant as I mostly cater for myself in my room, rarely eating out. Lastly, a semblance of security, preferably 24 hour reception, cctv and a good, solid room door.

Health Insurance

Previously, I've never bothered with any type of insurance, health or travel. Flight delays, cancellations, disruptions, lost luggage, getting dengi-dengi, malaria, yellow fever or being run over by a bus or bitten by a rabid dog, these were part of the adventure. However, with Covid 19 and all its variants, many countries are insisting on proof of insurance. Currently, Thailand is not requiring proof of insurance or Covid certificates for British citizens to enter the country, but the rules can change overnight without warning. Just a few days ago, it was announced that visitors from China and other Asian and African countries where there are increased infections must provide proof of cover. Given that, I do have all my covid certificates, four to date and, not to get caught out, health insurance for 60 days, the requirement being cover for the length of stay plus ten days.

Finding a health insurance provider to cover people beyond 75 years is almost impossible and then exorbitantly expensive, running into four figures. However, I found one in Thailand that would cover a 77 year old, so that is what I did. I was surprised that despite answering all the questions honestly and completely, the price was only £180, including Covid cover. All confirmed in further extensive email documentation adding to the growing file of paperwork, often needed instantly, for airline and immigration or anyone wanting a quiet read.

Packing

For my last holiday to Cyprus, I had to purchase a medium sized suitcase as I had only a small backpack with all my worldly possessions in when moving to Latvia, never anticipating that I would ever again have enough money to travel beyond Latvia's borders. Both are now packed full, almost all my clothes, mostly shorts and tee shirts, shoes and some formal wear along with my ever-growing collection of smelly bathroom things - aftershaves, soaps, deodorants, hair gel and other stuff I have never owned before. Wherever I book, I prepare to be, as far as possible, self-sufficient.

The hotel I am going to has some 250 rooms. It is a concrete tower block with a seating / cafeteria area at street level, a place to smoke and watch the world go by. It looks fine. However, it seems to have had access to balconies closed off. I have experienced this before. I suspect it's either because of concrete cancer or guests wanting to end it all.

Given the cheap price, one can expect that not so much is going to be provided in the way of guest comfort. No tea or coffee making supplies, limited linen changes and shabby decoration. So, it's important that, for a stay of a month in one place, I am as self-sufficient as possible. Included in my luggage therefore are: a heating element for teas and coffees, wooden knives and forks, paper plates, a sturdy mug, an air conditioning controller (truly), an extension lead, international power converters to charge my gadgets and a tea towel, everything necessary to make my stay comfortable. Whilst I am out on my jaunts, all these things are locked in my suitcase with a sturdy lockable strap, hopefully to avoid prying eyes or the light-fingered. I don't mean staff but, as often happens, dolly-with-trolley servicing will leave doors open as they flit around. Anything left in sight is temptation for other guests to whip in, out and away. Nor would I want to think that the maid has had a quick slug of my gin.

The rooms have no safes in which to store valuables or passport. Knowing how easy it is to get into most hotel room safes, I have an assortment of bags that can be worn beneath my clothes, hidden from sight. These allow me to travel as I do, looking every bit like a street dweller without attracting attention - other than for my gorgeous looks.

Location

There are plenty of fast easy transport options in Bangkok, my preferred being the metro blue line. It circumnavigates the city, lots of stops to explore at each station. No bargaining with tuk-tuks or taxis, although the taxi company Bolt operates there with a fixed price, which is perfect for exploring places far from the metro.

I chose my hotel by looking at clusters around metro stations until I found one that was close enough to a station, in this case a ten minute walk, on the periphery of the city centre, close to the main railway and bus station, too. It's still a busy location with local eateries and supermarkets and 7/11s. A short and quick way to get to the bright lights of the city centre safely, should I overstay my jaunt beyond dusk.

Outward

Just a couple of days to go now; all packed, documentation in order. Tomorrow, I will clean my home and leave it tidy and welcoming for my return. No harm in planning ahead. I will switch off the fridge freezer, unplug the TV and other gadgets but will leave the heating and water boiler on minimum as the temperatures next week are predicted to drop to minus 6. The only part I cannot prevent freezing is the loo pipe below the floor. I returned from my last trip to find that it had frozen solid. It took two weeks to thaw it out by boiling water on the log burner and pouring it down the loo a couple of times a day. Fortunately, it thawed enough to allow partial solids, if you get my drift, to be swept away, albeit with a lot of gurgling.

On arrival in Bangkok

My flight lands at a sensible hour, around 9 a.m. Plenty of time to get to my hotel for a 14.00 check in. I must be one of those unusual people who slowly I amble, watching all this activity, usually talking to others in the line, shuffling forward inch by inch. The immigration officials rarely smile or even acknowledge you as they fumble your passport and papers, only stopping to look you in the eye before looking down. Then comes the stamp and a nod and you carry on through. Last time, a few weeks ago at Riga, the official, in his 30s, I guessed, looked severely at my British passport and my Latvian ID for what seemed an age. Several times he looked me up and down, comparing my picture on both documents. It could be intimidating, but he was cute and I had to resist telling him so.

Once through immigration, on to the baggage carousel watching the scramble amongst those fighting to get their cases off first, being jostled by those insisting on getting their trolley to the front. Hopefully, it won't come through as it did the last time, with a big red 'Priority' label. Perhaps the baggage handler had a bad morning.

Through customs and out into a Bangkok airport melee, a sea of people holding up placards, taxi drivers, relations, tour groups, lovers and the tribes of those wanting to whisk you and your luggage to a taxi as you desperately but politely try to shrug them off. Once past this, it will become easier, taking in the sights and sounds of the airport at a slow pace to the metro station, stopping for a coffee and to rest on the way.

No need to stop to change money. I have already done so in Riga to avoid another long line of people. I purchase a ticket for the few stops where my line from the airport intersects the blue line but not before I buy my monthly pass; thirty euros. The blue line stop is nearest to my hotel. I emerge from the station, navigating my way slowly using mobile sat nav, at the same time memorising the locations I pass for the ten-minute walk. I intend to arrive unhurried, refreshed and casual.

Next report from Thailand, that's if I make it, of course.

Brian

BANGKOK

(https://m.facebook.com/story.php?story_fbid=1545038192641009&id=576872938)

It's me again. This is a special message to my special friends. I know, after yesterday, where I had a fabulous time, I might add, with my new-found friend. I will tell you more. First of all, I'm completely safe. As I was going out of my hotel, I met the hall porter, or the man who does all the ferrying about, looking after guests and their luggage. We chatted and he asked if I wanted a motor bike ride to the station. I told him I wasn't sure yet and was thinking about where to go. There was another man hanging around, well presented, called Sunam. The porter went off to do his job but he must have told Sunam who I was because he came over to me and asked me if I was on holiday and why I'd come to Thailand.

"Nothing in particular," I said. "I'm kind of freaky and like travelling. I like going into villages, meeting people and stuff like that."

He suggested a Buddhist monastery. I told him I wasn't religious, that I quite liked to look at these things from the outside. I don't need to go inside. I certainly don't need to pay exorbitant fees to go in and have people trying to sell me all kinds of trinkets and rubbish. I'm happy just to see them and move on. He suggested a safari park. That sounded interesting so he offered to take me there. I thought that was a jolly good idea and what a nice man. He asked when I'd like to go and I replied, "Well, now's a good time," and off we went!

It was about thirty miles away. He had his car over the road, a green one with official Thai writing on the side. I couldn't read any of it, of course, but I got in and we had a brilliant day! I wondered if he was he going to drop me off at the gate to the safari park then whizz off, which would be fine because I could find my way back, but he said he would come in with me and show me around.

"Well, that's marvellous," I said. "Obviously, I'll pay for you." Actually, the entry fees are quite expensive, but I'm not completely stupid and am always wary. He's a pleasant man and we got on well, chit chatting all the way, but I could not find out what his work was. I asked him what he did for a living and he replied, "Oh, we can go to the elephant enclosure or…" and other evasive answers.

"Right," I said, "You're not going to tell me what you do for a living, then?" and told him not to worry about it. He could tell me whatever he wanted, I wouldn't know if it was true. I'd believe anything so it was a bit pointless asking stuff like that. He avoided it completely. Anyway, that was okay.

When we arrived, he told me that the entry fee was about 1500 dollops (*Ed. Brian's expression for money*). Don't ask me how much that is in pounds or euros – maybe forty? Quite expensive. He told me to wait there while he went over to the counter, but I didn't because I wanted to see what he was doing. I like to see how it all works. He chatted with the woman behind the counter then told me it was indeed 1500 barth so I took out 3000 to pay for both of us. It's the holiday of a lifetime so I can't miss the opportunity. I've never been in a position to do these sorts of things before. He said, "No, you pay for yours, you don't need to pay for me." Bla bla bla. At the same time, he handed over an ID card and another card to the woman who was tapping away at the computer thingy. She said bla bla bla and he said bla bla bla and I got my change and I didn't have to pay for him. I thought, 'Hang on, you're not just a random stranger at the hotel, you're a tour guide, but do I care? No.' I was pleased about it in one way although it's hardly full of integrity. He could have said, 'I'll take you to the safari park and it will cost you this much and I'll show you all the way around because that's my job.' I'd have still agreed. It was just a subterfuge. But they all have a living to make, I know that. I enjoy having someone show me around even if it might be under false pretences. It means I'm safe. They're not going to let me go or lose me.

Anyway, we had a good day. We got to lunchtime and there was an hour's pause between shows. I went to the loo and Sunam said he'd wait for me, but when I came back, he was gone. I waited an hour and was getting ready to call a cab to take me thirty miles back to the hotel when he suddenly reappeared saying that he'd been sitting in the car! He asked me what I wanted to do the next day and suggested a boat ride and a restaurant and it all sounded fine so I agreed. At the end of the day, he'd bought me something to eat, which was the first proper meal I'd had since arriving, so I was a bit peckish. Well, there'd been all these extras to pay for during the day.

"Sunam," I said, "you need to tell me how much I owe you. You've been buying things and doing things and you've got a living to make."

"Oh," he replied, "I'll leave it to you."

"That's not right, is it," I said. "Alright, I'll give you twenty barth, which is five pence. How about that?"

He looked at me blankly, so I suggested fifty barth, a hundred, a thousand, ten thousand? I was making the point that he had to tell me, but he left it to me. I'd already seen the cost of these trips by looking online, but it's the process of making a booking, turning up somewhere at the right time, having the right paperwork etc. So, it worked in my favour on the basis that I already had an idea of the cost through travel agents of doing it properly. But this was a door- to-door personal service. There was another vehicle of the same description, all part of the same company, so I knew, aha, this is what they do, they hang around outside hotels and randomly suggest to guests places to go or ask if they can help. Now this is their business, which is fair enough, but I'm not that keen when they try to hide that fact. Anyway, that's the scenario. But's interesting to observe and see how the business works. I actually feel safe doing it like that rather than somebody randomly taking me around when I don't know what they are up to.

Sunam lives close to the hotel - I can see it from my window. He has chickens everywhere and cannabis growing all over the place. Well, it's legal in Thailand. They've completely decriminalized it, so I guess everyone's taking advantage. I found that out when I came back. I checked because I thought they might be using me as a drug mule! You know, taking me back to his place, asking if I could carry a few bags of cannabis back to the UK - No, I don't think so! They invite you to join in a smoke, but I say no. I'm strong on that. Maybe in the past, but I'm too old for that now. The cannabis might keel me over forever. Best not to risk it. Again, friendly, but a two-edged sword. He wants to do his job as a tour guide but he also has to look after his family. I know, because I've filmed them, his wife and children, his father, his brother and a friend from down the road. And he's the only bread winner. I understand that and I never try to short change them. I'm always generous to a fault. But there's a line to be drawn and that is when they think I'm being generous because I'm stupid. I've been around the block a bit.

I have friend in the Philippines. It's the same thing there. The whole village want me to go back as I could support whole families. It's not like they truly want to look after me. They just think, being old, I might expire quicker so they can get all my worldly wealth or live off my pension which, out there, would serve a whole family. I did consider this seriously a few years ago. I thought, well, if anything happened, I could go to the Philippines, but they don't want me, they want my pension. Isn't that awful! Anyway, I'm not that stupid.

Today's jaunt to the safari was absolutely marvellous. Sitting around the family, watching them with their chickens and preparing food. A friend down the road arrived bringing strange tubes with smoke billowing out of them, then he was crunching and grinding and rolling cigarettes. They're only around the corner so I'd be quite happy to pop around and have a beer with them.

Now I'm telling this to my special friends – well, I don't know how many, you're all special. You all worry a bit about what I get up to, but please don't because I do know what I'm doing. Although I'm rather stupid and happy-go-lucky, I have radars at the back of my head to know where I'm going. There comes a point, if I think someone is taking advantage of my good nature, then I'm quite happy to cut them dead. Gone, without any thoughts. That makes me a bit of a psychopath, I guess (*this in jest, trust me – Ed.*).

Tomorrow I'm going on a road trip again… oh, one other thing, I went yesterday to the gay quarter in Bangkok. It was lunch time, so nothing happening, just business people doing their thing. Good to say that I've been there. I'd like to go back at night, although I don't normally do that, certainly not on my own. But Sunam, I could happily ask him to take me there and he'd agree, for a fee, then I would be quite happy to go. I'd have a Thai person with me to make sure I'm not ripped off, robbed or have people approaching me for services that I don't want. That could be good. I'll play it by ear.

Well, I'd better go now. I've got to go to bed. Bye. Have a lovely time. I miss all of you, as it happens. By the way, Sunam asked me, "Have you got a wife?" No. "Have you got children?" No. "Have you got any family?" No. "Are you all on your own?" I said, yes, absolutely. I felt a bit guilty about that because I'm not on my own; I've got three people in Latvia that I feel are family. Anyway, love to you all. I'd better stop now otherwise I'll go on all night and there'll be people knocking on the walls saying, "Will you stop jabbering!"

Bye bye!

Yesterday was supposed to be my day off, resting, the only plan to go for my suit fitting in the evening. Except. However tired I might have been the night before, I still awoke early and wanted to be out exploring again. So, it was off on to the metro, alighting at a random station, this time to emerge at a flower market. Plus, a few hundred metres to a ferry pier where I decided to take a two-hour trip along the river to see the floating markets, feed the fish and do other tourist delights, as you may have seen on my videos. Just myself and one other family, the whole long boat to ourselves.

So many tourist boats on the waterways with so few tourists. However, the tranquillity, if you can ignore the sound of the engine, was so relaxing. There was a wonderful cooling breeze as the boat chugged its way past houses and once vibrant communities, many now falling into the river, dilapidated and abandoned. An eerie sight, but fascinating.

At the conclusion of my trip, I jumped aboard a normal passenger ferry and with the aid of google maps, found the closest pier to where I was supposed to be for my suit fitting. Thirty minutes later I got off, surprised that it was exactly the location I wanted to be; no walking. Sounds easy, but with many different boat companies - tourist, passenger and even hotel boats - boarding the right one is an art. They stop for a brief time, ten seconds at most, allowing passengers to alight and reboard. There's a frenzied surge in all directions whilst a man, hanging on to the mooring rope, blasts out instructions then blows a whistle and off we go again at break-neck speed.

It's rush hour. The boats fill to maximum, people sitting and standing like sardines. The noise of the engine, a woman rattling her money box, yelling at the top of her voice for people to pay, the inaudible announcements - you have to count or know the stops so you're ready to alight, working your way through to the stern to jump off.

I see a fabulously swanky hotel, reaching for the sky. An hour to spend walking around the designer jewellery, art and fashion shops. There no prices shown anywhere at all, definitely not for the crass plebs such as I. A Pepsi and a cigarette outside and time for my fitting.

Now in the shop with Sundram, Aman and yet another affable older brother, all assisting me to try everything on, pinning on the sleeves, measurements retaken for final instructions to the seamstresses. Time passes and I am off again with Aman for another trip by motorcycle to see Bangkok by night and some more shops of course. This time he is not working but browsing himself. We look at clothes, shoes, wallets and the like. He has expensive tastes. He sees a microwave.

"For my mother in India," he says. "You buy for me?" he asks with a smile.

"Only if you buy me that eighty-inch TV first," I reply.

No joy there, so we are soon back on the streets again.

Whilst we are dashing through the traffic of Chinatown, he asks me,

"Would you like a massage? A nice young girl?"

No and no, but I say that it's now 8.30 p.m. so he should drop me off at the metro for my journey back to the hotel. He decides on the way to go through a gloomy area to small park/open space nestled under and between fast roads, empty of people save for a man at an entrance counter collecting motorcycle parking charges. We sit in a shadowy place opposite, underneath a string of dim bulbs. He says that you can come here and see people kissing sometimes. "Well, where are they?" I ask with a laugh.

A chance for a couple of selfies on his phone and it's off to the metro. We wave goodbye, but not before I pay him for his time. He implores me not to tell his brother about the payment, should I be asked, but I cannot agree to this. They are supposed to be sharing my largess. I walk the last part of my journey. The cafe opposite is closed so it's into a 7/11 for some snacks before bed.

PATTAYA

Massage parlours and toyboys, German concert pianists and Polish furniture manufacturers - my second day in Pattaya.

Nine in the morning and I took my first motorbike taxi ride into the city centre, just for the fun of it. Too early for the shopping mall to be open so a walk around another covered market, stopping for a crushed ice melon drink to cool me down. The motorbike ride was rather scary, racing away at full throttle for a few seconds and then throttling back fully, only to open it at full speed again, like a learner driver doing kangaroo starts, all accompanied by worrying rattles. I was relieved to get back to my hotel. I've also had enough of markets so no more of them for a while.

In the hotel lobby, a frail old man with a white striped walking stick was sitting alone, watching people come and go. I'd seen him there before and stopped to talk to him. He told me that he had tunnel vision in one eye and could see little from the other. He'd been diagnosed with senile dementia and suffered with gastric reflux. After eight years coming to the hotel, this would most likely be the last time. He is 76 but looks 96. So sad. He is German and was a concert pianist playing for the Berlin Philharmonic. Fortunately, he has a friend coming to see him next Monday who lives here.

He asked my advice regarding his gastrointestinal problems whilst clutching a half white sliced loaf of bread. He said that was all he ate during the day. I told him that was not a good idea. If he insists on eating just bread, change to wholegrain. An hour later, he follows me into the restaurant next door. They knew him well as he always ate there over the years. Standing by my seat, he asks the waitress if she could exchange his half loaf of white sliced bread for brown bread, looking to me for support. She heads to the kitchen, returning with brown bread in a bag and he leaves happy. The waitress was so kind and sympathetic.

Following my almost all-day breakfast, around two in the afternoon, I decided to perambulate the area, eventually coming across the gay streets that I missed yesterday. Empty, save for staff setting up tables for the evening. I saunter past a massage parlour with around six or more beautiful young men sitting outside, all inviting me for a massage. These places are everywhere, quite professional looking, offering to massage back, feet, shoulders and other parts of the anatomy. As it happens, after all my walking, my feet were sore, and my left shoulder was still painful from an incident in Cyprus, dragging luggage from under a bus. Another story. The shop looking clean, I acquiesced, maybe influenced by the gorgeous young male masseuses. Another first for me. Two hours of feet and shoulders massaged with Tiger Balm. It was glorious! Air conditioning, piano music gently playing in the background - and it appears to have made a great difference, especially to my shoulder. All the time, those young men sitting outside popping in to talk and take pictures with me. I promised that I would return, and I will.

Around eight in the evening, I plucked up courage to revisit Walking Street. It was still quiet but nevertheless vibrant and lively enough to get a feel for what it would be like later. I say hello to a middle-aged man sitting alone with a beer. He invites me to join him for a chat. He is a Polish furniture manufacturer taking a couple of weeks break from the wife and daughter; apparently, they do not get on too well. A pleasant chat. Half an hour later we say goodbye and go our separate ways.

Almost at the end of the street, I passed a young man who asked if I would sit and have a drink with him. It turned out not that he was 39 but looked half his age. To me, he was good looking, not a prima donna or fashion queen, polite, no touchy feely, no suggestive innuendo. His smile was great and he appeared genuine. “No, thank you, young man, but I appreciate the offer,” and I strolled slowly on to stand against the road closure railing for a cigarette. I mused to myself that if I were to fully experience this adventure, then I should be brave enough to at least have a drink with him and talk. I knew that I would be buying a brief friendship, maybe half an hour, but a few moments of pretend love without physical contact?

Finishing my cigarette, I saunter back, which I would have had to do anyway. There he is, looking up at me, smiling.

"I've decided," I said, "that I need to sit down and rest for a while. I will be happy to buy you one of your expensive drinks."

The usual arrangement at these places is that you order your drink and the same for your companion, except that his is twice or three times the cost of yours. The bar sells more expensive drinks and the young man gets commission. He's happy of course. I make it clear immediately that I don't want sex, just a friendly chat over a drink and that is just what we did. He had a good sense of humour and we laughed a lot. I relented and bought him another expensive non-alcoholic beer. He asked if I had eaten. I had, but I would happily buy him something to eat. "Oh, yes please. It's my break now," at which, we headed off.

I had already eaten twice, but I still couldn't let him eat on his own, telling him that I have to return to my hotel. He offers to walk me back - he knows the hotel, of course. We arrive and he asks to use my toilet. No problem. I open the curtains and balcony doors for my own security.

"You come to the bar tomorrow?" he asks.

"No. I've seen the street and have no wish to see it again. It's too expensive for me to drink there."

He is disappointed. He tells me that on the sixth of this month, in just a few days, it's some religious festival. The bar will be closed. He asks if he could come and see me. We could spend some time together as friends. Well, that I could not refuse. He has to return to work now, so we part with a warm hug. I kiss his neck and he kisses me on the lips.

This is the continuing story of Brian's slide into into rampant debauchery, purely for research of course. Not for the faint hearted, a genuine exposure of my thoughts, feelings and motivations, spurred on by B…, my friend in Latvia, who commented, after my last missive, that I deserved to enjoy life. I intend to do just that before I slip into senility. As always, I have no secrets and I continue to be just me. I hope that I am pure of heart and deed. Until now, that is.

So many fears of men lumbering over me, terrible memories from childhood. I cannot and will not reveal all that happened to make me feel this way. Yet I still have a predilection for strong men to hold me and keep me safe. Sandy is strong but gentle. I can't move without him being there, taking my shoes off, putting them on, finding me cushions, helping me up and down the steps with constant hugs and kisses, even following me closely to the toilets and standing outside waiting.

I've had an incredibly busy few days and have made new decisions. My plans to go to the elephant sanctuary and various other places went awry as my guide was too busy and did not tell me. I waited a long time for him to contact me but he let me down. The only free time he had was two days before I'm supposed to leave for Latvia, and one of those would be taken up in his office, seeing what trips I wanted! That wasn't helpful. Anyway, that's by the by.

I've decided to go to Laos with Sandy, and that's what I'm going to do, tomorrow. We're going to stay there for a few days. His family are desperate to meet me, and he's excited about it. As for the bar where he works, I would like to get him away from it completely. My God, it's incredible what goes on there! For someone who people watches, like me, to see what they are getting up to with all the different characters, it's a book on its own. You know, how the whole thing works and who gets the money and so on.

I will get a month's visa as a tourist, returning to Bangkok after a month, then home to Riga. Maybe. I'm not sure. Anyway, I'm going to make sure that everything is covered there, and everyone is happy, that I pay my dues and all that sort of thing. So do not worry. Sandy and I get on beautifully. He is the only one I sat and talked with and bought drinks for. He didn't make any untoward moves, he wasn't inappropriate in any way, and I told him, and he respected it, that I don't do sex, and it was fine. We had a marvellous time, talking and laughing. Occasionally, boys came along and I bought them drinks because I feel sorry for them. It's a desperate situation.

What happened is that Sandy said he wanted to visit his parents in Laos at some time, maybe the beginning of next month, and he said it would have been great if I could have gone with him and he could have introduced me to his family and all this sort of thing, so I said to him last night, 'We'll go tomorrow, then!'

He couldn't believe it. So that's what we're doing. I already had a taxi booked that was going to take me to the airport on Friday, so I just rebooked it for tomorrow.

We went to his room to sort out luggage. The room is incredibly small. It's got a mattress on the floor and just one wooden box that represents furniture, like a dressing table, and a dressing rail. Nothing else. When you go to the building, you go through an entrance into a dark, damp corridor, stone walls in between drains. Going backwards and forwards you've got to be careful where you walk. There are all these rough old doors with padlocks on. And the room itself is absolutely appalling. As for heat, all it has is a big fan on the floor. You really want to save them and take them away from all that.

We leave in the morning. What transpires, we will have to wait and see. Sandy's parents are coming to meet us at the airport along with his brother, his cousins and his friends. They all speak English and some are married to Westeners. Some are teachers in Laos. They all want to meet me. We spent the afternoon talking on the phone. The plan is a bit fluid, and until I'm there, I won't be able to decide what I want to do, but it seems a shame not to take the opportunity as I'm so far into Asia already. I've been to Vietnam and the Philippines, and now Thailand, so it seems a shame not to visit Laos, perhaps have a splash about in the Mekong River.

His parent's house looks presentable. Typical wooden building with chickens and other animals roaming about. On the river itself they've got canoes and boats of all kinds, so quite excited to see all that. As for my hotel here, I've asked them to keep the room a few days just in case there are hold ups or problems. You can see the balcony and Walking Street, which is just around the corner. My god, it's a hotbed of vice and all kinds of fierce things. It's not my scene and I would not voluntarily come back to see it again. And Pattaya, without anyone to show you other places, is tacky. I would like to take Sandy away from all that if I can. Anyway, I will stop now, so from me, Brian, in the backstreets of Pattaya, goodbye. I will keep up with you again in the fullness of time. Bye bye everyone. Oh, doo-de-do…

BACK TO BANGKOK

A few days later, Bangkok again. Ah, good day everyone. Well, here I am at the departures area of Vientiane International Airport. This morning I was driven on a motorbike to Vientiane, not far away, on a motorbike, and I booked a flight back to Bangkok. Sandy is inside. He's ordering something to drink, something to eat and so on. In about half an hour, my flight will be available for checking in. In a moment, I will say goodbye to Sandy and to Ventiane. The reason is that I am going back to Bangkok to catch my original flight to Riga, as planned. I will then decide what happens next. I've got a month's travel visa booked so I could apply for a one year's visa and return to Laos. I need to learn whether Sandy is up to that. Although he says it's a great idea, I have yet to ascertain amongst all his dreams, what it is that he wants. I need to be careful, and although you think I'm reckless, and I suppose I am in a way - I was hoping to save him from a life of selling his body in those bars, which I hate. Sandy has been there seven or eight years, so even if I decide not to come back, at least I've done the right thing by him, bringing him home to his family – and buying him a motorbike. That was a way of saying that I appreciate everything, that I like him – well, love him really - but I have to be cautious because it's my future and my money at stake, and while I appear to be a reckless, I'm not. By flying back, it will not only give me a chance to test his resolve and integrity, but also to make a decision for myself.

Yesterday, we went to a Buddhist Temple. Sandy said his prayers and the motorbike, my gift to him, was covered in religious rope or string that went from outside to where the priest was seated inside so he could bless it. Sandy spent about half an hour in front of the Buddhist priest, in prayer, then came out with what looked like a colostomy bag – it wasn't, of course, it was just water. When we got back to the hotel, he sprinkled water all over the bike to bless it again. The priest had done the same thing to a car, sprinkling water all over it while the headlights were flashing and the indicators going. Everyone was happy.

I continue my adventure now. In about twenty-four hours' time I will be boarding my flight back to Riga, via Stockholm. Overall, Bangkok has been fantastic. Just so much to see and so much to do. Now I've given myself an opportunity to think about things. I loved Laos. Just the sort of scene that I like. It's about ten years behind Bangkok. I did some videos yesterday and in one of them I was dancing. No, I wasn't on drugs. It's just so great, I enjoyed every minute of it. It really has been the holiday of a lifetime. It's been so much fun, so many dangers, so many risky things, and at the same time, I've tried to help. I can't pass a beggar without giving them money. And to try and help people like Sandy to change their lives, a naive thing to do! As if. But I made the attempt, and I'm pleased at that. And I'm pleased to be coming back to Latvia still innocent for the most part and unsullied, for the most part. But certainly, I haven't shamed myself, apart from the dancing, and my private parts remain unmolested. And I've not molested other people's private parts either. What I do next, I shall decide in the next week.

My email to the hotel in Laos where I stayed:

Good day to you sir.
For reasons that I will not divulge here, I have checked out early.

Sandy was my guest and he will also be required to check out immediately.

All my luggage if Sandy does not take it, you can dispose of at your leisure.

Should you allow him to stay longer, that is your decision.

Please be advised that I will not be responsible for any charges that he incurs should you allow him to stay beyond today.

He has funds to pay the laundry charges, I suggest you hold any luggage until he does so.

Thank you for your kindness and good will shown to us, you have a truly magnificent establishment and I would be happy to recommend it to anyone.

I do not seek a refund for the following three weeks but hope that you can at least benefit by re-letting the room.

Kind regards

Brian C...

EMAIL TO LADAVANH

My dear Ladavanh,

Firstly, I have to say that I was and still am in love with Sandy. He is such fun to be with and I would wish for nothing more than to be with Sandy forever. However, I will now be brutally honest with you both about my concerns. I was prepared to embark on a life changing adventure which would involve finding accommodation for us, a long-term visa in the weeks ahead and a bank to finance some form of business. We could have worked together and lived together. The only criteria, that we could happily enjoy each day in our own home. Sadly, whilst posing these questions to Sandy, they brought little response.

One idea was to live along the Mekong River with a small holding breeding chickens and the like, a good idea I thought. However, Sandy said he would like to build apartments to rent out, but he had no idea where or how. I am not rich, just a single building would use up all my capital. My intention was to live comfortably for as long as possible.

Now for the more personal stuff, very personal as it happens. Sandy is loving and caring, says all the right things, talks about love, fabulous, but not about what we are going to do to formulate a plan for life. And time is short. Sandy, without asking me, used my mobile to invite himself as a friend. My trusted friends could then see Sandy's profile and some of his clients with pictures of them together. I was bombarded with warnings of this being a well organised scam, reeling foolish old men into disaster. I would be stripped of money and left stranded and penniless in a foreign country. Sandy went to great pains to assure me how honest and open he was. However, a pair of sunglasses I had given him were mentioned the next evening by Peter, Sandy's most ardent client, who told me he had given

Sandy 350 dollars to buy them as a gift. As much as I found this amusing, and served Peter right, I was disappointed that Sandy could lie and take money in this way. The problem is one of integrity and honesty. Sandy without fail will say he has no money for food or to do anything, constantly asking for more. He has already told me that he had managed to save enough to visit his family in Laos for the festival next month on the 10th and wanted me to visit at the same time and meet the family. When I said that we could go next day and that I would pay all expenses, he was delighted and thankful.

I knew Sandy had at least 350 dollars from Peter who regularly bought him gifts and would probably continue to do so. Sandy also had the money he'd saved for his trip home next month. When I told him that I had to go back to Latvia to for a while, Sandy again wanted more money. "How am I going to eat? How can I buy fuel for the motorbike?" This question has been asked and asked again, even whilst waving me goodbye at the airport, "I still need some money from you."

At the monastery, when the motorbike was blessed, Sandy took money for the flowers, candles, robes and donations from my own wallet. I saw him do it. Not much maybe, but I was disappointed as he did not ask before nor tell me after. My belief that he would never lie and is as honest as the day is long was seriously challenged. But I was, and still am, besotted by him, hence my taking time to be open and honest with you. He is, as you must know, HIV positive, but I was so fond of him, it would not have mattered to me. He even preferred to sleep alone and would keep his distance. I suspected that he did not enjoy intimacy. This did not fill me with confidence.

That is a snapshot of my feelings. I wanted to show Sandy respect and love, to take him away from the sordid environment he is in, but this is not possible, for all kinds of reasons. I, too, am sad, but realistic. I am an old, lonely man searching for his dream, but with integrity.

I hope you now understand my reasons for leaving.

Brian

HAPPILY BACK HOME IN RIGA

Following my long, tortuous, thirty-six hour journey from Vientiane, Laos, via Bangkok and Helsinki, it was a great relief to be back in Riga. Three days later, having fully recovered from that journey, I appreciate my home, even more so as the landlady had put my heaters on and lit the log burner for my return. With nothing to un-pack, as I had left everything behind in Vientiane, in an hour or two I had switched my sim card, carefully hidden in a dark corner of my wallet, and was back on-line. The first task that evening was to block my

Facebook and Messenger account. I did not want any further contact with the numerous people that I'd met, and was unlikely to ever meet again, especially Sandy. I do not want to be harassed to return post haste into his arms, stretched out in love for me and my wallet.

A friend of his did manage to send me an email. I was not aware anyone had my email address, but Sandy must have made a note of it from the hotel booking form in Laos. It was a heart tugging missive to say Sandy was crying in his room all the time, was not eating and felt distraught that I had left him. I replied to this email in depth and honestly, recorded above in another of my missives. I then blocked that avenue to further communication, ensuring that I could not be persuaded to do anything foolish.

So nice to be back in familiar surroundings - the log burner, my lounge, garden and close friends, few but so important to me. Now more than ever I appreciate where I am, in spite of the cold weather and the awful Latvian administration services.

Time to open all my posts after more than five weeks away. Two letters from the UK government, one to tell me my pension was increasing from next month and another to tell me they owe me £1200 from overcharging me with all the letters and demands over the past two years. Wow, that is, good news!

My landlady told me about a gay bar that has just opened in Riga so I shall make time to visit it, perhaps one evening this week. It may not be as vibrant as some of the bars I have been in recently but closer than Asia! Looking forward to that, always in the hope of being able to talk to other gay people. After two and a half years here in Riga, I know no other gay people. 'So what?', you might ask. If you're not looking for sex, what's the difference whether they're gay or not? In reply, there is so much banter you can have with another gay person without offending anyone, which is easy for me at the best of times. Even being in a gay friendly environment and observing others feels good, whether I talk to anyone or not.

My friend B... asked me if I had spent too much and did I have any money left. As it happens, I budgeted for my 'holiday of a lifetime' and stayed more or less within that, no fancy hotels, most of my sightseeing on foot or public transport, no fancy restaurants dining out and, prior to Pattaya, no drinking in bars. My excesses in Pattaya's bars, paying for my extremely short-term love affair (including a motorcycle), giving money to beggars, hotels, travel, all remained in budget and worth every penny. I was pleased to tell B... that I still had many holidays left in me. Other adventures await soon.

Despite Latvia warming up, I need to plan some insulation of my home in readiness for next winter. For now, it's off to the charity shops to replace the clothing I left behind in Vientiane, and to check my mobility chair for future forays into Riga.

I had a lucky escape from being beguiled into possible disastrous scenarios, but thanks to my friends and their advice, which I listened to, even if I did not appear to, I made the right decision returning to Riga. Holidays, wherever they may take me, and whatever temptations befall me, I must remember this last trip and restrict my largess to a gin and tonic.

Good to be back home!

MORE FROM RIGA

To my friends.

Like me, I guess your minds are swimming and all consumed with the current crisis. As some sort of diversion for me, and I hope you, I will talk about what I do to de-stress and enter my own dreams to blot out everything, for a while.

Today is beautifully sunny, almost warm. It was a dilemma whether to light the log burner or not, but I did, and now the room is a little too warm. Still, I refuse to open the window and let the heat escape. Today, I must rake the lawn, which is a daunting task. Whilst my landlady and her mother would do it, I feel it is a way of helping them and showing my love of what is a huge garden. After a year and a half here, I seem now, in their absence, to be responsible for cutting the grass, caring for the allotment and watering the flowers.

With no skills or tools, I maintain, in the most rudimentary way the fences and gates, proud of my paltry efforts nevertheless. Just pleased I do not have to dig a path out through the snow to go shopping anymore now.

Longingly I look at the pub bench set in the middle of the lawn, given to me by B..., sadly only twice to be used by visitors as yet, each time the visitors got totally inebriated.

Luckily for me, I don't have to work. My basic state pension is enough to keep me warm and fed. Every other day I cook with a crockpot, thirty or more years old, given to me by my friend A…, filled to the brim with vegetables and diced meat. The other days, it's crinkle cut chips and pork chops, my favourite. I buy a large lump of pork that will just fit into my small freezer along with bags of chips. The pork, I slice and dice. A repetitive diet, but a cheap and filling one.

Mostly, settling down in my armchair, watching the news, smoking, maybe the odd can of beer. This gives me a warm, secure and comfortable feeling of decadence, forgetting what is happening out-side of my boundary fence. In the evening, a couple of friends will, as one would say, 'for his daily dose of Brian', call me on a Facebook video call where I can talk my drivel, sharing laughter and ridiculousness, interrupted only by Doris the microwave, Henry the beer shelf or Charlie the stable boy (a bucket) in charge of briquettes. Maybe I am too polite. I always ask by name for whatever I want and thank them profusely, then back to the chat. One of my friends did ask, amused, why I talked to the toilet or the sink whenever I used their loo! The joy of being barmy. Everyone should try it! Sometimes, or in my case always, it is therapeutic to talk to people without an agenda, the only rules being, not to denigrate anyone else, not to get angry but laugh a lot and explore experiences.

One of the benefits of not going out during winter, other than a monthly shopping trip, is that I am confined to my beautifully warm kitchen. As with many old people, I wear a tee shirt and shorts all the time, which means my washing machine is only used once a month, saving on electricity and water. Pretty disgusting, I hear you mumbling, but my general aroma is that of roses and daffodils.

I am usually completely hidden from the world, except for my landlady and her mother who, on seeing me brave the minus temperatures to get some briquettes from the shed, will phone or message me to insist I put a coat and scarf on. She is not impressed when I tell her that I am superman and continues to give me a stern talking to.

I am eagerly looking forward to the summer sun, exploring in my electric chair more secret paths that few foreigners know exist. Despite the slippery slopes and steep embankments, I charge through bushes, wooded glades, along streams, working out where and how to cross the railway lines as the workers wave - so friendly. First, I have to super-glue a lump of plastic back onto the front mudguard that shattered in my crash negotiating at speed the barriers in the snow at a level crossing. The ignominy of using it with a chunk missing! Oh, my pride and joy! Too much to bear.

Time for a beer and another briquette for the log burner. Bye bye for now, assuming anyone is still reading…

SUDDENLY, I BURST INTO LIFE AGAIN!

I know that I have been silent here for a while.

Since returning from my holiday of a lifetime and all those new experiences, I have felt a tad lonely and decided that I should, for the first time, embark on trying a couple of dating sites to look for a permanent man. It was with absolutely no expectations at my age, but fun to explore. That was three days ago. I have now filled out the following profile:

Old, fit, erratic, crazy, self-sufficient, shy, funny, a tad lonely missing the love. Loves to travel, loves talking and talking and talking, with lots hugs and cuddles too. Needs a lover/carer, younger, fit and equally funny, full time to share the life with. Not looking for casual sex, a toy boy or a prima donor, fortune hunter or just plain lazy for an easy life. Just needs a truly caring and sharing partner to mutually care for and hugs and cuddles of course. As a lifelong gay, have never been drawn to bi-sexual partners, after all, it's twice the competition. Not interested in relocating to Asia or where the supposed action and lovers are. Europe is fine and even better someone from Latvia or the UK. Bit of a long shot I know and don't really have any expectations of finding anyone. However, if you have read this far, thank you and I hope that you find your own special dream one day too.

My age and wants, as well as what I did not want, followed. A picture uploaded and off it all went, expecting to hear nothing. As profile details go, mine did stand out for being longer than most and without any sexual content or innuendo. Astonishingly, within an hour, the first reply arrived, from a young man, swearing undying love and care for me in my old age. He just needed a couple of thousand dollars to get him out of a financial jam and he would be on his way:

The Reply:

Hi, I am a genuine guy, and I understand what you're saying. If you're interested in companionship in return or helping me financially insane by being like my sugar daddy, I'd be more than happy to support you regarding what you are saying. We can move forward by doing many enjoyable things at whatever you suggest. I'm a caring honest and truthful person and would be interested in being by your side if you was willing to help me in financial situation.

My reply:

Hello C..., I appreciate your directness, I was looking for a life partner to share the life and fun with. Not sure what your expectations are regarding a sugar daddy. Certainly, I would need to know much more about you to consider that. I would have proffered a life partner but would not expect to be pushing you out of the door to go to work. I have to go for a while, you can get back to me however.

A reply to my reply:

I appreciate you coming back to me and sorting things out due to my ex taking me for £120,000 and leaving me pop broke is something seriously not helping me moving forward wear I got myself into some trading that I need to pay off a tax bill that £2,300 to a crypto I understand the directness of of coming forward and what have you but I'll be more than happy to be life partner and go from there and do whatever you so wish he was to help me on a financial level and go from there but obviously me going out to work in the other reason why I do what I do because of me being disabled and I used to do this is the job and all I haven't been used to is just doing escorting and being in business for number years so so you're more than welcome 2 to speak with me in Great lengths but I would be immensely grateful if you can help me on this financial situation that I need to become to try and sort it out which is £2,237.77 and then I will be able to sleep better at night which I'm struggling with at the minute. What do you think to what I said and would you be willing to help me in this regard.

My reply to his reply to my reply:

Wow, that is just such a mess you are in and far beyond my resources. I liked your profile and thank you for being so honest, but really it really is too far for me to consider. I do wish you luck in putting your life together again. A number of questions spring to mind and I will ask but you do not have to answer if they are uncomfortable for you. What is your disability? Are you in your own home? Are you working? Are you mobile with a vehicle? Are you claiming benefits? Can your family not help with your financial situation? What are your long-term goals and aspirations for the future?

His reply to… etc.

What my disability is rheumatology arthritis, and since the issue of my ex's done giving me nothing, burst a cyst in the brain and leaving me now in a situation where I'm trying to better myself moving forward. All I do is hit a brick wall and then Bouncing Back.

Next was a student nurse, along with photos from Dublin. Then a young Russian man, wanting me to help him escape Russia from persecution for being gay. He did look gorgeous and would also look after me forever.

I decided to up the age range I was seeking, mainly to stop all these obvious fortune hunters. That would slow them down, I thought. But no! An avalanche of older guys arrived from Germany, Hungary, Spain, Canada, America and of course the UK including Devon, Shropshire, Lincolnshire, Derbyshire, Kensington and more. I had five hundred likes with dozens of direct messages to read, and I replied to all of them, kindly, despite what some of them wanted to do to me. I was flabbergasted.

I had pointed out that I smoke, but most of those who didn't smoke said that it was no problem, one even suggesting that I would look sexier with a pipe. I had to point out to all of them that sex was not my main motivation and advised them to re-read my profile in case they were responding to the wrong person. Whilst thanking them for their interest, I would pose a barrage of questions to gauge how genuine they might be. I was able to dismiss 95% immediately. A few, I am still in dialogue with. My personal security being a concern, I set up an email address specifically for this, plus some security features. My true identity should remain hidden.

It was, and still is, fun to do, and perhaps a knight in shining armour may come along. For now, I am enjoying all the attention and looking at some of the personal videos they put up. Whilst writing this post, another ten messages have appeared, so I must go. People are wanting my body.

CHILDHOOD MEMORIES

People sometimes ask, are you really gay? I am. I may not indulge as many do, but yes, I am really, truly gay. They ask if I am healthy. My health is fine for my age. I still walk and talk, travel and care for myself, and I am active. My few friends here in Riga know how isolated and lonely I am, hardly helped by not speaking Latvian, which is why they check up on me if they don't hear for a while.

I have gay dreams - a strong man, a loving man, someone to cuddle up to, warmth and hugs - but forget the rest. This is the most I have ever revealed. It doesn't matter too much any longer, not at the end of my life. And there is so much more that even now I cannot speak about easily, or at all.

As I grew up, I would fall in love with other boys and young men. Some would pull me onto them in play fights. I knew what they wanted but was too scared of being hurt physically. Those moments were pure lust, but for me felt threatening. I would fight free when anyone wanted to show me their private parts. Just to look at them terrified me. It was a time when one could never reveal secret thoughts or strange sexual encounters to anyone. The guilt was overwhelming. Many times, I would lay in bed, trying to hold my breath, hoping to die.

I have never accepted gifts. They make me feel indebted, almost like a bribe, and I do not trust people. Times have changed, but I still feel the effects of what happened to me in my childhood. I was pulled in the nick of time from a man bundling me into a van at the age of four. Almost every week, for four years from the age of seven, a neighbour took me to the toilets in a park, forced me to sit on his lap, tied me up and fondled me. I would have to do other things he asked me to do, then I'd get ten shillings. I hated it. Yet each year, he remembered my birthday, which no one else did, even in my family. He would ask to see my school reports and reward me similarly with another ten shillings. So, interspersed with acts of kindness were acts of evil monsters.

In later years, I would give advice to groups of teenagers about staying safe. I'd suggest never going home to someone else's house without telling a friend or parents, not accepting more than one drink and most importantly being able to run fast. All else failing, I taught a few self-defence moves. Even at my age, I feel competent defending myself.

Going to a cinema, especially on Waterloo and Victoria railway stations, was risky. There were many men looking to take advantage of children. Twice I remember being saved by adults sitting nearby realising what was happening. I blamed myself and still do, because I did not run fast enough, and even enjoyed the attention. It was nice to receive gifts just for being cuddled. Perhaps it was my cheerful and trusting disposition that attracted these people. I thought that that was what love was. I was happy to sit on their laps, enjoying the caresses. You see, home was violent in the extreme with knives, guns and police, all part of the mix. So, love, which is how I thought of it, was comforting.

There were genuine, caring people that wanted me to keep them company, listening to their stories, sharing laughter and no more. I remember once, an old man sitting late at night in his roadside tent, guarding the materials for digging the road works in St Johns Wood, London. It was a green tent lit by red lamps, by his side a hot brazier with the kettle boiling on top. I stopped to warm my hands. He offered me tea and an up-turned bucket to sit on and we talked for an hour or two before I began my walk back home in the early hours of the morning.

As a teenager, after finishing work at an off licence around 10.30 at night, I would go to an almost derelict shop in a back street where the tenant, a Canadian ex-soldier, who had been there since the end of World War Two, lived in absolute squalor. The shop window was stacked high with old televisions and other rubbish, obscuring all daylight. He had neither carpets nor furniture, save for his ancient rocking chair. He always wore the exact same clothes, never changing, never washing. He did not have a bath nor any cleaning facilities other than an old sink and cold tap. He had no official papers and subsisted by purchasing hundreds of defunct television sets, ex-rentals that could not be repaired. For years, I would help him until two in the morning, breaking them down, salvaging every part - screws, valves, aluminium chassis and so on. He would then sell these for scrap at street markets and finally burn the cases in an open fire at the back room. They would lie half in, half out of the fireplace and we would kick the wood into the flames, piece by piece. The smoke in the room was horrendous. Using that, and the gloomy light from a 25 watt bulb, he made coffee in a black, battered pot loaded with coffee and salt. Yuk! It was vile. I never got paid but I would accompany him to the scrap yards to sell his scrap and a treat for a fry-up in a café. His van was equally ancient, not an undamaged panel, several paint jobs over the years and bald tyres. The engine always needed coaxing and there was much bad language before it would start. No road tax or insurance of course.

Sometimes, I would come across televisions and radios that I could get going again and took them home. I loved playing with electrical goods. I kept many of them in the bedroom which I shared with my father who would not sleep with my mother because he had emphysema and was often unable to breath. I tied a cylinder vacuum cleaner to the top of an open window, the hose reversed, which I used to force air into my father's mouth when he thought he was dying. It was surprisingly successful.

I'd installed a fuse-box, extension leads and breakers and always had at least four televisions and a couple of radios that I'd be working on. If I was able to fix them, I would give them away to anyone that did not have one. Whilst I was breaking them down in the Canadian's back room, he would be rocking away in his chair singing old cowboy songs.

He was an ex-rodeo rider from Calgary in Canada, his legs horrendously scarred from that occupation. Before he was called up to the army, he worked on the roads leading into the Canadian wilderness, not tarmac, just dirt. His language was the coarsest I'd ever heard. His toilet was down the drain in the backyard, his bed in a room above, no lights or curtains, only an old iron bedstead covered in shabby clothes and worn blankets. No wardrobe or drawers but a pile of unwashed, ragged clothes in the corner.

Eventually, he had to leave to avoid the Inland Revenue's demand for unpaid rent. He had told me where he was going which was around thirty-five miles away. He wanted me to visit him, saying that I could stay the night in his derelict caravan. The last time I saw him was when I cycled over to his new 'home'. By the way, I rode an old bone shaker, onto the handlebars of which I'd tied a huge portable radio with an equally huge battery. It seemed to take forever to cycle there, but I had the radio at full blast all the way. Classy. He was living in half of a crashed caravan with no end, other than a tarpaulin. It was in a breaker's yard for old commercial vehicles which he was employed to cut up. At the time of my visit, he was cutting up old dust carts from the local council. I loved helping but it was too far for me to cycle. Anyway, sleeping over in the caravan was so spooky with the only light being from oil lamps and rain coming in through the sides of the tarpaulin. I was the only person in the world that he knew. He expected me to undertake any task, however dangerous, then scream and shout at me if it wasn't good enough, saying how useless I was. He was every inch a remnant from a bygone age.

We would sit for hours, in the gloom, and when he was not singing, he would be talking about his time building roads, riding the rodeos, etcetera. He treated me as an equal, never touched me, hugged me or said anything affectionate, but guarded me with a passion if anyone commented on our friendship. He would rustle up food that was generally ghastly - dirty tins of beans on slices of bread decorated with oily fingerprints.

I have had a long life, filled with many adventures, met many people around the world, always with a sense of propriety, even prudery. However, it has not stopped me enjoying the activities and joyful participation of young people, be it teaching or adventures, rock climbing, trekking and so on. I am not unaware of what goes on. I have indeed written a book of gay sexual activities, sometimes witnessed, laced with my sense of humour. Maybe that is what keeps me sane, together with a realistic nod to the foibles of The Human Race.

I had a partner for twenty-six years and another for twelve, but I have never liked physical sex or seeing people naked. We never even slept in the same bed or room, unless for a cuddle and comfort. Nevertheless, these were wonderful years. Much of my behaviour and predilections can be traced to childhood, being abused in a violent family, quizzed as to why I did not have a girlfriend and ostracised for not liking girls. I have been invited to parties in the best places in London and met film stars. However, I mostly declined attention. I enjoyed the adventure of stepping into other worlds and did attend some auspicious, secretive events and gatherings, but managed to slip away before the hosts or guests became too amorous. With age, slower reactions and many wrinkles, the chasing no longer happens. In short, I knew I was gay from a young age, but the pain and hurt both before and since has made me scared of looking at a naked man.

Until now that is.

REFLECTION

So many have made contact with me and I am so frightened that they all seem to offer and want what it is I am not looking for. My biggest fear at the most vulnerable time of my life is to lose everything and find myself living on the streets. Now I am trapped as what to do. The clock is ticking. Do I keep travelling for no particular reason or sink back into my armchair and let whatever life is left in me ebb away? I have met so many beautiful people in so many countries and never taken advantage of any, as much as they might have wanted me to. But I must come to a decision.

MY 2023 PROFILE

A lonely soul, living in a strange land, home sold and wanting to find a partner here in Latvia or the UK. To be cared for and be loved, not for most people's prime motivation for being here, "sex", but for who I am, were that sex just happened to come along, was gentle, caring and only motivated by love, then OK but not important at all. Seeking that illusive person to offer everything to. Someone to sometimes just hug and cuddle, sit close to, hold hands. More to share a caring, monogamous partnership with, a home and great fun holidays and a future together, rich or poor, it matters not.

Where you might live, own or just rent. For the truly right person, I will care share and relocate being financially self sufficient.

Now as I get older I have not the wish nor mental agility, and time especially to go through all the hoops and expenses of relocating to another foreign land, unless it was in the EU and my man would assist me in going through all the processes. I live and am a resident, at the moment in Latvia Finding any one here in Latvia would be great but unlikely. Maybe better to return to the UK, if I can't find anyone here in Latvia, where I know what I am doing but not to be alone either.

I am just a simple, uneducated working class guy, liking the simple unsophisticated life. No especial skills or intellectual prowess, but not a moron either. Dress conservatively, eat simply.

Enjoy laughter, humour and travel. Someone out there needs someone soft and gentle to cuddle surely!

Given my age, I don't want to waste what little time I have left, in being just someone to chat to endlessly on line, feeding the nosey, the bored and the dreamers for ever.

So please do not respond if you are not serious.

I have to keep trying.

PUBLISHER'S AFTERWORD

I'm going to stop here. If I keep waiting for Brian to settle down, find love and end this memoir sensibly, I'll be waiting forever. He still documents everything and I'm sure the musings will continue for a long while. He thought he'd met the man of his dreams, but this changes on a regular basis. Maybe so, maybe no. He is currently living in the south of England, enjoying a 'domestic relationship'. Well, that was when I started this sentence.

As stated in the introduction, there's something touching about the way he approaches each day, communicating so openly and positively, unfettered by woke, wake, cancel or counsel. He just does his own thing, speaking with everyone, laughing at everything, dealing with the struggles of life in an original way.

As the publisher, I've asked myself during the extremely heavy edits whether it has been worth the effort. I think so. It may not be a best-selling celebrity autobiography, but I felt there was something deeply human buried in the atrocious grammar, something about our need for companionship and love in a world that seems to conspire against emotional fulfilment, even with the extraordinary potential and often dramatic deceptions of online dating.

You might be able to follow the author's further ramblings on his Facebook videos, though how long he will maintain them is anyone's guess.

To conclude, as Brian might say, "Have a lovely weekend everybody!"

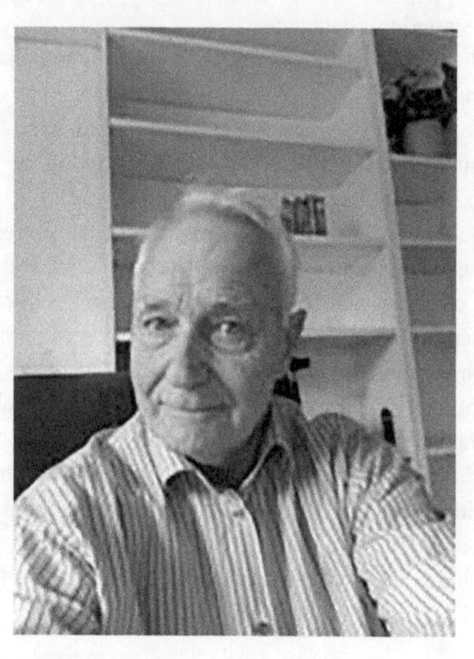

Colour Your Reading

8 to 12:	Green
YA:	Red
Adult:	Magenta
Poetry:	Blue
Non-Fiction:	Gold

Hawkwood Books 2024